P9-CFB-561

100 IDEAS THAT CHANGED FILM

David Parkinson

100 IDEAS THAT CHANGED FILM

David Parkinson

Laurence King Publishing

Introduction

As this alternative history of cinema illustrates, 'film' is a very loose term. It can be applied with equal validity to the earliest silent short and the latest event movie, to a cartoon and a documentary, to a serial and a newsreel, to an avant-garde experiment and a piece of pornographic exploitation. Yet these variations on the moving image all largely derive from a core set of ideas that have determined how films have been produced, distributed, exhibited, consumed and appreciated for some 120 years. Whether you're new to studying film or a dedicated cineaste, you may be surprised by how many concepts and techniques are shared by flickers and blockbusters.

Film is often called the seventh art. Compared to sculpture, architecture, painting, music, poetry and dance, it is still in its infancy. But such has been its rate of evolution, few who attended the first cinema show at the Grand Café in Paris on 27 December 1895 would recognize the affinity of the simple scenes projected by the Cinématographe with the Hollywood spectacles whose generic tropes and computer-generated effects currently enthral audiences worldwide.

Nobody knows who first had the idea of creating moving pictures and no one person can lay claim to having invented the means of recording or disseminating them. Long before Louis and Auguste Lumière secured their place in film history, writers, scientists and entrepreneurs had been intrigued by the artistic and commercial potential of images that appeared to replicate life for the entertainment and edification of paying customers. However, none of those responsible for such devices as magic lanterns and optical toys or notions like persistence of vision could have foreseen that the movies would become the most accessible, popular and arguably the most socially, politically and culturally significant art form of them all.

This book seeks to identify the key theories, techniques and strategies that enabled film to progress from sideshow to institution. Even though cinema has always had a global dimension, the majority of the ideas were hatched in Europe and the United States. While many were devised to solve technical and commercial problems, others sought to extend aesthetic or dramatic parameters. Consequently, what follows is as much a chronology of business opportunism and technical pragmatism, as a celebration of artistry, social commitment and showmanship. Indeed, without the backing of financiers, the ingenuity of boffins and the intervention of administrators, film may never have developed beyond being just another nineteenth-century curio.

It is also interesting to speculate how different the course of film history might have been had the Great War not caused the closure of national industries across Europe and allowed the nascent community in Hollywood to assume control of the international market. During cinema's first two decades, pioneers in America, France, Britain, Germany and Italy had made equally crucial contributions to the evolution of screen storytelling. But the remainder of the silent era was dominated by the ascent of the Hollywood studio system, whose conveyor belt approach to film-making and reliance on bankable genres and stars gave it a hegemony over world cinema that it has yet to relinquish, despite the rise of more prolific rivals in India (Bollywood) and Nigeria (Nollywood).

Indeed, it was Hollywood's business model, as much as the quality of its now-talking pictures, that enabled the Big Five studios of MGM, Paramount, Warner Bros, Twentieth Century-Fox and RKO to introduce the block booking and vertical integration practices that provided guaranteed outlets for their products and allowed American cinema to survive the Depression and World War II. However, the golden age could not last forever and a combination of suburbanization, anti-trust laws, Communist witch-hunting and television prompted the studios to resort to colour, widescreen, 3-D and stereophonic sound in a bid to arrest a near-ruinous postwar slump in attendances.

The decline of the studio system coincided with a resurgence in European cinema. While Continental film-makers had challenged the conventions of Hollywood classicism throughout the silent era, a period of stagnation had followed, during which authoritarianism limited freedom of expression and industries across Europe struggled with dubbing and subtitling practices. Spelling the end of this despondency, a new determination to depict life as it was lived resulted in the advent of Neorealism in postwar Italy. Soon afterwards, a French rebellion against polished pictures with literate scripts and lavish production values led to the coining of auteur theory and the eruption of the new waves that not only transformed the European and American scenes, but also prompted the rise of Third Cinema that finally enabled film to become a genuinely global medium.

Europe also had much to do with the appearance of film schools, museums, archives and the festival circuit. But, from the early 1970s onwards, the big film ideas came predominantly in the business and technological spheres. The multinational conglomerates that began acquiring the Hollywood studios in the 1960s recognized that young people were the new target demographic and started producing blockbusters in the sci-fi, fantasy and adventure genres that were packed with state-of-the-art effects and backed by massive media advertising and merchandising campaigns to lure audiences into the modern multiplexes.

Some critics have identified a consequent infantilization of American mainstream cinema and have lamented the synergist dependence on pre-sold sources, sequels and remakes that has sapped its originality. But the corporatization of Hollywood has also provoked a backlash by independent directors inspired by the exploitation mavericks of the 1950s and '60s and their willingness to tackle topics the studios shy away from has afforded opportunities for female, African-American and queer film-makers to find their arthouse niche alongside foreign-language cinema.

It is impossible to predict where film will be in a decade's time. The gaming revolution has sparked rumours of interactivity ending movie-going as a communal pastime. Yet, even if cinema does divide into distinctive experiential and intellectual formats, many of the ideas discussed here will remain relevant, as the basics of film content and form have essentially remained consistent over the past century. Styles, techniques and processes may come and go. But films continue to play on universal emotions and it's to be hoped that audiences will long be challenged, charmed and consoled by them, whether they reflect the everyday or provide an escape from it.

Projecting illusions, promoting escapism

MAGIC LANTERNS

These optical lanterns contained the principal elements later found in film projectors: a source of illumination; a mechanism for moving frames through the light-proofed casing; and lenses for condensing and projecting images onto a distant screen. As an early form of mass entertainment, they also anticipated the storytelling experiments of later film-makers.

A single lens lantern, made in Liverpool around the late 1880s by Archer & Sons.

The names Christiaan Huygens, Athanathius Kircher and Thomas Walgenstein will mean little even to dedicated cineastes. Yet these seventeenth-century scholars figured prominently in the development of the magic lantern, an early type of image projector with which anonymous Savoyards and Auvergnats astounded kings and commoners across Europe from the early 1700s to the late 1860s. But while these activities primed audiences for a communal form of projected entertainment, it was left to later innovators such as Henry Langdon Childe and Abbé Moigno to devise the storytelling techniques that eventually shaped the first moving pictures.

The likes of Étienne-Gaspard Robert's Phantasmagoria in Paris (1798–1837) and the Royal Polytechnic Institution shows in London (1838–81) attained considerable sophistication. Indeed, such was the intricacy and artistry of the full-colour lantern spectacles available in 1895 that many considered the first black-and-white films to be coarsely gimmicky by comparison.

After all, lanternists had been projecting photographic slides (or 'life models') since the 1860s. The first slides had been simple, single illustrations. But, as techniques were refined, they started to come in sets or strips that told tales from across the generic range in an elliptical manner that often required captions, commentaries or accompanying ballads. Some even cut between parallel storylines set in different locations.

Designed to educate and entertain, and veering between the realistic and the romanticized, the factual and the fantastical, lantern slides could be comical, inspirational, shocking and occasionally pornographic. Most slides were hand-painted (which prompted the move to colour the earliest films), while others were fitted with pulleys, gears or levers to provide intra-image movement. The use of multiple lanterns or lenses enabled practitioners to create transformations, substitutions, disappearances, apparitions and dream inserts. They could also dissolve or fade between views, while lanterns mounted on wheeled carriages could enlarge or diminish subjects in scale in anticipation of cinema's later long, medium and close-up shots.

Wheels of life (pairs of counter-rotating discs containing sequential images) and choreutoscope strips gave the impression of continuous movement, while chromatropes, eidotropes and cycloidotropes produced shifting shapes and colours that presaged the concerns of experimental film-makers with form, texture and rhythm. Furthermore, the combination of fixed background slides and those with moving elements foreshadowed cel animation, while Paul Philipstal and Étienne-Gaspard Robert (or 'Robertson') pioneered back projection in casting ghoulish images onto gauze screens and smoke clouds in the first gothic horror shows.

Eadweard Muybridge, Émile Reynaud and Georges Méliès were among the many film-makers inspired by the magic lantern. But its greatest legacy lay in the way it provided the uneducated masses with a brief respite from their arduous lives, as this escapist populism was harnessed by the first cinema entrepreneurs, whose itinerancy lives on in the travelling picture shows that continue to enthral audiences in the remoter parts of Africa and Asia. ∎

'Designed to educate and entertain … lantern slides could be comical, inspirational, shocking and occasionally pornographic.'

Images from a set of 24 glass slides based on Sir John Tenniel's original drawings for Alice in Wonderland.

ABOVE: *Motion studies by Eadweard Muybridge published in* Animal Locomotion *(1887).*

BELOW: *This equine sequence by Muybridge was projected using a zoopraxiscope under the title* Sallie Gardner at a Gallop *(1878).*

Now you see it, now you ... still see it

ABOVE: *This 1840s* disque magique *was a variation on the phenakistoscope, which created the illusion of moving imagery.*

BELOW: *Jules Cheret's poster advertising a scene from Émile Reynaud's 1892 Théâtre Optique animation,* Pauvre Pierrot.

IDEA № 2
PERSISTENCE OF VISION

In the century prior to their first projection – and for decades afterwards – it was believed that a rapid succession of still images could be viewed as a single continuous motion thanks to the perceptual phenomenon known as persistence of vision. Numerous scientists and psychologists have since discredited the concept, but it continues to spark debate.

Persistence of vision was first noted by the Roman poet Lucretius in *De rerum natura* (65 BC) and demonstrated with the whirling firebrand experiment by the Irish mathematician the Chevalier Patrick D'Arcy in 1765. It was defined by Peter Mark Roget (of Thesaurus fame) in 1824, and his theory that an image fleetingly lingers on the retina after it has been removed from the field of view inspired a series of optical toys that created an illusion of movement from static illustrations, among them John Ayrton Paris's thaumatrope ('magical turning'), Joseph Plateau's phenakistoscope ('deceitful view') and William George Horner's daedalum, which was rebranded as the zoetrope ('live turning') by William F. Lincoln in 1867.

However, from the moment Plateau fitted his phenakistoscope with posed photographs in 1849, the race was on to capture actual movement. The endeavours of locomotion specialists Eadweard Muybridge and Étienne-Jules Marey resulted in the development of chronophotography in the 1880s, which was appropriated and refined by Thomas Edison and the Lumière brothers for their respective Kinetograph and **Cinématographe** machines, which both seemed dependent upon persistence of vision.

As the mechanics of recording and projecting moving images scarcely changed between the 1890s and the digital era, the significance of this psycho-perceptual misconception is incalculable. Yet psychologists remain puzzled by the actual neural and cognitive processes involved in the perception of intermittent movement.

Persistence of vision in isolation certainly seems a spurious hypothesis, as audiences see movies as smooth action not a superimposition of stills. However, it makes more sense taken in conjunction with the 'phi phenomenon', or stroboscopic effect, which was revealed by Gstalt psychologist Max Wertheimer in his *Experimental Studies on the Seeing of Motion* (1912) and which explains why the individual blades of a rotating fan appear as a single circular form.

While the phi phenomenon creates movement between frames at optimal projection speeds of between 12 and 24 frames per second, persistence of vision prevents the viewer from seeing the dark spaces between the individual images by causing 'flicker fusion' when the projection beam is broken at a frequency approaching 50 times per second. However, other experts reject this theory in favour of the notion of 'apparent motion', which suggests that certain cells in the eye and brain responsible for analysing motion can be duped into sending the wrong signal by stimuli resembling movement.

Wherever the truth lies, in order to eliminate flicker, the rotating shutter within the projector has to allow each image to be flashed upon the screen twice. Thus, whenever we watch a film, we spend half the time gazing at an optical illusion and the other half sitting in the dark in front of a blank screen. ∎

Edison's pre-projection brainchild

Patrons paid 25c to see five films at the Holland brothers' Kinetoscope parlour, which opened at 1155 Broadway, New York in April 1894.

IDEA № 3

THE KINETOSCOPE

This early device for exhibiting motion pictures – spectators viewed films individually through a peephole in the Kinetoscope's casing – has often been seen as one of cinema's dead ends. But, despite being superseded by projection in December 1895, it played a key role in the medium's technical, industrial, aesthetic and commercial evolution.

Thomas Edison had been inspired to create 'an instrument which does for the Eye what the Phonograph has done for the Ear' before meeting pioneering sequence photographer Eadweard Muybridge in February 1888. But, having filed a caveat for the Kinetoscope, he entrusted the project to William Kennedy Laurie Dickson, who shot some tests using John Carbutt's sensitized celluloid. Edison himself, however, provided fresh impetus after encountering Étienne-Jules Marey at the 1889 Paris Exposition, although the ideas of intermittency to exploit **persistence of vision** and perforated film strips came from Ottomar Anschütz's Electrical Tachyscope and Émile Reynaud's Théâtre Optique respectively.

Switching to George Eastman's 35mm celluloid strips in 1889, Dickson prototyped the Kinetograph camera, and a party from the National Federation of Women's Clubs became the first to sample the Kinetoscope in May 1891. But it wasn't until May 1893 that *Blacksmith Scene* was shown to the public at the Brooklyn Institute of Arts and Sciences, and April 1894 that the Holland brothers opened the first Kinetoscope parlour at 1155 Broadway in New York.

Dickson and his assistant William Heise made their 20- to 40-second kinetoscopics in the first film studio, the Black Maria, with *Fred Ott's Sneeze* (1894) becoming the first movie comedy. Footage of strongman Eugene Sandow, dancer Annabelle Moore and sharpshooters Annie Oakley and Buffalo Bill Cody linked the moving image to other forms of popular entertainment. Edison also recorded sporting events, as did his rivals. A boxing bout staged by the Latham family prompted the invention of the Latham Loop, which permitted longer films. The Lathams also drew up the first star contract when they exclusively signed heavyweight boxer Gentleman Jim Corbett in 1894, the same year that Senator James A. Bradley's objection to a view of dancer Carmencita's stockinged ankles resulted in the first screen **censorship**.

The Lumière brothers and R.W. Paul were among the many Europeans

ABOVE: *Inside Edison's Kinetoscope, Phonograph and Graphophone Arcade, managed by Peter Bacigalupi at 946 Market Street, San Francisco.*

BELOW: *Erected for $637.67 in the grounds of Thomas Edison's West Orange laboratory, the Black Maria was the first purpose-built film studio.*

to be inspired by the Kinetoscope. Indeed, Edison's failure to secure international patents cost him dear, while the strict enforcement of his domestic copyrights led to the Patent and Trust wars (see **Feature Films**) that proved so crucial to shaping the structure of the Hollywood film industry (several of whose major players had run Kinetoscope parlours).

Edison continued to tinker with projecting Kinetoscopes until 1914. By that time US cinema was dominated by D.W. Griffith, who had helped refine film grammar at the American Mutoscope and Biograph Company, which Dickson had joined after acrimoniously parting company with Edison's Enterprises. Edison mistakenly believed that films should be made by technicians rather than artists. But the Kinetoscope's legacy lives on in the viewing of films on television, video, DVD, computers and mobile phones. ∎

1896 poster by Henri Brispot demonstrating the cross-class appeal of the Cinématographe.

The 'flickers' flicker into life

ABOVE: *Marcellin Auzolle's classic poster for* L'Arroseur arrosé *(1895).*

BELOW: *Mischievous Benoît Duval gives gardener François Clerc a soaking in the same scene as the one also being enjoyed by the audience in the film's poster (above).*

IDEA № 4
THE CINÉMATOGRAPHE

This hybrid camera, printer and projector holds a unique place in screen history since it facilitated the event that has been designated as marking the birth of cinema: Louis and Auguste Lumière's ten-film presentation to a paying audience at the Grand Café, Paris on 28 December 1895.

Thirty-five patrons paid one franc each to attend the first show. But the Lumières were soon selling 7,000 tickets a week and the so-called 'flickers' became a craze. Their success marked the end of the age of inventors, which had witnessed scientists, showmen and mavericks including Muybridge, Marey, Jules Janssen, Louis Le Prince, Jean Aimé LeRoy, William Friese-Greene, Birt Acres and the Skladanowsky brothers (Max and Emil) laying claim to recording motion. However, it was Edison's Kinematograph camera and **Kinetoscope** viewer that prompted the race to project.

Filmed with the prototype Cinématographe, *La Sortie des Usines Lumière* was the first footage shot specifically for **projection**. It debuted privately on 22 March 1895. Emulating the compositional style of contemporary photography, Louis Lumière set the trend for records of everyday happenings that would continue into the early 1900s. Indeed, the camera's lightness suited it for outdoor filming and its placement for *L'Arrivée d'un train en Gare de La Ciotat* not only exploited the kinetic power of the approaching locomotive, but also made innovative use of **off-screen space** by having figures

enter the frame from behind the lens. Lumière also produced the first film comedy, *L'Arroseur arrosé*, in which a boy soaks a gardener with his own hose.

However, many early Lumière efforts like *Repas de bébé* (1895) were essentially home movies and it was left to the employees they dispatched across the globe to refine shooting techniques. The first film show in just about every country was given with a Cinématographe, as operatives such as Alexandre Promio enticed the curious by recording local landmarks in footage that was then marketed as travelogues back in Europe.

Borrowing its mechanism from the Kinematograph and its name from a flawed sequence camera patented by Léon-Guillaume Bouly, the Cinématographe, perfected by the Lumière siblings and engineer Jules Carpentier, established the basics for recording and projecting motion pictures that would remain largely unchanged for several decades. It operated at 16 frames per second (fps), which remained the norm until **sound** forced a change to 24 fps. Popular makes like the Pathé Professional (1905), the Debrie Parvo (1908), the Bell & Howell Studio (1912), the Arriflex (1937) and the Éclair Cameflex (1948) appropriated its

winding mechanism that intermittently sent a negative film strip from a feed reel towards a lens and an aperture, where it was held in place long enough for a shutter to open and admit light focused by the lens from the target object to be fixed by the chemical emulsion on the celluloid's surface.

Louis Lumière ceased production in 1900 and devoted his energies thereafter to widescreen, colour and stereoscopic processes. However, he missed a trick in not accepting a 10,000-franc offer for a Cinématographe from a member of his first-night audience in 1895, as the spectator in question, magician Georges Méliès, would become cinema's first commercially successful narrative artist. ■

Towards a bigger-than-life, communal experience

IDEA № 5

PROJECTION

The fascination with cast forms predates Plato's Cave of Shadows. Though it was only at the end of the nineteenth century that moving images finally flickered on a screen, at every stage of cinema's prehistory, machines and processes were invented with mass audiences in mind.

TOP: *Projecting reality: Louis Lumière's* L'Arrivée d'un train en Gare de La Ciotat *(1895).*

ABOVE: *Robert Donat in the Boulting brothers biopic,* The Magic Box *(1951), which claimed William Friese-Greene as the inventor of the first practical camera-projector.*

In 1420, Giovanni da Fontana's *Bellicorum Instrumentorum Liber* included an illustration that suggested how a lantern could be used to terrorize enemy troops by projecting demonic images into the air. In the mid-nineteenth century, T.W. Naylor and Franz von Uchatius attempted to project images from optical toys, while Henry Heyl, Thomas Ross, Eadweard Muybridge and Ottomar Anschütz all sought to project moving images from posed or hand-copied photographs. Yet, having perfected cinematography, Thomas Edison failed to recognize the commercial or communal benefits of projection and paid the price as the Kinetoscope parlours he supplied were replaced by the **nickelodeons** in which urban audiences of all ages, classes and ethnicities learned the basics of screen storytelling.

The famous anecdote about viewers diving for cover during a screening of Louis Lumière's *L'Arrivée d'un train en Gare de La Ciotat* is almost certainly apocryphal. But it's not as far-fetched as one might suppose, as pioneering film-makers such as ex-magician Georges Méliès exploited the audience's collective sense of wonderment to dazzle, delight and disconcert, and this eagerness for shared sensation explains the success of Saturday matinees for children, late-night double bills of suspense and horror movies, and singalong versions of musicals like *The Sound of Music* (1965) and *Grease* (1978).

Projection helped make cinema a socially acceptable pastime. In order to meet demand, the production process was industrialized and genres emerged to shape audience tastes and reduce the risk of box-office misfires. New technologies and narrative strategies were also devised to satisfy the public's need for novelty and spectacle. But popular entertainment could also be used as a form of social control, with censorship suppressing certain ideas while promoting others more conducive to those bankrolling the studios or providing state subsidies. This proved particularly useful in times of national emergency, as the **propaganda** messages in features,

documentaries, **newsreels** and instructional shorts could be guaranteed to reach the widest possible viewership.

However, attendances dropped sharply in the period following World War II, in the face of competing leisure activities such as television. But even though the studios eventually sold their films for domestic broadcast, they invested heavily in widescreen, colour and stereophonic technology in the early 1950s to lure people away from their living rooms. Hollywood also experimented with 3-D, drive-ins and **exploitation** genres to attract the younger generation, and this emphasis on enticing juveniles into giant-screen multiplexes with effects-laden event movies has sustained the **blockbuster** era since the mid-1970s.

Despite the deployment of digitization, projection has changed little since 1895. However, it remains to be seen what impact the long-rumoured advent of interactive cinema will have on the traditional communal experience. ∎

The hills are alive: Julie Andrews in The Sound of Music *(1965), which has become a cult favourite with audiences at special singalong screenings.*

A prank with pepper causes cross-town chaos in Lewin Fitzhamon's trick comedy, **That Fatal Sneeze** *(1907).*

Cinema makes a spectacle of itself

TOP: *Ingenious trickery, as a car returns to Earth after speeding around Saturn's ring in R.W. Paul's* The '?' Motorist *(1906).*

ABOVE: *Fantasy, trickery and an exquisite eye for detail combine in Georges Méliès's sci-fi fantasy* A Trip to the Moon *(1902).*

IDEA Nº 6
TRICK FILMS

The trick film marked the advent of special effects and captured the public imagination as the initial novelty of moving images was beginning to wane. Moreover, the magical transformations it featured allowed film-makers to develop the show-stopping techniques that would prove essential to commercial narrative cinema.

The first flickers were Lumière-style shots of daily life, travelogues, records of sporting and showbiz celebrities, and reconstructions of historical and topical events. However, given the number of magicians among the movie pioneers, trick films were almost an inevitability. The French siblings Émile and Vincent Isola, Britons David Devant and John Nevill Maskelyne, and Americans Billy Bitzer and James Stuart Blackton variously experimented with stop-motion, cranking speeds and in-camera effects like masking and multiple exposure. But the doyen of trick films was the former stage magician Georges Méliès.

Despite Méliès's claim to have stumbled across cinema's trick potential when his camera jammed while filming on the Place de l'Opéra in 1896, the technique of substitution splicing – in which the camera stopped while the objects involved in the trick were exchanged – was actually devised for Edison's *The Execution of Mary, Queen of Scots* in the previous year. Whatever the technique's origins, it suited Méliès's prestidigitatious style in *scènes à trucs* –

transformation scenes – such as *Conjuring a Woman at the Robert-Houdin* (1896) and *The One-Man Band* (1900), in which figures disappeared or were duplicated with a true illusionist's flourish. Indeed, he often bowed and gestured to viewers to ensure they missed none of his ingenuity.

Méliès similarly recycled old stage business in *The Astronomer's Dream* (1898), which set the trend for *féeries* (fairy plays) such as *Cinderella* (1899) and fantasies like *A Trip to the Moon* (1902), which broke the nascent medium's reliance on what critic André Gaudreault has called 'monstration' and transformed it into an exhibitionist 'cinema of attractions', which film scholar Tom Gunning has suggested followed the example of the fairground, the circus and vaudeville in seeking to entice, thrill, shock and delight audiences with its unique use of spectacle and surprise.

Fairy plays were an established French theatrical tradition and filmic *féeries* were invariably photographed frontally against painted backdrops. However, many were enhanced by

stencilled colour and concluded with an extravagant grand finale. Yet while examples such as Albert Capellani's *Aladdin* (1906) prioritized ostentation over plot logic and character, they still sought to marry drama and display, and directors gradually discovered how to integrate such special effects into their story-lines, with D.W. Griffith learning his trade as an actor in trick films like *The Sculptor's Nightmare* (1908).

Despite the popularity of the likes of Edwin S. Porter's *Dream of a Rarebit Fiend* (1906), America could not compete with European tricksters such as Segundo de Chomón and Cecil Hepworth, who initiated a cinema of sensation with *How it Feels to Be Run Over* (1900), the eccentric humour of which presaged **slapstick** and **Surrealism**. By the time Méliès released *The Conquest of the Pole* (1912), trick films had become passé but their emphasis on magical moments sparked cinema's continuing dependence on eye-catching sequences in comedies, musicals, swashbucklers, science fiction and horror. ∎

'Directors began conveying the psychological state of their characters with head shots and atmospheric inserts.'

ABOVE: *In her sole screen role, Renée Falconetti endures the agony of interrogation in Carl Theodor Dreyer's* The Passion of Joan of Arc *(1928).*

BELOW: *If looks could kill: Charles Bronson as Harmonica in Sergio Leone's spaghetti epic* Once Upon a Time in the West *(1968).*

Getting inside a character's head

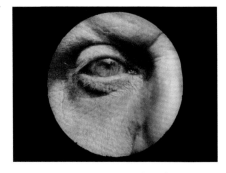

A circular mask is used to suggests a boy's eye view in G.A. Smith's short, Grandma's Reading Glass (1900).

IDEA № 7
CLOSE-UPS

Close-range shots tightly framing an actor's face only emerged as a familiar part of screen technique after they became a status symbol among Hollywood stars of the 1920s. But film-makers have subsequently used close-ups to suggest a character's interiority and to draw attention to a particular expression, gesture or prop.

There were plenty of precedents for the close-up in painting and photography, as well as in magic-lantern slides. Indeed, one of the most famous Kinetoscope shorts, *Fred Ott's Sneeze* (1894), focused predominantly on the subject's face. G.A. Smith also made innovative use of close-ups in dividing scenes into multiple shots. In *Grandma's Reading Glass* (1900), for example, he used a black circular mask on his lens to simulate the extreme close-up perspective of a boy with a magnifying glass.

Although some film-makers resisted such increased intimacy, few continued to insist on full-figure shooting by the end of the decade. The French actor-director Max Linder used 'bust shots' (presenting characters from the waist up) to implicate viewers in his comic antics, while in 1918 Lev Kuleshov juxtaposed an image of Ivan Mozhukin with various emotive objects to reveal the close-up's centrality to associational montage. This became a key technique in the silent era and beyond but it wasn't until Scandinavian and German directors began conveying the psychological state of their characters with head shots and

atmospheric inserts that the close-up became a cinematic staple.

Meanwhile, despite D.W. Griffith's increased use of close-ups after *The Lonedale Operator* (1911), Hollywood primarily opted for objectivity and only fully embraced cutting in to tighter shots in the late silent era, as the star system exploited soft-focus poses to convince fans of the dash, glamour and stature of their idols. However, close-ups also had a storytelling value, as they drew the audience into the narrative by highlighting key elements within the **mise en scène**, such as a prop a slapstick clown was about to trip over, a weapon a gangster was about to fire or a secret that was about to be revealed. **Point-of-view shots** were often additionally effective, as an image filling a 50-foot screen could have a significant emotional impact upon an audience empathizing with a protagonist's plight.

Film-makers use camera distance to create patterns and rhythms and establish motifs and themes. Height and angle are equally important. Context is everything, but low-angle shots often suggest a character's power, while those looking down tend to

emphasize vulnerability. Canted or Dutch angles imply a world out of kilter, as in Carol Reed's *The Third Man* (1949), although Alfred Hitchcock used overhead shots to similarly disconcerting effect in *The Birds* (1963).

In the early 1950s, directors struggled to accommodate close-ups in widescreen compositions and often used scenery and shadows to occupy unwanted space. However, close-ups suited the smaller television screen and TV directors graduating into features made extensive use of them. Furthermore, the growing need to compress key action into the so-called 'safe area' for **home-entertainment** formats enabled the new generation of blockbuster superstars to demand sizeable close-up quotas in their contracts. ∎

From fades to freeze-frames

Jean-Pierre Léaud faces an uncertain future as Antoine Doinel while the final frame freezes in François Truffaut's The 400 Blows *(1959).*

IDEA № 8

OPTICAL TRANSITIONS

The switch to digital editing has seen the cut become the dominant editorial mode. However, the first moving images required a more varied syntax, and many of the optical techniques devised to guide the first viewers through silent storylines remain valid to this day.

The fade and the dissolve were relics of magic-lantern shows. Indeed, audiences were so used to such smooth transitions that many pioneering film-makers avoided the straight cut, as it was deemed too abrupt and distracting. However, it could also be thrillingly effective, as Alfred Hitchcock proved in *The 39 Steps* (1935). The dissolve became an essential part of Georges Méliès's technique after *Cinderella* (1899). But such transitioning quickly became clichéd and dissolves were reduced to being alternative edit points or harbingers of **flashbacks** until the 1920s, when Marcel L'Herbier's *Eldorado* (1921) spurned intertitles to use dissolves to suggest elapsed time and E.A. Dupont's *Variety* (1925) ushered in the Hollywood montage with its exhilarating overlapping sequences.

The dissolve was also used for transformations such as Brigitte Helm's metamorphosis into the robot in Fritz Lang's *Metropolis* (1926). However, the opening of Orson Welles's *Citizen Kane* (1941) demonstrated that it could also serve as a lyrical variation on the cut, while Michelangelo Antonioni gave it a metaphysical purpose in dissolving

David Hemmings from the scene after he fails to solve the mystery in *Blow-Up* (1966). The change to **colour** photography and the greater immediacy of Nouvelle Vague and television editing might have made the lap dissolve seem staid, yet it still retained a valuable temporal remit.

Another signifier of passing time, the fade, can also be used to draw the viewer into a film's world, as in the opening shot of Frank Tuttle's *This Gun for Hire* (1942). It can also emphasize significant plot developments, as with the fades to red in Ingmar Bergman's *Cries and Whispers* (1973), which allow the audience to contemplate what has just occurred before the story resumes.

The iris offers a similar facility. Favoured as a bookending gambit by D.W. Griffith, this has become something of an archaism since Orson Welles used it to conclude the motoring episode in *The Magnificent Ambersons* (1942). The wipe has also fallen from favour, with the dramatic power it possessed in Victor Sjöström's *He Who Gets Slapped* (1924) being lampooned by Laurel and Hardy in *Thicker Than Water* (1935). However, it too now has a

nostalgic charm, which persuaded George Lucas to utilize it in *Star Wars* (1977) in homage to Akira Kurosawa's *Hidden Fortress* (1958).

Finally, there's the freeze-frame. Joseph L. Mankiewicz flashes back from one at the start of *All About Eve* (1950), but these static shots usually act as dramatic full stops, as in George Roy Hill's *Butch Cassidy and the Sundance Kid* (1969) and Peter Weir's *Gallipoli* (1981). However, they can also convey ambiguity, as in the frozen zoom of Jean-Pierre Léaud on the beach at the climax of François Truffaut's *The 400 Blows* (1959). ∎

ABOVE: *Ingmar Bergman uses red fades to reinforce the colour's symbolic link with blood, passion and the soul in* **Cries and Whispers** *(1972).*

Friend or foe? Artist Xavier Lafitte's viewpoint while pursuing Pilar López de Ayala in José Luis Guerín's In the City of Sylvia *(2007).*

Seeing the world through someone else's eyes

IDEA № 9
POINT-OF-VIEW SHOTS

Mirror image: a rare glimpse of Philip Marlowe attempting to crack a murder case in actor-director Robert Montgomery's Lady in the Lake *(1947).*

Whether depicting aristocratic prying in Ernst Lubitsch's *Lady Windermere's Fan* (1926) or Ted Levine's night-vision stalking in *The Silence of the Lambs* (1991), point-of-view (POV) shots – where viewers see the action through a character's eyes – intensify the immediacy of a scene and draw the audience into the film's world.

The earliest subjective images were the so-called 'phantom rides' filmed from the front of moving vehicles in the 1890s. Following G.A. Smith's *Grandma's Reading Glass* (1900), POV shots were invariably vignetted with blurring or darkness at the edges to replicate the view through a telescope, binoculars or a keyhole. Non-masked shots soon became common, however, and were first used to convey physical sensation in Vincenzo Denizot's *Tigris* (1913).

The French Impressionists also recognized the potential of subjective shots for expressing psychological states, with Germaine Dulac and Jacques Feyder using anamorphic lenses to suggest the heroine's anguish in *The Smiling Madame Beudet* (1922) and the old man's ennui in *Crainquebille* (1923) (see **The Narrative Avant-garde**). But F.W. Murnau employed a freely roving camera, fades, dissolves, super-imposition, montages and distorting mirrors in *The Last Laugh* (1924) to show both the physical perspective of Emil Jannings's demoted, demoralized and occasionally inebriated doorman and what he saw with his mind's eye.

That film was hugely influential and POV shots soon acquired prospective and retrospective uses. Exploiting cross-cutting and eyeline **matches,** film-makers also devised continuing, discovered, delayed, multiple, open and forged perspectives.

However, creating entire films in the subjective mode proved difficult, with Orson Welles abandoning a POV adaptation of *Heart of Darkness* to make *Citizen Kane* (1941) and Robert Montgomery being forced to rely on visual gimmicks to present *Lady in the Lake* (1947) entirely from the standpoint of shamus Philip Marlowe.

Alfred Hitchcock made frequent use of POV shots, often shifting character perspective within a scene. Yet while these provided psychological insight (and perhaps reflected Hitchcock's voyeuristic personality), their primary purpose was usually visceral. Brian De Palma similarly utilized subjective **tracking shots** to generate suspense in *Dressed to Kill* (1980), while Ruggero Deodato's *Cannibal Holocaust* of the same year instigated what has since become the horror cliché of revealing the fate of missing persons through their 'found' POV film footage.

As the influence of video games grew, POV shots became increasingly familiar in action blockbusters, 3-D features and digital animations. **Computer-generated imagery** also made it possible to approximate non-human perspectives, as in James Cameron's *Terminator 2: Judgment Day* (1991), as well as those of flying projectiles such as bullets in Hong Kong's heroic bloodshed genre.

Yet POV shots aren't solely employed to enhance spectacle. Vittorio De Sica and Agnès Varda included subjective tracks in *Shoeshine* (1946) and *Cleo from 5 to 7* (1962), while Alain Resnais used POVs to explore the interaction of time, memory and imagination in *Last Year at Marienbad* (1961). But subjective images primarily allow viewers to enter a character's temporal and spatial reality. However, as José Luis Guerín demonstrates in following an artist who is pursuing a young woman in *In the City of Sylvia* (2007), it's not always possible to gauge the precise nature of their thoughts. ∎

The camera gets wheels

TRACKING SHOTS

Details from the bravura continuous tracking shot occupying the first three minutes and 20 seconds of Orson Welles's Touch of Evil *(1958).*

Mounting the film camera on a wheeled platform that ran along tracks gave it the ability to move not just from side to side, but also physically towards, away from or around its subject – and in the process endowed cinema with a whole new dynamism.

Ever since Alexandre Promio had the idea of placing a Cinématographe in a Venetian gondola in 1896, the film camera has rarely been still. Camera movements provide narrative information, reveal and conceal space, direct attention and create expressive effects that alter the viewer's perception of the world of the narrative and the psychology of its characters. They can also enhance spectacle.

Devised by R.W. Paul for his coverage of Queen Victoria's Diamond Jubilee in 1897, panning and tilting – the horizontal and vertical movements of an otherwise fixed camera – were employed to retain focus on the principal action within the frame. As the first cameras came without viewfinders and had to be hand-cranked, most movements in cinema's first decades were basic pans and tilts, although they eventually became more adventurous with the whip pan in Rouben Mamoulian's *The Song of Songs* (1933)

and the 360-degree pan in Gene Kelly and Stanley Donen's *On the Town* (1949).

But it was the travelling shot that gave movies genuine visual dynamism. As many early film-makers disliked calling attention to technique, they were initially limited to the parallel tracks employed by D.W. Griffith for his last-minute rescue scenes. However, the diagonal tracking shots in Giovanni Pastrone's *Cabiria* (1914) proved so influential in taking the viewer into the heart of the scene that so-called 'Cabiria movements' came to feature in such diverse pictures as Yevgeni Bauer's *The Child of the Big City* (1914), Charlie Chaplin's *The Vagabond* (1916) and William J. Bowman's all-but-forgotten *The Second-in-Command* (1915), whose extensive use of tracks anticipated masterpieces like Marcel L'Herbier's *Money* (or *L'Argent*) (1928), Lupu Pick's *Sylvester* (1924) and F.W. Murnau's *The Last Laugh* (1924), which perfected the unchained point-of-view shot.

The coming of the talkies briefly curtailed movement, as cameras were suddenly confined to soundproofed ice-boxes. But Mamoulian's *Applause* (1929) restored parallel tracks and devices muffling the motor noise called 'blimps' soon enabled cameras to reframe and follow the action once more. Elevated shots – which had been improvised in Griffith's *Intolerance* (1916) and Harold Lloyd's *The Kid Brother* (1927) – became more common after the wheeled crane was invented for Pal Fejos's *Broadway* (1929), although its use was largely restricted to musicals and swashbucklers.

The handheld methods pioneered for **Cinéma Vérité** and the Nouvelle Vague brought a new authenticity and immediacy to camera movement, which became smoother with the introduction of Steadicam in 1976. A range of mounts and remote control rigs have since been introduced to facilitate tracking, crane and aerial shots, while digital technology has significantly extended the potential length of takes. Thus, even in an age of fast-cut shakicam, there's still a place for the well choreographed travelling shot. ■

ABOVE: *Ewan McGregor being filmed by a light-weight Arricam camera on the set of Roman Polanski's* **The Ghost** *(2010).*

RIGHT: *Busby Berkeley's signature was the top shot looking down on kaleidoscopic patterns of chorines. But he settles for an elevated track in this scene from* **42nd Street** *(1933).*

Motion and emotion

Mack Sennett typically treats his stars as human props, as the Keystone Kops race to bungle another case.

IDEA № 11
CHASE SEQUENCES

The chase sequence may now seem a clichéd facet of the action genres. But, along with the last-minute rescue, it was crucial to teaching the first film-makers how to structure a story and present screen incident in a cogent and involving manner, and it continues to provide some of the biggest thrills in twenty-first-century blockbusters.

In *A Practical Joke* (1898), G.A. Smith's one-shot remake of Louis Lumière's *L'Arroseur arrosé* (1895), an irate gardener pursues the boy who has soaked him around a tree. The advent of one-reelers, however, afforded directors the opportunity to depict more intricate and expansive action. Yet while the tableaux they employed unified action, time and space, they mostly stood as individual units that presented scenes in their entirety before moving on. This emphasis on the discrete shot even affected early chase films, as all participants had to evacuate the frame before the shot was considered complete. However, the need to inject pace into the pursuit prompted film-makers on both sides of the Atlantic to fashion a new way of linking shots that would retain narrative logic while also eliciting an emotional response from the audience.

Initially, films such as Edwin S. Porter's *The Life of an American Fireman* (1902) attempted a greater linearity by repeating whole passages from different perspectives. But Porter's *The Great Train Robbery* and British pictures like Frank Mottershaw's *A Daring Daylight Burglary* (both 1903) cross-cut between simultaneous events to produce elliptical continuity. As shot lengths shortened, directors imported the comic chase from vaudeville. But romps from Biograph Studios such as *The Escaped Lunatic* and *Personal* (both 1904) also introduced such key concepts as a sense of depth, rhythmic cutting, matched action (in which the action depicted at the end of one shot continues in the next from a different perspective), consistent screen direction and off-screen space.

Such was the clarity of the chase sequence that audiences could readily grasp meaning without recourse to an accompanying lecturer or narrative song, which in turn encouraged directors to attempt more complex scenarios. Drawing on the sensationalist strain current in dime novels and stage plays, D.W. Griffith exploited the spatial and temporal relationships defined by parallel editing to generate suspense in the last-minute rescues that became a leitmotif in his work after *The Fatal Hour* (1908). Moreover, his use of a moving camera added momentum to sequences that were further propelled by live musical accompaniment.

The chase also became a crucial component of slapstick, with Mack Sennett's frantic location careens inspiring knockabout clowns and Surrealists, as well as the race and caper comedies of the 1960s and beyond. But chases and rescues eventually became more associated with excitement than hilarity, whether they occurred in serials, B-movie Westerns, crime dramas or adventures.

The horseback charge was particularly exhilarating and even foot pursuits like the Viennese sewer climax in *The Third Man* (1949) could be thrillingly tense. But the car chase perfected in *Bullitt* (1968), *The Italian Job* (1969) and *The French Connection* (1971) confirmed the younger generation's need for speed and spectacle, which has continued to impinge upon the blockbuster, with everything from the James Bond and Indiana Jones series to *Star Wars* (1977) and *Avatar* (2009) counting a chase sequence among their highlights. ∎

ABOVE: *Two of the three Minis making their getaway across Turin following the robbery in* **The Italian Job** *(1969).*

BELOW: *Archaeologist Indiana Jones (Harrison Ford) flees a rolling boulder in a Peruvian temple in* **Raiders of the Lost Ark** *(1981).*

'The car chase … confirmed the younger generation's need for speed and spectacle.'

For a seamless viewing experience

CONTINUITY EDITING

Continuity through cross-cutting, as a heroic canine tracks down a kidnapped child in Rescued by Rover *(1905).*

The basic principles of continuity editing – which sets out to make cinematic storytelling as smooth and natural-seeming as possible – have changed little in the century since they were established. However, some of cinema's most exciting and significant developments have involved revolts against the narrative linearity of classical screen syntax.

Continuity editing is so efficient that most audience members barely notice it. The first film-makers quickly outgrew the single-shot format, with Georges Méliès notably linking self-contained tableaux to tell stories such as *A Trip to the Moon* (1902). However, the **chase sequences** in Edwin S. Porter's *The Great Train Robbery* (1903) and Cecil Hepworth's *Rescued by Rover* (1905) introduced the notion of parallel action – the cross-cut depiction of simultaneously occurring incidents – that was refined by D.W. Griffith during his prolific spell at Biograph (1908–13). By breaking scenes down into shots taken from different distances and angles, Griffith was able to accentuate

the drama and explore the psychology of his characters. He also varied shot lengths to achieve rhythm and mood, and gave **optical transitions** like fades, dissolves, irises and wipes both diegetic and expressive meaning.

Griffith also cut on movement to disguise reframing with meticulous matching. But seamless editing was perfected in Germany by F.W. Murnau and G.W. Pabst, and its unique ability to convey causal, temporal and spatial information ensured that it became a key component of the standard Hollywood grammar that would extend across the genres and the globe from the 1920s.

Yet while cross-cutting was an aesthetic impulse, it also made

economic sense, as it allowed directors to shoot out of sequence, and afforded them and their editors the opportunity to salvage misfiring scenes and mediocre performances by constructing prints from the best takes. Indeed, editors often employ 'cheats' to solve blocking, matching or continuity problems and ensure that pictures adhere to such conventions as the 180-degree rule fixing the axis of action and the 30-degree variation between images, even in shot-reverse-shot sequences. Moreover, editors can also expand and contract shots by exploiting techniques such as slow motion and jump cutting.

Clarity has always been the primary goal of invisible cutting, particularly

where commercial entertainment is concerned. However, such narrative sequencing hasn't always suited makers of documentaries and experimental films. Moreover, it was viewed with open hostility by the Soviet film-maker Sergei Eisenstein, who devised an aggressive form of dialectical montage to counter its 'capitalist tyranny'. The French Impressionists and German **Expressionists** also challenged its hegemony, as did the auteurs of the Nouvelle Vague, although they were as likely to employ long **mise en scène** takes as ellipsis and non-linearity.

American cinema eventually assimilated subversive discontinuity in the late 1960s, although point-of-view editing remained the norm until a combination of televisual technique and digital editing packages fostered a mesh of **handheld** shots, **close-ups** and quick cuts that critic David Bordwell calls 'intensified continuity'. By the late 2000s, the shot length of the average Hollywood feature had decreased by 10 per cent, from 5.15 to 4.74 seconds. As most viewers take up to 3 seconds to adjust to each new image, they are being coerced into responding emotionally rather than intellectually to rapid **montages** that scarcely allow an appreciation of the artistry of the cast and crew. Ironically, this prioritizing of graphic and rhythmic relations over spatial and temporal ones has made mainstream movies more abstract. But audiences worldwide still prefer stories with a beginning, a middle and an end. ∎

The secret of continuity

MATCH SHOTS

ABOVE: *Alfred Hitchcock boldly uses eyeline matches in* Rear Window *(1954) to allow the viewer to share James Stewart's perspective and, thus, increases the tension.*

BELOW: *In* Carrie *(1976), Brian De Palma employs graphic matches to link Sissy Spacek's trauma to telekinetic power, domestic abuse and religious fervour.*

Imagine a dialogue in which a close-up of a woman declaring her love cuts to a shot of a listening man's knees. If the next cut focused on the woman's shoulder before switching to the man's chin, the viewer would quickly become disorientated, as the cross-cuts would defy the visual logic of eye contact conversation. Match shots ensure spatio-temporal consistency by suggesting a character's eyeline view. They should barely be noticed, but they are key to the conceit of invisible editing.

The technique of matching shots took time to evolve. Reverse angles only became commonplace in the 1910s and directors started using eyeline matches that suggested a character's perspective to link shots taken from different positions and angles. As most sets were constructed in an 'L' shape to save money, reverse shots were usually limited to exteriors and, even after Arthur Mackley introduced the over-the-shoulder shot in *The Loafer* (1912), it remained rare until Ralph Ince made it a staple in pictures like *His Phantom Sweetheart* (1915).

D.W. Griffith disliked the shot-reverse-shot method and his resistance retarded its usage in both Hollywood and Europe into the 1920s. However, its ultimate acceptance prompted a shift from cuts along the lens axis to those on a 180-degree line of action, which ensured that each shot within a sequence preserved the spatial relationship between the camera and the action and that relative positions within the frame remained consistent. Directional continuity also adhered to the 180-degree rule, while a 30-degree convention arose to create a suitable angle of difference between sequential shots.

Yasujiro Ozu frequently breached this 180-degree axis to comment on characters or emphasize an incident's dislocatory impact within the film's world. Yet audiences didn't seem unduly disconcerted by either this technique or the jump cuts popularized by the Nouvelle Vague. Moreover, filmmakers everywhere found shot-reverse-shot such a convenient way of constructing scenes that they rarely felt the need to contravene it. Thus, it continues to be widely used to establish group dynamics, build suspense, stage fight sequences, capture reactions and record conversations in a semi-subjective and more visually arresting manner than a standard two-shot.

In order to disguise edits, it became customary to cut on action, with re-establishing shots being employed to reorientate the viewer before the reverse-angle strategy resumed. However, cheat shots are sometimes needed to imperceptibly mismatch the position of figures and objects within the mise en scène. Another tactic was point-of-view cutting, a variation on eyeline matching that Alfred Hitchcock used to ingenious effect in *Rear Window* (1954).

Hitchcock also excelled at match cuts and disciple Brian De Palma

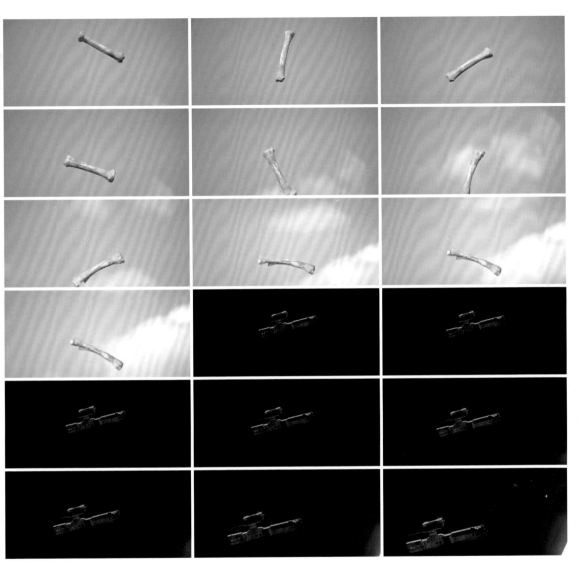

similarly demonstrated how they could juxtapose images to shock effect in the psionic chiller, *Carrie* (1976). Graphic cuts, or raccords, also serve a metaphorical purpose, such as the bone used as a weapon by the ape in Stanley Kubrick's *2001: A Space Odyssey* (1968) transforming into a spacecraft with a nuclear payload as it flies through the air.

Conversely, Alain Resnais utilized graphically discontinuous editing in the Holocaust documentary *Night and Fog* (1955). This method of conceptual connection has since recurred in avant-garde films like Bruce Conner's *A Movie* (1958) and Kenneth Anger's *Scorpio Rising* (1964), as well as poetic Godfrey Reggio travelogues such as *Koyaanisqatsi* (1982) and found-footage compilations like Gustav Deutsch's *Film Ist. A Girl & a Gun* (2009). ∎

An iconic match cut across millions of years of human evolution, as a prehistoric bone becomes an orbiting satellite in 2001: A Space Odyssey *(1968).*

MABEL NORMAND

A thriving nickelodeon in Waco, Texas, the home of Thomas Tally who opened Los Angeles's first movie venue, the Electric Theatre, in 1902.

INSET: Silent star Mabel Normand started out as a model for the illustrated song slides that accompanied the singalongs that were popular with nickelodeon audiences

Perfecting the supply of entertainment for the masses

IDEA № 14

NICKELODEONS

Anticipating the modern theme park ride, Hale's Tours presented travelogues from 1906 in theatres designed to resemble railway carriages.

Moving theatres were largely an itinerant novelty before Harry Davis opened The Nickelodeon in Pittsburgh in June 1905. Such was its success it soon had 42 city rivals; by the end of 1906, 2,500 nickelodeons had opened nationwide, leading to a revolution in the way films were viewed, distributed and produced in America

Within four years, 26 million Americans were going to the movies each week and, by 1914, there were 14,000 'nickelodeons' – from the slang for a five-cent coin – in competition with the emerging **dream palaces**. Some were dirty and disreputable, but the majority were well maintained and varied in size from 99-seaters to converted music halls capable of accommodating several hundred people at a time.

Despite Louis Lumière's conviction that moving images would be a passing fad, they remained a profitable attraction well into the 1900s in vaudeville theatres, fairground booths, church halls and anywhere else opportunistic showmen could secure a booking. From around 1902, however, travelogues, news items and **trick films** were used as 'chasers' in American vaudeville theatres to disperse malingerers and cinema only regained its popularity through a combination of narratives and nickelodeons.

Future moguls like Adolph Zukor, Carl Laemmle, Louis B. Mayer and the Warner brothers were among the first nickelodeon owners, and they turned film-going into a national habit by opening 16 hours a day, so that shoppers and workers as well as those seeking some evening escapism could pop in to catch the 20- to 30-minute programmes. Immigrants relished entertainments that didn't tax their language skills, but the bulk of the audience was made up of children and women over 30. Proprietors sought to entice middle-class families by leavening their programmes with illustrated songs and vaudeville acts.

The films themselves were silent, but most were accompanied by live renditions or recordings of popular songs that interpreted the complexities of their nascent storytelling style. Larger venues offered narrators or actors playing out scenarios in the wings. Some even invested in machines to provide sound effects, but most relied on their pianists to produce atmospheric accompaniment and film-makers responded by incorporating musical action into their pictures.

On Thanksgiving Day 1908, William Fox's Dewey Theatre in New York sold 12,000 tickets. The need for regular programme changes in order to maintain such numbers had led to the formation of film exchanges that rented out the latest releases. But while output trebled in the early part of 1908, the trust controlling American cinema – the Edison Trust comprising Edison, Biograph, Vitagraph, Lubin and Selig Polyscope – couldn't cope with demand and two-thirds of the films shown in the States had to be imported, mostly from France and Britain.

Indigenous newcomers rose to the production challenge, among them Kalem, Essanay, Nestor and Champion. The French companies Pathé and Eclair also founded US studios, as did the first female director, Alice Guy Blaché, and the first named film star, Florence Lawrence, well in advance of the formation of United Artists in 1919 (see **US Independent Cinema**).

The nickelodeon boom ended with the coming of features. But by then it had already laid the foundations that would enable Hollywood to dominate the global market after European production collapsed during the Great War. ∎

The imposing Babylonian set for the Belshazzar's Feast sequence in D.W. Griffith's Intolerance (1916).

A better class of entertainment

FILM D'ART

A poster for Queen Elizabeth *(1912), the film d'art that helped change American audiences' attitudes to cinema.*

Many critics have blamed films d'art for retarding the development of cinema as an autonymous art form by forcing it to accommodate existing literary and theatrical orthodoxies. But the historical adaptations and reconstructions of classics earned cinema a new social and moral respectability with middle-class patrons and launched the superspectacle.

Moving pictures were still primarily the preserve of fairgrounds and **nickelodeons** when a company called Le Film d'Art sought to increase their aesthetic and intellectual appeal by presenting France's leading thespians in a series of prestigious literary and theatrical adaptations. Featuring members of the Comedie Française, André Calmettes and Charles Le Bargy's *The Assassination of the Duc de Guise* (1908) was scripted by Academician Henri Lavedan and boasted a specially commissioned score by Camille Saint-Saëns. As it was photographed with a static camera in medium shots against painted backdrops, the film has usually been dismissed as stagily grandiloquent. However, the restrained acting and deft use of period props, off-screen space and cutting on action impressed producers across Europe and America, who imitated the Film d'Art style to adapt works by Shakespeare, Hugo, Dickens and Tolstoy, as well as numerous operas and ballets.

The new audience was not only willing to sit through longer films, but was also prepared to pay extra for the privilege. This fact was not lost on Adolph Zukor, who acquired the American rights to Louis Mercanton's 50-minute four-reeler *Queen Elizabeth* (1912) and charged $1 for a ticket to see the divine Sarah Bernhardt in action. Indeed, Zukor made such a handsome profit that he launched the Famous Players Film Company, which became the cornerstone of Paramount Pictures, one of the founders of the Hollywood **studio system**.

Yet it was in Italy that the film d'art reached its peak. With its breathtaking chariot race and Roman conflagration, not to mention its 5,000 extras and Colosseum sequence with real lions, Enrico Guazzoni's *Quo Vadis?* (1913) could lay claim to being the first blockbuster. However, it was quickly surpassed by Giovanni Pastrone's landmark feature *Cabiria* (1914), which cost over one million lire and took over six months to shoot on lavish, three-dimensional sets in Turin, as well as on location in Sicily, the Alps and Tunisia.

The scope and scale were imposing. But, most importantly, Pastrone and Spanish cameraman Segundo de Chomón shattered the film d'art's enclosed theatricality by experimenting with lighting designs, special effects, crane shots and slow tracking shots. Moreover, they took the viewer into the heart of the action (in anticipation of the mise en scène technique refined by Jean Renoir, Orson Welles and Max Ophüls) and goaded D.W. Griffith into attempting to top these Italian superspectacles with his Civil War epic *The Birth of a Nation* (1915) and *Intolerance* (1916), whose episodes in ancient Babylon, biblical Judea and sixteenth-century France render it the most ambitious film d'art of them all.

The readiness of lauded stage divas such as Bernhardt and Gabrielle Réjane to appear before the camera did much to raise the status of screen acting, while the bourgeois acceptance of flickers prompted the construction of the first dream palaces. But film d'art's most significant contribution was the inspiration it afforded directors determined to escape the proscenium and produce pictures that were wholly cinematic. ∎

Size matters

DEATH OF DAN KELLY & STEVE HART

FROM LEFT TO RIGHT: *Gun-toting desperadoes: Dan Kelly (Sam Crewes) and Steve Hart (Mr McKenzie) in the first feature film,* The Story of the Kelly Gang *(1906), and McTeague (Gibson Gowland) and Marcus (Jean Hersholt) in Erich von Stroheim's butchered masterpiece,* Greed *(1924).*

IDEA № 16
FEATURE FILMS

It's hard to imagine the impact that Australian Charles Tait's hour-long *The Story of the Kelly Gang* (1906) had on audiences accustomed to ten-minute one-reelers. If the first movie-goers were content to marvel at actualities and trick films, film-makers reared on novels and stage plays had grander artistic ambitions.

The transformation of the flickering novelty into a sophisticated narrative medium would not have been possible without the Latham Loop, which prevented intermittent camera and projector mechanisms from tearing celluloid strips exceeding 100 feet in length. However, Thomas Edison disputed the Latham family's ownership of the patent and sparked a war between his Motion Picture Patents Company and a loose cabal of independent producers, who eventually established a base in Hollywood.

The impetus to switch to longer films, however, came from Europe. Presenting 30 tableaux in some 14 minutes, Georges Méliès's *A Trip to the Moon* (1902) was almost three times longer than its competition. But it was a combination of films d'art such as *Queen Elizabeth* (1912) and Italian superspectacles like *Quo Vadis?* (1913)

that not only inspired D.W. Griffith to move into features with *Judith of Bethulia* (1913), but also prompted entrepreneur Adolph Zukor to form a distribution company and persuade exhibitors to rent pictures instead of purchasing them outright and abandon their nickelodeons for the more opulent dream palaces that attracted a better educated clientele.

The switch to features just as Europe was being engulfed by the Great War enabled Hollywood to forge its enduring hegemony over world cinema. Film-making became a business, with shooting schedules being drawn up around the screenplays that replaced the more improvisatory approach to making shorts. Built with the profits features generated, studios gave directors greater control over décor, lighting and technique as they refined screen grammar to form a

universal silent language that could tell stories across the generic range in the most visually innovative and accessible manner.

Yet few Hollywood film-makers had complete artistic freedom, as features formed part of cinema programmes that screened a certain number of times each day to ensure optimum ticket sales. Consequently, Erich von Stroheim had his nine-hour, 42-reel masterpiece *Greed* (1924) slashed to ten reels by MGM. In the sound era, A features averaged out at 90 minutes and **B movies** at around an hour. But Victor Fleming's 226-minute *Gone with the Wind* (1939) demonstrated the commercial potential of roadshow specials, which allowed the studios to charge inflated prices for screenings in prestigious venues. Extents grew even more epic as the studios came to rely on scale to arrest declining attendances.

ABOVE: *Scarlett O'Hara (Vivien Leigh) among the wounded Confederate soldiers at the Atlanta railroad depot in* Gone with the Wind *(1939).*

BELOW: *While Phil Jutzi's 1931 version of Alfred Döblin's* Berlin Alexanderplatz *ran for 85 minutes, Rainer Werner Fassbinder's 1980 version (shown here) lasted 931 minutes.*

Running times continued to increase into the blockbuster era. But there have been arthouse and avant-garde behemoths, too, with even Rainer Werner Fassbinder's 931-minute *Berlin Alexanderplatz* (1980) and Jacques Rivette's 773-minute *Out 1: Noli me tangere* (1971) finding themselves dwarfed by Gérard Courant's *Cinématon* (1978–2009), a silent aggregation of 2,269 vignettes that sprawled over the years to 151 hours. ∎

A little middle-class luxury

IDEA № 17

DREAM PALACES

Still Europe's biggest cinema chain, the British Odeon company was founded in 1928 by Oscar Deutsch, who claimed the name stood for 'Oscar Deutsch Entertains Our Nation'.

By the mid-1910s, going to the flickers had become a national pastime in America. Exhibitors were so eager to provide patrons with unrivalled escapism that architects were designing movie theatres in imitation of 'the most palatial homes of princes and crowned kings for and on behalf of His Excellency – the American Citizen'.

The earliest audiences had done their viewing in the far less salubrious surroundings of fairground booths, circus tents and vaudeville houses. Even the nickelodeons that had proliferated after 1905 offered little more than a hard bench and an accompanying pianist. But while these storefront venues were deemed adequate for immigrants and proletarians, they failed to entice the middle classes who had been impressed by theatre screenings of spectacles like *Queen Elizabeth* (1912) and *The Birth of a Nation* (1915). Realizing that this new, respectable clientele was willing to pay inflated prices for features, exhibitors rushed to emulate the first supercinema that had opened in New York in 1913, Thomas W. Lamb's 1,845-seat Regent.

Four thousand movie theatres were built over the next decade, as Lamb, John Eberson, George Rapp and Charles S. Lee plundered architectural styles from Europe and Asia to give ordinary folks a taste of luxury. Samuel L. Rothapfel took Broadway by storm with the Strand, Rialto, Rivoli and Roxy, which were surpassed in exoticism by Sid Grauman's Million Dollar, Egyptian and Chinese theatres in Los Angeles. But cities across the States – and, indeed, the world – had their own dream palaces, complete with marble foyers, chandeliers, gilded plasterwork, carpets, tapestries, murals, sweeping staircases, fountains and air-conditioning. Many had liveried staff and their own orchestras, which would accompany the live acts that enhanced the evening's entertainment.

But most Americans saw their films in smaller venues and, reflecting the burgeoning consumer culture, they demanded value for money. Consequently, Hollywood began producing live-action and animated **shorts**, **serials** and **newsreels** to offer balanced programmes before the main feature. As Art Deco became the dominant building style and the Depression began to bite, the B movie appeared, along with intermissions to boost concession takings. In other bids to arrest slumping receipts, studio-owned chains and independents alike introduced Saturday matinees for kids, 'midnight rambles' for African-Americans, and bingo and raffles for the impecunious. Weekly admissions still dropped by a third in 1932 and 8,000 venues closed nationwide.

However, it wasn't just the small exhibitor saddled with block booking and the cost of converting to sound who perished. The chains belonging to the Big Five studios – MGM, Paramount, Warners, Fox and RKO – were also decimated before they were finally sold after the imposition of the 1948 Paramount Decrees which prevented the studios from owning their own cinemas. As the viewing habits of a newly suburbanized populace changed, dozens of gaudily grand edifices were demolished or refurbished. But the manner in which they had promoted and presented pictures made them pivotal to Hollywood's Golden Age, as their grosses kept the studios active and dictated generic output. Moreover, they instigated the moviegoing habit that has sustained American cinema through subsequent downturns and enabled it to retain its global supremacy by generating commercial successes for export. ∎

Opened in 1928, John Eberson's French Renaissance-style Paradise Theatre in Chicago closed in 1956, as its domed ceiling made the acoustics unsuitable for talkies.

'The majority of scripts are organic documents that can be amended throughout the shoot.'

John Turturro as the intellectual struggling to script a Wallace Beery wrestling picture in Joel and Ethan Coen's Hollywood satire, **Barton Fink** *(1991).*

The undervalued writer's craft

IDEA № 18
SHOOTING SCRIPTS

Cinema started out without scripts and it's still possible to make a film without one today. As a result, the writer's status has been much contested over the last century. But as running times grew longer and budgets larger, the script became the keystone of the Hollywood factory system.

In 1909, the Motion Picture Patents Company decided that all movies should run for a single reel of 1,000 feet. This standardization transformed the American film industry by simplifying existing systems of distribution and exhibition. However, it also had a major impact on the way that pictures were made, as producers like Thomas Ince began insisting on the use of shooting or scenario scripts, which not only provided a narrative outline for the director to follow, but also a logistical breakdown that allowed schedules to become rationalized so that costumes, props, equipment and performers were always on the optimum location or set in order to save time and money.

Despite Jean-Luc Godard once saying that a film should have a beginning, a middle and an end, but not necessarily in that order, the classical American screenplay has usually adhered to Aristotelian principles and operated within generic guidelines to pitch the main protagonist(s) into a dramatic or comic situation that compels them to become better people in resolving a conflict. Equating one page with a minute of screen time, the majority of scripts are organic documents that can be amended throughout the shoot by the omission of scenes or the addition of new material on numbered and colour-coded pages. A script or continuity clerk maintains a record of changes made during production to ensure that information within the frame remains consistent between edit points. Yet while shooting scripts are as essential on most sets as storyboards, Hollywood writers haven't always been treated with much respect.

Scenarios weren't copyrighted until 1912 and silent credits rarely reflected a writer's input. Even after the studios invited pre-eminent novelists, journalists and playwrights to California on the coming of sound, they were often poorly paid and had to endure their work – much of which was adapted from pre-sold sources – being revised by in-house hacks and script doctors. The Writers Guild was founded in 1933, but it was powerless to prevent writers (many of whom were women) from repeatedly being consigned to genres in which they had a proven track record or specialisms such as story progression, dialogue and gags.

As directors contributed more frequently to their screenplays in Europe, the writer's art was better appreciated there. Nevertheless, François Truffaut still denounced the 'Tradition of Quality' that emerged in postwar French screenwriting and his positing of **auteur theory** encouraged more film-makers to imbue scripts with their own personality. Yet while some directors prefer improvising or working from treatments, most still rely on the annotated shooting script, despite the old Hollywood maxim that nobody ever bought a ticket to see a screenplay. ■

Boris Karloff studies the shooting script for Karl Freund's The Mummy *(1932), in which he plays both Ardath Bey and the reanimated Imhotep.*

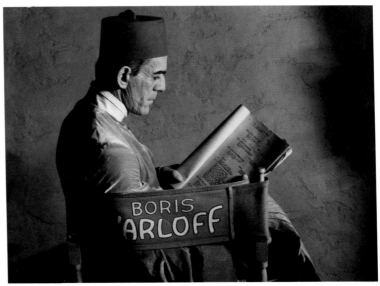

Making magic live on set

ABOVE, LEFT: *Stumbling in the dark: Robert Krasker's masterly use of light and shade plunges Holly Martins (Joseph Cotton) into confusion in* The Third Man *(1949).*

ABOVE: *Peter Jackson combined effects techniques from the silent and digital eras in the* Lord of the Rings *trilogy (2001–03).*

IDEA № 19
IN-CAMERA EFFECTS

Imagery composited in post-production may seem more authentic to modern eyes, but considerable artistry and ingenuity went into the in-camera effects – from shutter shifts to the use of matte paintings to conjure bygone or imaginary worlds – that were produced on set during cinema's first few decades.

Visual effects have been entrancing audiences since the days of the Kinetoscope. Georges Méliès was quick to recognize the potential of trick techniques and his use of stop-motion and multiple exposures in *Cinderella* (1899) and *The One-Man Band* (1900) demonstrated that moving images could do more than record realism. However, Edwin S. Porter gave effects a dramatic function in *The Great Train Robbery* (1903) and D.W. Griffith and the French Impressionists were prime among those to show how fades, irises, dissolves and superimpositions were as central to the language of silent cinema as the movement and positioning of the camera.

Devised by Norman Dawn, matte paintings conjured such illusory environments as the Emerald City in *The Wizard of Oz* (1939) and the Statue of Liberty beach in *Planet of the Apes* (1968).

Equally effective at reducing set construction costs or overcoming the difficulties of runaway shooting outside the studio was the Schüfftan process, which used a semi-transparent mirror at an angle of 45 degrees to the camera to reflect images of landscapes or miniature buildings to create the illusion of actors in apparently vast settings. Perfected by German cinematographer Eugen Schüfftan on *Metropolis* (1926), it was much used by Alfred Hitchcock and revived by Peter Jackson for *The Lord of the Rings: The Return of the King* (2003).

The Dunning-Pomeroy self-matting bipack, which facilitated a primitive form of blue-screen shooting, offered a variation in *Tarzan the Ape Man* (1932). But both systems were rendered obsolete by rear projection, which utilized translucent screens to embellish street scenes, travel sequences and chases after the advent of sound made outdoor shooting more problematic. The introduction of a triple-projector format allowed colour backdrops, but front projection became the standard after Douglas Trumbull achieved bigger, brighter and more detailed images for *2001: A Space Odyssey* (1968). Yet despite the subsequent efficacy of front projection systems, compositing has almost exclusively become a digital domain.

Spectacle and speed are the hallmarks of the blockbuster, but filmmakers have long been tinkering with velocity. Undercranking gave silent slapstick its distinctive faster-than-life pace when the footage was projected, while the likes of Jean Cocteau, Akira Kurosawa, Martin Scorsese and John Woo have employed the opposite effect, slow motion, either to heighten drama and suspense or to increase set-piece viscerality. Although primarily used comically, reverse motion can also have a disconcerting impact, as can rack focus, dolly **zooms**, slit scans, speed ramps and time-lapse and bullet-time sequences. So always look closely, not every cinematic *trompe-l'oeil* is CGI. ∎

Martin Scorsese used close-ups and slow motion to emphasize the brutality of the boxing bouts in **Raging Bull** *(1980).*

Betty Hutton relives the glory days of the silent serial in **The Perils of Pauline,** *a 1947 biopic of the legendary chapterplay heroine, Pearl White.*

The rise of the cliffhanger

IDEA № 20
SERIALS

ABOVE: *Buster Crabbe with Frank Shannon (Dr Zarkov) and Jean Rogers (Dale Arden) in* Flash Gordon's Trip to Mars *(1938).*

BELOW: *Poster for Edward Sedgwick's 20-part* Fantomas *(1920), which references French serial master Louis Feuillade's 1913 original.*

Over 470 serials were produced in the United States between 1912 and 1956. In telling continuous stories in 10–15 weekly episodes of 15–25 minutes each, chapterplays, as they were also known, helped turn cinema-going into a habit. Moreover, their legacy lives on in the Hollywood blockbuster.

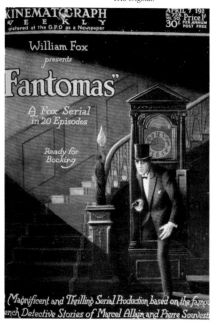

Serialization had been a standard literary practice long before Edison released *What Happened to Mary?* in conjunction with *McClure's Ladies' World* magazine in 1912. But it was *The Adventures of Kathlyn* (1913) that instigated the silent serial boom by melding the sensationalism of dime novels, populist theatre and movie melodrama into an episodic format that pitted feisty heroines against fiendish villains and their infernal machines. The plots relied more on contrivance, coincidence and convolution than continuity and character. But each instalment promised copious action and a cliffhanging climax, and serial queens such as Kathlyn Williams, Grace Cunard, Ruth Roland and Pearl White became so popular that production rose from six titles in 1914 to 28 in 1920.

Coinciding with the nascent feature film, American serials exploited forces of nature, technology, chase sequences and last-minute rescues to create spectacle across the generic range. Cut-price imitations were produced in Britain, Norway, Denmark, Germany, Italy and Spain. But nothing could match Louis Feuillade's *Fantômas* (1913), *Les Vampires* (1915) and *Judex* (1916), which introduced a so-phistication and psychological depth that Hollywood made little attempt to emulate as sound turned the chapterplay into an escapist format that was aimed primarily at Saturday matinee audiences and saw the plucky heroine being replaced by action men in jungle, aviation, espionage and crime adventures, as well as Western, science-fiction and superhero sagas.

Minor major studios like Columbia and Universal and Hollywood's low-budget Poverty Row outfits such as Republic dominated the scene. With Roy Rogers and Gene Autry among its stars and William Witney and John English as its principal directors, Republic could also call upon the services of special effects wizards Howard and Theodore Lydecker and stuntmen like Yakima Canutt to keep titles thrilling, on deadline and within budget. By contrast, Universal could splash out $250,000 on *Flash Gordon* (1936) and cash in by re-editing it and its sequels as features.

During the 1930s, troubleshooters such as Buster Crabbe, Ralph Byrd, Tom Tyler and Kane Richmond took their roles as seriously as cowboys Buck Jones, Johnny Mack Brown, Ken Maynard and John Wayne. But once serialdom had finished battling the wartime Axis powers, brawn replaced brain and an element of camp began creeping into action increasingly dependent upon clichéd situations and stock footage. An attempt was even made with Frances Gifford, Kay Aldridge and Linda Sterling to revive the imperilled heroine rubric. But the Paramount Decrees impacted heavily upon the serial, as did television, which adapted the chapter format for its long-running series. Consequently, studio production ceased with Columbia's *Blazing the Overland Trail* in 1956.

Yet the influence that chapterplays exerted on directors such as George Lucas and Steven Spielberg is readily evident in the similarity between Darth Vader in the *Star Wars* films and The Lightning in *The Fighting Devil Dogs* (1938), and Indiana Jones and the eponymous hero of *Don Winslow of the Navy* (1942). Moreover, corporate Hollywood's enduring fixation with superheroes also has its antecedents in serials featuring Superman, Batman, Captain America, the Green Hornet, Buck Rogers and the Lone Ranger. ■

ABOVE: *An accident waiting to happen: Stan Laurel and Oliver Hardy about to reduce calm to chaos in* **The Finishing Touch** *(1928).*

LEFT: *The master and the student: Charlie Chaplin's Little Tramp character was dubbed a shabby version of Max Linder's dandy.*

From knockabout to gross-out

IDEA № 21

SLAPSTICK

Screen comedy comes in many forms but the most enduring is slapstick. This did much to popularize moving images with the first audiences worldwide since the physical antics of characters striving to retain dignity – as everything around them descended into chaos – were much less culturally specific than verbal humour.

ABOVE: *Showcasing their brand of verbal slapstick,* Duck Soup *(1933) was the last Marx Brothers comedy featuring Groucho, Chico, Harpo and Zeppo.*

BELOW: *Oh behave!: Mike Myers laced the action of* Austin Powers: International Man of Mystery *(1997) with both slapstick and double entendres.*

Slapstick was named after the *battacio*, or 'slap stick', which made a dramatic popping sound when actors hit one another with it and which was used in the Commedia dell'arte, an Italian stage tradition whose blend of stereotype, sketch and shtick was passed down through circus and pantomime to vaudeville and burlesque and into cinema. Many early gag films plagiarized popular variety turns and comic strips, but the fast-moving knockabout also reflected everyday experience in increasingly mechanized urban sprawls. Silent slapstick invariably contained an element of social commentary.

Louis Lumière's *L'Arroseur arrosé* (1895) cracked the first screen joke and several French comedy series proved vital to the development of film grammar and technique. Moreover, shorts featuring André Deed as Boireau (1906–09), Charles Prince as Rigadin (1909–20) and Ernest Bourbon as Onésime (1910–14) also allowed their stars creative input, with Max Linder virtually becoming a slapstick auteur in the shorts he made between 1910 and 1917, which considerably influenced Charlie Chaplin in Hollywood.

Chaplin debuted in 1914 for Mack Sennett, whose Keystone Studio had launched Mabel Normand, Fatty Arbuckle and Harry Langdon. Dubbed 'the King of Comedy', Sennett advocated a fast, abrasive style known as 'socko' that pitched his seemingly indestructible Keystone Kops and Bathing Beauties into breakneck chases, high-rise perils, encounters with recalcitrant props, and all manner of pratfalls and assaults.

However, Chaplin found such frantic buffoonery crude and shifted the emphasis to character and situation, while still using knockabout to humanize and subvert his Little Tramp's travails in a hostile society. Harold Lloyd similarly adopted a more genteel approach in creating his trademark go-getter, and his comedy of thrills was surpassed only by Buster Keaton's mastery of outsize props, which was integrated into the narrative with a fluency and precision that allowed him to headline self-generated features, while early comedy stars such as Ben Turpin, Chester Conklin and Snub Pollard drifted into walk-on obscurity.

However, Keaton was one of many clowns to struggle in the sound era, with only the Hal Roach duo of Stan Laurel and Oliver Hardy, and their Danish counterparts Carl Schenstrøm and Harald Madsen, making an entirely successful transition. The Marx Brothers, W.C. Fields, Charley Chase, Abbott and Costello, and the Three Stooges incorporated slapstick into their films. It also became a mainstay of cartoons such as *Tom and Jerry*.

Yet, despite the efforts of Jacques Tati, slapstick became just another

comic component in madcap romps such as *It's a Mad Mad Mad Mad World* (1963) and the films of Jerry Lewis. Jim Carrey exaggerated Lewis's divisive brand of mugging in the 1990s. But as physical comedy grew more infantile in the *Home Alone*, *American Pie* and *Austin Powers* franchises, as well as in the gross-outings of the Farrelly brothers, the slapstick contained in Bollywood masalas and Hong Kong chop-socky continued to hark back to more innocent times. ∎

Doubling up for daredevilry

IDEA № 22
STUNTS

The Hollywood maxim 'pain is temporary, film is forever' is a little glib. But it could stand as an epitaph to the stuntmen and -women who have lost their lives bringing spectacle and authenticity to movies since Frank Hanaway was shot off his horse in Edwin S. Porter's *The Great Train Robbery* (1903).

The first stuntmen – there were very few stuntwomen in the early days of cinema – were acrobats, rodeo riders, athletes and body builders, who relied as much on physical courage as technique. The same was true of cowboy Tom Mix and Keystone's slapstick clowns. By contrast, Mack Sennett's high-speed antics were meticulously staged, by ex-racing driver Del Lord, and both Buster Keaton and Harold Lloyd planned their stunts to the last detail to ensure they were as safe as they were hilariously prodigious. Douglas Fairbanks similarly spent hours rehearsing his swashbuckling bravura. But shorter schedules meant greater risks for those stunting in serials. Moreover, stuntmen were rarely credited since producers wished the thrill-seeking public to think that the daredevilry of stars like Pearl White and Charles 'the Thrill-a-Minute Stunt King' Hutchinson was all their own work.

During the silent era, stuntmen such as Gene Perkins and Harvey Parry braved fire, water and wild beasts to keep the action as sensational as possible, while Al Wilson and Dick Grace took to the skies in aerial adventures like the first Oscar winner, *Wings* (1927). In the process of satisfying their audience's craving for cliffhangers, mid-air rescues, punch-ups and chases, 10,794 injuries were sustained shooting Hollywood films between 1925–30, with 55 of them being fatal. Many horses were also killed by the pit fall and Running W trip methods, which were outlawed in 1940 after the American Humane

Wire fu techniques allow Nameless (Jet Li) and Sky (Donnie Yen) to duel in mid-air in Zhang Yimou's wuxia classic, Hero *(2002).*

Association secured access to sets to ensure that no animals were harmed during filming.

Beyond Errol Flynn actioners, stunts were largely the preserve of B movies and serials during the 1930s. But masters of the stunt performer's art like Yakima Canutt and B. Reeves Eason also enlivened prestige pictures such as *Stagecoach* and *Gone with the Wind* (both 1939), and the daring set-piece became a key element of widescreen epics such as *Ben-Hur* (1959). As the studio era ended, however, the emphasis shifted away from classical antiquity and the Wild West and onto the modern metropolis, where Cary Loftin perfected the car chase in *Bullitt* (1968) and *Vanishing Point* (1971) after 30 years of devising blow-outs, skids, rolls and crashes.

The Bond movies set new standards for stunt work which were sustained into the blockbuster era by the likes of Hal Needham, Glenn Randall, the Corbould brothers, Jeannie Epper and Yuen Wo-Ping. Moreover, despite insurance pressures, Sylvester Stallone, Jackie Chan and Tom Cruise maintained the tradition of stars doing their own stunts. The emergence of new breakaway, squib and pyrotechnic processes, as well as such techniques as wire fu, demonstrates the continuing ingenuity and vibrancy of physical stunting. But the audience's insatiable demand for ever more recklessly spectacular stunts has prompted the development of indestructible synthespians, whose simulated derring-do looks set to be limited only by the human imagination. ∎

RIGHT: *In* Steamboat Bill, Jr. *(1928) Buster Keaton repeats a stunt he had already performed in* Back Stage *(1919) and* One Week *(1920).*

BELOW: *Yakima Canutt doubling for John Wayne in John Ford's* Stagecoach *(1939), in which he performed another daring horse leap as an Apache.*

'Cliffhangers, mid-air rescues, punch-ups and chases.'

MOVIE STARS

MOVIE STARS PARADE   SEPTEMBER 25c

JAMES DEAN—DYNAMITE!

PDC

MARILYN'S BIG SCENES

The most iconic movie star? Marilyn Monroe boosts The Seven Year Itch *in the September 1955 issue of* Movie Stars Parade.

Selling the dream

THE STAR SYSTEM

By controlling and even reinventing actors' personas, the Hollywood star system ensured matinee idols provided proof that dreams could come true. But over the past 60 years, the freelance spirit, media prying and the rise of the internet have significantly diminished studio-controlled star mystique.

Most early screen performers were amateurs. But the switch from novelty to narrative prompted American film-makers to assemble stock companies of actors to meet demand from the nickelodeons. Stage stars deemed the early flickers beneath them and many appeared anonymously. However, a year after Thomas Edison introduced French import Pilar-Morin and the film studio Kalem identified its principal players, Independent Moving Pictures chief Carl Laemmle faked the death of Florence Lawrence to boost *The Broken Oath* (1910) and in the process launched the star system.

Such was the commodification of star identities that names were changed, biographies concocted and looks transformed in order to establish fan bases and sell tickets. Matinee idols became ideals of beauty and role models. But while every national film industry had its stars, none could rival **Hollywood** for its diversity and depth of talent. Most stars either played variations on their screen selves or became the personification of their genre. In addition to the A-listers, there were stars of B movies, series, serials and shorts as well. Children, animals and cartoon characters also found fame as the **fan magazines** colluded with studio publicity departments to glamorize the Tinseltown lifestyle.

However, Fatty Arbuckle's notorious manslaughter trial and the shocking deaths of William Desmond Taylor and Wallace Reid led to a code of 'Don'ts

and Be Carefuls' being imposed upon Hollywood in the early 1920s and the studios became much more protective of their assets. Signed to lucrative but restrictive deals (which often included morality clauses), bankable talkie stars traded their individuality for plum roles, soft-lit close-ups and covert support if their private lives threatened to become too public. Thus, while Clark Gable and Myrna Loy reigned contentedly as the King and Queen of Hollywood, more intransigent icons such as Bette Davis and Olivia de Havilland found themselves on frequent suspension for refusing roles.

During World War II Davis played a prominent part in the Hollywood Canteen for service personnel, while the likes of James Stewart saw action in Europe. Stewart was also one of the first stars to go freelance, as agents grew more powerful and packages and percentages replaced contracts and coercion. Moreover, as older stars drifted into television, newcomers such as Burt Lancaster and Kirk Douglas set up their own production companies, while Marlon Brando – who was neither typically photogenic nor studio-fashioned – introduced the **Method acting** style and African-American Sidney Poitier landed mainstream leads.

At the same time, the rise of rock'n'roll created a rival form of stardom and, although movie stars like Tom Cruise and Julia Roberts retained their commercial value into the block-

BELOW: *The keeper of the flame: Bollywood superstar Aishwarya Rai in Sanjay Leela Bhansali's* Devdas *(2002).*

BOTTOM: *Rescued from a war zone, German Shepherd Rin Tin Tin made 26 pictures for Warners between 1922–31 and saved the studio from bankruptcy.*

buster era, concept and spectacle came to matter more than celebrity in the new cinema of CGI attractions. Event movies now open as much through internet buzz as stellar presence, and while movie royalty continues to exist, it is now more prominent in Bollywood than Hollywood. ∎

Hooray for Hollywood!

IDEA № 24

HOLLYWOOD

Without Hollywood, there would be no Bollywood, Lollywood (in Pakistan) or Nollywood (Nigeria). There also wouldn't have been variations on the studio system in Britain, France, Germany and Japan. But the American movie capital might just as easily have been Jacksonville, Florida or even Cuba.

Frankly my dear: Rhett Butler (Clark Gable) and Scarlett O'Hara (Vivien Leigh) in David O. Selznick's Gone With the Wind *(1939).*

Despite the myth, this former orange-growing backwater some seven miles north-west of central Los Angeles was not chosen for its proximity to Mexico to permit independents defying the Motion Picture Patents Company (see **Feature Films** and **Shooting Scripts**) to slip across the border to avoid enforcer gangs. More persuasively, it offered long hours of sunshine and mild winters to guarantee the all-year production required to keep the thriving nickelodeons supplied. Hollywood's other attractions included a low tax base, plentiful labour, limited union interference, cheap real estate and a diverse landscape within a 50-mile radius that could stand in for anywhere in the world.

Selig Polyscope led the way, shooting *The Count of Monte Cristo* there in 1907 and establishing the first permanent studio in 1909. Within six years, 60 per cent of all American pictures were being made in Hollywood. Thomas Ince's industrial rationalization of production and Adolph Zukor's systems of vertical integration, by which a studio owned the means of production, distribution and exhibition, and **block booking** enabled the Wall Street-backed studios to churn out the star-driven, generic features that captured the global market in the wake of the Great War. Moreover, this commercial dominance allowed the Big Five studios to introduce technical innovations such as sound, colour and widescreen that became integral to film-making everywhere and helped Hollywood survive the economic crises wrought by the Depression and the post-World War II combination of suburban migration, television, rising costs and the Paramount Decrees.

Lasting from the early sound era to the coming of television, Hollywood's fabled Golden Age was comparatively short, but what André Bazin called 'the genius of the system' enabled it to expedite a switch from mass production to creative co-operation and the collective control of distribution. As the studios were then swallowed up by multinational conglomerates, they began sponsoring pictures developed by independent producers, directors or stars, packaged by talent agencies or **co-production** partners, and made on leased soundstages or at runaway locations. Yet the Hollywood brand retained its potency, which was reinvigorated by the blockbusters that caught the international imagination and reinforced its box-office hegemony through post-production special effects that no other industry could afford on a similar scale, let alone generate to such a high standard.

Reaganomic deregulation further enhanced Hollywood's ability to react to changing circumstances, and the corporations governing the studios since the 1980s have exploited the shift in audience demographics, the home-entertainment boom and the opening up of the old Soviet bloc and China by adopting the synergy strategy that ties movies into soundtrack albums, video games, meal deals, toys, TV and cartoon series, novelizations, comic books, stage shows and theme-park rides. Indeed, Hollywood is now less a film community than a business opportunity, and its reliance on pre-sold properties like adaptations, remakes and sequels means that it takes increasingly fewer artistic risks. Yet even though it is now only the world's third-largest film industry in terms of output (behind Bollywood and Nollywood), its cultural and commercial predominance will remain unchallenged for the foreseeable future. ∎

'Hollywood is now less a film community than a business opportunity.'

Erected on Mount Lee in 1923 to advertise a real estate development, the famous 450ft-long sign read 'Hollywoodland' until 1949.

The men behind the magic

Scriptwriter-turned-executive,
Darryl F. Zanuck supervised
production at 20th Century-Fox
between 1934–56 and 1962–71.

IDEA № 25
MOVIE MOGULS

Few men were more revered or reviled than the moguls who ran Hollywood during its Golden Age. Despotic, temperamental and poorly educated, these opportunistic showmen nevertheless had an instinctive grasp of popular tastes and used the vertically integrated structure they imposed upon the American film industry to entertain the world.

Having scratched livings in various trades, the majority of the moguls – most of whom were of Eastern European Jewish descent – stumbled into movies as the owners of penny arcades, nickelodeons or distribution agencies. William Fox and Carl Laemmle turned to production in a bid to break the Edison Trust (see **The Kinetoscope** and **Nickelodeons**), with their immigrant experience teaching them the value of universally accessible pictures, which became a Hollywood hallmark. Laemmle also recognized the importance of stars and ballyhoo to the longer features that he pioneered in the wake of Adolph Zukor's success with the imported film d'art *Queen Elizabeth* (1912). He also founded the Universal City studio complex in 1915, which confirmed Hollywood's hegemony over an increasingly industrialized business.

Indeed, Laemmle, Fox, Zukor, Samuel Goldwyn, Louis B. Mayer, Harry Cohn and the four Warner brothers were tantamount to front-office auteurs, who not only managed the daily operation of their studios, but also set the tone for the kind of pictures they produced. Laemmle encouraged a Germanic influence at Universal, while Zukor's approach at Paramount was more chicly continental. Mayer's MGM

became renowned for opulent, star-studded family sagas, in which virtue was rewarded during the happy ending. Cohn attempted something similar on tighter budgets at Columbia, as did the doggedly independent Goldwyn, whose polished features had an intelligence that belied his malapropistic reputation – 'Our comedies are not to be laughed at'. Jack L. Warner, however, opted for a trenchant, pacy social realism that often brought him into conflict with the guardians of the Production Code, which strictly regulated the content of all Hollywood films from 1934 and to which the moguls had assented to prevent external interference following a spate of scandals in the 1920s (see **The Star System**).

Such co-operation typified the way the studio heads tackled social, economic and technical issues. They supported practices such as block and blind booking, as well as accepting a common sound-on-film process to facilitate the introduction of talkies. Furthermore, they shared the stars, writers and directors they controlled through iron-clad contracts, and united in protecting their investments by resisting the demands of craft guilds and trade unions and by collaborating controversially with the House UnAmerican Activities Committee (see

The Blacklist). Consequently, through a combination of gall, gumption, luck, nepotism, persistence and ruthlessness, these inveterate survivors were able to steer Hollywood through the Depression and World War II.

The moguls also occasionally exhibited artistic insight and responded with alacrity to changing trends in fashion, music, language and manners. Being of migrant stock, they also accommodated foreign talent and used their knowledge of European culture to appeal to the widest possible audience. But they had no answer to the postwar financial problems that were exacerbated by television, spiralling costs and the Paramount Decrees. However, the brand names they established enabled their studios to weather the vicissitudes of New Hollywood and flourish once again in the less romantic era of globalized multimedia conglomerations that began in the 1980s. ■

'A combination of gall, gumption, luck, nepotism, persistence and ruthlessness.'

ABOVE: *Louis B. Mayer (front centre) proving MGM's boast to have 'more stars than there are in the heavens' at the 1943 Academy Awards.*

RIGHT: *Robert De Niro headlined Elia Kazan's adaptation of F. Scott Fitzgerald's* **The Last Tycoon** *(1976), which was inspired by MGM's 'Boy Wonder' producer, Irving G. Thalberg (1899–1936).*

'Selling blocks of unseen films was inspired by traditional wholesale methods.'

The end of block booking prompted Hollywood to produce epics like **Cleopatra** *(1963), which cost $44 million but only took $26 million at the box office.*

It's a seller's market

BLOCK BOOKING

The Hollywood studio system was built on block booking. Selling blocks of unseen films was inspired by traditional wholesale methods and designed to ensure that venues always had enough product. Initially, it was considered a flexible and mutually beneficial arrangement. However, protests eventually resulted in a drastic structural realignment that transformed American film-making.

In the nickelodeon era, films were sold by the foot. But the shift to feature production necessitated the introduction of exchanges to optimize circulation. In 1914, Adolph Zukor's Paramount Pictures was formed from the merger of several exchanges and its links with Famous Players-Lasky saw production, distribution and exhibition unified within one company for the first time. Ultimately, MGM, Warners, RKO and 20th Century-Fox came to be similarly vertically integrated and, when revenue-sharing with exhibitors was introduced in the early sound era, they began to operate at full capacity and shifted the risk of production by supplementing their standard star vehicles with B movies that were guaranteed outlets at a flat rental fee by full-line forcing.

Elsewhere, minors like Universal and Columbia were heavily reliant on block booking, while Poverty Row made do with the 'states rights' regional distribution scheme of selling films on a state-by-state rather than nationwide basis. But even though United Artists abjured block booking, many independent producers felt discriminated against. Also, conservative pressure groups claimed that the system had fostered an increase in morally dubious titles. Faced with the prospect of external censorship, the studios agreed to adhere to the 1934 Production Code, forgo seasonal bookings for smaller blocks and provide exhibitors with detailed synopses of unmade movies. Nevertheless, having survived the Depression under President Roosevelt's protection, Hollywood was soon beset by crusading senators, the US Justice Department and the newly formed Society of Independent Motion Picture Producers; only World War II delayed the Supreme Court's imposition of the Paramount Decrees in May 1948, which not only outlawed block booking, but also forced the Big Five to divest themselves of their cinemas.

The timing of the decision could not have been worse, since not only were audiences declining as Americans moved to the suburbs to pursue rival pastimes like watching television, but production costs had also begun to spiral. No longer assured of sales, the studios made staff cutbacks and dispensed with programmers (see **B Movies**), cartoons and live-action shorts. They also began concentrating on prestige pictures that had to stand on their own merits. But not even widescreen, colour and stereophonic sound could prevent expensive flops such as Joseph L. Mankiewicz's *Cleopatra* (1963), and the tyranny of the bottom line turned Hollywood into a place of **sequels**, copycats and focus groups as risk-free homogeneity replaced artistic innovation and diversity.

Ironically, exhibitors were also hit by the drop in output, and the closure of smaller theatres ushered in the current age of multiplexes and block-busters, which indulges a modified form of block booking and the studio ownership of cinema chains. It also allows a film's fate to depend almost entirely upon its opening weekend takings before it is rush-released into the home-entertainment market. ■

Art as industry

THE STUDIO SYSTEM

The RKO studio on Gower Street, which was acquired by Lucille Ball's Desilu TV company in 1957 before merging a decade later with its near neighbour, Paramount.

Americans didn't invent the studio system, which integrated so many of the different operations of film-making and distribution, but they made the most effective use of it. By industrializing film production, Hollywood was able to satisfy domestic demand, dominate the global market and reinvent itself in the face of periodic setbacks.

Primarily managed by moguls of European descent, the Hollywood studios were divided into five majors (Metro-Goldwyn-Mayer, Paramount, Warner Bros, 20th Century-Fox and RKO), three minors (Universal, Columbia and United Artists) and the various 'B-hives' of Poverty Row. Most had been formed by merger in the 1920s, and New York financiers had not only kept the studios solvent during the Depression and the transition to sound, but also imposed operational and ethico-political constraints to ensure that Hollywood up-held the American Way and made money. To this end, the majors devised vertical integration, which allowed them to produce their own films, screen them in their own theatre chains and distribute them to non-aligned exhibitors through block booking.

Creative power essentially lay with the studio heads and their trusted unit producers, who developed projects with the writing and craft departments before roles were cast and directors appointed. Tight budgets and shooting schedules limited scope for spontaneity, yet auteurial talents did emerge alongside the journeymen who stuck to their scripts and storyboards in manufacturing prestige pictures, B movies and serials, as well as live-action and animated shorts.

A handful of stars were also allowed to demonstrate their versatility, but many became identified with the genres that were the staple of a conveyor-belt process that churned out common-denominator entertainment designed to eradicate the risks attendant on art films. Much production took place within the controllable studio environments of soundstages and backlots, although the diverse Californian landscape also allowed for location shooting.

Each studio had its own personality, but Hollywood was a community bound by co-operative rivalry and shared ideals and practices. Consequently, the vast majority of the 7,500 features produced between 1930 and 1945 utilized cause-and-effect linearity and invisible **continuity editing** to ensure the accessibility of action whose content was governed by the self-regulatory Production Code that was enforced between 1934 and 1968 by the Motion Picture Producers and Distributors of America to prevent interference by outside pressure groups.

However, the studio system began to unravel as the effects of television, spiralling costs, the House UnAmerican Activities Committee and the Paramount Decrees were felt in the immediate postwar period. Colour, stereo, widescreen and 3-D were all introduced in a bid to win back audiences, while mass production was abandoned in favour of leasing facilities in return for distribution rights, as part of package deals with independent producers, talent agencies and free-lance stars. Nevertheless, RKO closed in 1957 and the failure of several all-star mega-productions in the following decade left the studios prey to multinational conglomerates.

Deregulation and the blockbuster boom prompted a second round of acquisitions in the 1980s, which re-positioned the studios within multi-media groups advocating marketing synergy. Yet the old names remained, and new technology and release strategies have enabled Hollywood to expand both its international influence and its share of the thriving home-entertainment market. ∎

With its famous Bronson Gate on Marathon Street, Paramount Pictures was the first vertically integrated studio and is now the only one still based in Hollywood.

Generic iconography: a hero
in a white hat (Charles
Bronson) confronts the man
in black (Henry Fonda) in
Sergio Leone's Once Upon
a Time in the West (1968).

Cinema's universal language

RIGHT: *Alfred Hitchcock so excelled at the thriller that he was nicknamed 'The Master of Suspense'.*

BELOW: *A typical example of Douglas Sirk's melodramas that became known as 'woman's pictures' because of their target audience.*

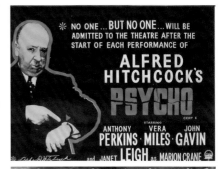

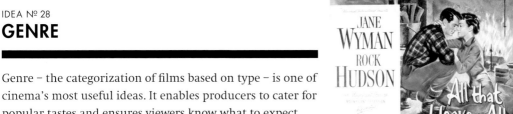

IDEA № 28

GENRE

Genre – the categorization of films based on type – is one of cinema's most useful ideas. It enables producers to cater for popular tastes and ensures viewers know what to expect each time they buy a ticket. It also allows critics to judge a movie's merits against a set of established criteria.

Although 'genre' is a literary term, its first application to film was purely industrial. The Hollywood studios ran as efficient factories and executives were keen to invest in the projects most likely to turn a profit. Genre took the guesswork out of production as core audiences existed for melodramas, comedies, Westerns, crime films, action adventures, horror, science fiction and, with the coming of sound, musicals. The recurring tropes made such generic features easier to produce and promote as they shared iconographies, techniques, settings, themes, musical motifs, characters and stars. Indeed, certain studios became known for specific genres: for instance, Warner for the gangster cycle, Universal for horror and MGM for the musical.

Genres could be broken down into sub-categories and hybridized. They could also extend into B movies, serials, documentaries, animation and the avant-garde. Yet, whatever form they took, genre films invariably reflected the socio-cultural conditions in which they were made. They were often exploited to reinforce civic values, but they could just as easily be used for escapism or disconcertion, as all genre pictures pose some sort of threat to the status quo, whether it comes in the

form of a vampire, an alien, a femme fatale or a screwball heroine.

Many film-makers found such formulaic patterns restrictive. But several auteurs flourished within the generic tradition. Howard Hawks mastered many styles, while John Ford became synonymous with Westerns, Douglas Sirk with melodramas, Vincente Minnelli with musicals and Alfred Hitchcock with thrillers. Subsequently, mavericks like Mel Brooks and Robert Altman delighted in subverting generic conventions and the dominant ideology they represented. Yet even though generic myths get burlesqued, they cyclically pass through phases of deconstruction and nostalgia back to reaffirmation, before inevitably being debunked once more.

Some Hollywood genres have slipped out of vogue, however. The Westerns and musicals that were box-office bankers in the classical era have now been replaced by effects-laden fantasies and many blame such fare for dumbing down American cinema.

Hollywood prompted the rise of genre film-making around the world as local producers sought to counter American commercial dominance. Some merely indigenized existing genres, most notably in the form of the

Spaghetti, Paella, Sauerkraut, Borscht and Curry Westerns that began appearing in the 1960s. But most had a stronger sense of national identity. Weimar Germany saw the emergence of the *Bergfilm* (mountain film) and *Heimatfilm* (homeland film), while the chic 'white telephone' comedies produced in Fascist Italy gave way to the *Peplum* (sword-and-sandal) and *giallo* (erotic, gory thriller) movie. Indian audiences revelled in historical and mythological variations on the masala musical format, while Mexicans preferred bawdy *chanchada* musical comedies and wrestling pictures. Martial-arts movies held sway in Hong Kong, while Japan's samurai and yakuza codes co-existed with such dramatic genres as the *jidai-geki* (period), *gendai-geki* (contemporary) and *shomin-geki* (common people). Anime is similarly awash with sub-genres and their influence is increasingly being felt in Hollywood's comic-book adaptations (see **Animation**). Genre has, indeed, become cinema's universal language. ∎

The thrill of the old

IDEA № 29
PRE-SOLD SOURCES

Cinema's reliance on other media for content and form has always been driven as much by commercial as by creative considerations. After all, basing a film on a pre-sold source – material that has already struck a chord with audiences in another format – significantly reduces the risk of a screen version's box office failure.

Having been translated into 67 languages and sold over 300 million copies worldwide, J.K. Rowling's Harry Potter franchise was one of the safest pre-sold bets in Hollywood history.

Proclaimed the 'seventh art' (after music, dance, painting, literature, architecture and sculpture) by Louis Delluc, cinema has never existed in aesthetic isolation. Literature played a crucial role in its evolution. The first one-reelers could only depict isolated scenes, but directors worldwide were soon attempting to précis entire novels in 20-minute dramas. By the mid-1910s, classics and bestsellers were not only aiding the development of features, they were also helping to attract a better class of viewer (see **Film d'Art**). However, critics often denounced cinema's cavalier attitude to adaptation as secondary characters and subplots were jettisoned in the process of compression. Indeed, the debate continues today as to whether a filmmaker's first duty is fidelity to their source or presenting their own unique vision of it.

Screenwriters have usually found it easier to expand upon a short story or newspaper article than to condense an entire novel; in the case of the latter, pulp crime and Western fiction has often proved easier to rework than more canonical titles. Nevertheless, devotees still complain if an adaptation is too free. Robert Bresson, Akira Kurosawa and Luchino Visconti excelled at capturing the essence of a source, yet the latter's *Death in Venice* (1971) was

denounced at the time for taking too many liberties with Thomas Mann's novella. Conversely, the **heritage** adaptations of Merchant Ivory and Claude Berri in the 1980s were attacked for illustrating rather than interpreting their source texts, although this was considered a virtue in the case of the *Harry Potter* series (2001–11).

Knowing when to retain the intimacy and immediacy of the proscenium and when to open out the action has been the primary problem facing those adapting plays. Dialogue is usually sacrosanct where master dramatists are concerned, but stylized stage speeches have tended to be toned down since the early sound era, when verbose photoplays were often dismissed as 'canned theatre'. But plays, operas and musicals are no longer filmed with such frequency and modern spin-offs are more likely to come from television programmes, comic books and video games.

Syndicated in daily newspapers, cartoon strips epitomized popular culture around cinema's inception. These comic cuts and ongoing adventures were soon inspiring **serials** and **series** in Europe and America alike. Comic books similarly hit the screen in Poverty Row adaptations in the 1940s. Since Richard Donner's *Superman* (1978), the superhero sub-genre has

become a cornerstone of Hollywood blockbuster production, with computer-generated effects thrilling fans and synergy and merchandising enriching the controlling conglomerates.

Japanese manga comics similarly sustain animated features, while European favourites like Tintin and Asterix the Gaul have made the transition from graphic books. Video games have also forged a reciprocal bond with cinema, but the lack of interactivity has meant that hit movies such as *Lara Croft: Tomb Raider* (2001) have been rare. But as features become increasingly expensive to produce and promote, and their fate remains dependent upon their opening weekend performance, film-makers will continue to rely on pre-solds, **remakes** and **sequels** to offset box-office caprice. ∎

'Critics often denounced cinema's cavalier attitude to adaptation.'

RIGHT: *John Mortimer and Truman Capote's screenplay for* The Innocents *(1961) owed as much to William Archibald's 1950 play as Henry James's 1898 novella,* The Turn of the Screw.

BELOW: *Adapted from a posthumously published novel by Giuseppe Tomasi di Lampedusa, Luchino Visconti's* The Leopard *(1963) won the Palme d'Or at Cannes.*

'Few child actors have enjoyed longevity.'

ABOVE: *Judy Garland was 16 when she began filming* The Wizard of Oz *(1939) and had to wear a corset to achieve Dorothy Gale's child-like physique.*

LEFT: *Life imitated art with the title of this 1936 picture, as Shirley Temple's banker father George squandered all-but $44,000 of her $5 million childhood earnings.*

A family, not a factory

Chosen from 300 Sicilian boys, eight-year-old Salvatore Cascio had never even been to the pictures before he was cast in Giuseppe Tornatore's Cinema Paradiso *(1988).*

IDEA № 30
CHILD STARS

Despite bringing winsomeness and authenticity to films for viewers of all ages, few child actors have enjoyed longevity. Indeed, several have led troubled and tragically short lives as they paid the price for parents, producers, the press, the audience and themselves failing to come to terms with their inevitable maturation.

Although children had long performed on stage, they rarely featured in early films. Consequently, Mary Pickford, the Gish sisters and Richard Barthelmess continued taking juvenile roles into their twenties. But seven-year-old Jackie Coogan's success alongside Charlie Chaplin in *The Kid* (1921) prompted each of the studios to find its own moppets, even though this meant providing educational facilities and adhering to strict labour laws. Kids on the lot reinforced the myth of Hollywood being a family rather than a factory. Moreover, films starring Jackie Cooper, Anne Shirley and Freddie Bartholomew made money, as did shorts and B series such as *Our Gang* and *The Bowery Boys*.

The Shirley Temple phenomenon proved even more lucrative, as parents clamoured to buy tie-in merchandise and stage mothers flocked to Hollywood. Ethel Gumm's daughter, Frances, was reinvented as Judy Garland for *Every Sunday* (1936), which co-starred Deanna Durbin, whose 'Little Miss Fixit' musicals saved Universal from bankruptcy. Both girls struggled with their weight, but Garland suffered most from the regimen of pills that most studios used to keep their child stars perky in pictures that sentimentally celebrated civic values, domestic bliss and the innocence of youth, even after the focus shifted from helping out the grown-ups and putting on shows to school scrapes and first love.

If the studios peddled the idealized vision of childhood demanded by their conservative backers, film-makers elsewhere offered a more realistic perspective, with Vittorio de Sica's *Shoeshine* (1946), René Clément's *Forbidden Games* (1952), and François Truffaut's *The 400 Blows* (1959) tackling issues such as war, poverty and broken homes. Yet while the youthful debutants in the aforementioned films, Franco Interlenghi, Brigitte Fossey and Jean-Pierre Léaud, went on to have decent careers, European cinema made less systematic use of child stars than Hollywood or Bollywood, where icons like Nargis, Madhubala and Meena Kumari started young.

There were fewer contracted kids in postwar Hollywood as the studio system began to unravel. The scampish teenager epitomized by Mickey Rooney was replaced by edgier types played by older actors such as Marlon Brando and James Dean, who better reflected the angst and alienation of adolescents moulded by the Cold War, rock'n'roll and exploitation movies (see **Teenpics**). Disney sought to stem the tide of delinquency, defiance and sexuality with several quaint Hayley Mills vehicles. But the provocative roles played by Jodie Foster, Linda Blair and Brooke Shields in the 1970s stressed the harshness, cynicism and debasement experienced by many children damaged by their environment.

As the careers of Macaulay Culkin and Haley Joel Osment testify, a child star's shelf life is now shorter than ever, with many only making headlines for their substance-fuelled antics on the descent from acclaim to celebrity and obscurity. Image is everything and the media delights in toppling pin-ups. But while talents like Leonardo DiCaprio and Natalie Portman continue to find fame and fortune, starstruck kids and their parents will keep dreaming. ∎

Essential reading for cinephiles

Magazines like Cine Arte, Cahiers du Cinéma, Sight & Sound *and* Premiere *variously assess film as an entertainment, an art, a business and an academic discipline.*

IDEA № 31
FAN MAGAZINES

The fan magazine is one of the clearest indicators of cinema's shifting demographic in its first 125 years. The earliest publications were aimed at increasingly emancipated females enticed by romance and glamour, while today's prozines are targeted squarely at geeky young males obsessed with genres and special effects.

Trade journals like *Moving Picture World* first appeared in the mid-1900s, offering a mix of business news, technical information and reviews. This formula was soon emulated by such enduring titles as *American Cinematographer* (founded 1921) and *The Hollywood Reporter* (1934), which became the film colony's first daily, in competition with the self-proclaimed showbusiness bible, *Variety* (1905). But the 1910 revelation that Florence Lawrence was the IMP Girl (see **The Star System**) ended the anonymity of screen performers and the onset of star mania meant that *Motion Picture Story* and its

ilk had to print more than just illustrated scenarios.

Readers now wanted to know about the personalities, opinions and lifestyles of their idols, and Hollywood producers quickly recognized the importance of magazines such as *Photoplay* (1911) to the success of the nascent studio system. Refusing to spread gossip or pry into private lives, pioneering editor James Quirk sold the Dream Factory image to two million movie-goers a month. Consequently, he secured the guaranteed access to the stars that enabled his successors to commission columnists of the calibre

Catering for cineastes and cultists alike, the film magazine market faces increasing competition from online ezines and specialist blogs.

of Hedda Hopper, Louella Parsons, Walter Winchell, Sidney Skolsky and Adela Rogers St. John. In doing so, he established a template that was copied by publications worldwide.

The slow decline of postwar Hollywood saw celebrity rags like *Confidential* exploit the growing inability of the studio publicity machines to control the news agenda and suppress scandal. Moreover, with mainstream circulations dropping, scholarly journals began to attract devoted followings. Indeed, *Sight & Sound* (1932), *Film Quarterly* (1945), *Cahiers du Cinéma* (1951), *Positif* (1952), *Film Comment* (1961) and *Movie* (1962) initiated the theoretical debates that led to the critical shift from stars to directors that sustained the new wave of glossies and fanzines fuelling the younger generation's enthusiasm for blockbusters and videos.

In contrast to serious but accessible titles such as *Bianco e Nero* (1937) in Italy, *Première* (1976) in France and *Empire* (1989) in Britain, the first fanzines were mimeographed or photocopied pamphlets that sold through subscription or at genre conventions and cult movie stores. Influenced by *Famous Monsters of Filmland* (1958) and *Castle of Frankenstein* (1959), they both reflected and reinforced the growing male fixation with the exploitation genres and, because they were less reliant on studio goodwill, contributors had much greater freedom of expression. Many went on to write for prozines – professionally produced magazines aimed at specific genre audiences – such as *Starlog* and *Fangoria*, while desktop publishing allowed the likes of *Gore Creatures* and *Garden Ghouls Gazette* to reinvent themselves as the more influential *Midnight Marquee* and *Cinefantastique*.

Despite the rise of fandom (which has spawned numerous indie and Z-grade directors), most titles were short-lived. Yet *Shock Xpress*, *Necronomicon* and *Flesh and Blood* have been anthologized in book form, while *Psychotronic* and *Video Watchdog* have found new homes online, alongside websites such as *Ain't It Cool News*, *Senses of Cinema* and *IndieWire*, which have helped exacerbate a print-media crisis that has cost many respected newspaper critics their posts and forced several movie magazines to close. ∎

Roll out the red carpet

IDEA № 32

THE OSCARS

Penélope Cruz became the first Spanish performer to win an Academy Award for Vicky Cristina Barcelona *(2008).*

The Academy Awards are the most prestigious prize ceremony in world cinema. They are popularly known as the Oscars, in honour of the 13½-inch alloy statuette designed by Cedric Gibbons and nicknamed 'Oscar' by either Bette Davis, Academy librarian Margaret Herrick or columnist Sidney Skolsky, depending on whose story you believe.

The awards were introduced in 1927 by the Academy of Motion Picture Arts and Sciences (AMPAS) in a bid to foster a new artistic and technical community within Hollywood that would also help limit the growing influence of the labour unions, ward off the censorial demands of religious and conservative pressure groups, and both legitimize and optimize the commercial prospects of talking pictures. Film prizes were nothing new, as the National Board of Review had already been making annual presentations since 1917. But, from the inaugural dinner at the Hollywood Roosevelt Hotel on 16 May 1929, the Oscars captured the imagination of the public, the media and the movie colony largely because they were bestowed by peers. This has remained an enduring aspect of their appeal, along with the opportunity they afford fans to witness Hollywood's A-list in all its finery. The ceremony is now televised live in over 200 countries worldwide. Indeed, such has been their international influence that the Oscars have spawned equivalents including the BAFTAs in Britain, the Césars in France, the National Film Awards in India and the Golden Roosters in China.

From the outset, Oscar buzz improved a nominated picture's box-office prospects and the studios quickly latched on to voter-friendly formulae. Films with lavish production values, a sense of historical or cultural significance, and a star braving hardship, disability or prejudice invariably proved irresistible. Consequently, titles likely to be Oscar bait were held back for the winter holidays so they would be fresher in the minds of AMPAS's 6,000-strong electorate than films released earlier in the year.

However, the verdicts of the ageing and highly conventional membership haven't always met with universal approval. Iconic figures like Greta Garbo and Alfred Hitchcock were repeatedly spurned, while Dudley Nichols (1936), George C. Scott (1970) and Marlon Brando (1973) famously refused their awards. Indeed, Oscar success has often been a curse rather than a blessing, with numerous winners struggling to live up to new expectations.

With sentiment and lobbying often counting for more than genuine quality, Oscars have frequently been given in recognition of entire careers rather than specific performances. Decisions haven't always been particularly enlightened, either, with a regrettable parochialism limiting the number of major awards won by either 'non-white' or non-English-speaking artists. It took until the 82nd edition, in 2009, for a woman – Kathryn Bigelow – to be named Best Director

A certain generic bias has also developed, with sci-fi, horror and comedy invariably being overlooked in favour of middlebrow adaptations and worthy social dramas. Some commentators have expressed concern that the Oscars risk losing their relevance by becoming stranded in the widening gap between the kind of films lauded by the critical establishment and those that top box-office charts. Over the years, categories for title writing, dance direction, original story and black-and-white cinematography have come and gone, and, following a series of backlashes and bungles, the Academy Awards may have to undergo further, and possibly more drastic, revision if they are to continue to reflect and reward the best in motion-picture art, science and commerce. ∎

BELOW: *Situated on Hollywood Boulevard, the Pantages Theater played host to the annual Oscar ceremony throughout the 1950s.*

RIGHT: *Marlon Brando accepted his Oscar for* **On the Waterfront** *(1954), but declined the award for* **The Godfather** *(1972).*

More than 1,700 special effects shots were required in **Pleasantville** *(1998) to produce images containing both black-and-white and colour segments.*

The continuing appeal of black-and-white

IDEA № 33
MONOCHROME

LEFT TO RIGHT:

Fast-reacting panchromatic film stocks allowed for greater control over artificial and natural lighting in pictures like **Seventh Heaven** *(1927).*

The celestial sequences were shot in monochrome in Powell and Pressburger's **A Matter of Life and Death** *(1946).*

Recreating the past with cutting-edge technology, as colour was digitally drained to achieve monochrome in **The White Ribbon** *(2009).*

Though colour tinting, toning and stencilling were widely used after 1895, film-makers often preferred to work in shades of grey. Many still do today; in fact, it would appear there has always been more to black-and-white than a mere absence of colour.

The classical Hollywood look balanced blacks, whites and greys. But several studios had distinctive visual styles. MGM and RKO achieved a pearly sheen by over-exposing film in the camera and under-developing negatives in the laboratory to produce low-contrast images that flattered the subject. At 20th Century-Fox, the aperture was reduced to increase the depth of field and attain sharper pictures. Warners opted for a grainier realism to suit its gritty themes, while Universal borrowed the high-contrast chiaroscuro of German **Expressionism** for its horror cycle of the 1930s and '40s, which proved so influential to **film noir**.

The Academy Award for cinematography was divided into black-and-white and colour categories between 1939 and 1966. Yet unreliable or expensive technology meant that most Hollywood movies remained monochrome until the mid-1950s. The transition was slower elsewhere and only partially for economic reasons.

Monochrome conveys less visual information than colour. Therefore, viewers are less distracted by spectacle and can concentrate on storyline, dialogue and character psychology. Owing to its popularity among arthouse film-makers who prefer to communicate through tone, composition and mise en scène, the myth arose that black-and-white was more authentic, serious and aesthetically valid than colour. However, the need to sell features to television, as well as on video and DVD, saw such a conclusive shift to colour that even pictures originally shot in monochrome were subjected to colourization to increase their marketability.

Despite the furore in the 1980s over computer-embellished bowdlerizations of early black-and-white movies disregarding the director's artistic integrity, colourized versions continue to emerge, with even fierce opponents such as Martin Scorsese pigmenting footage for *The Aviator* (2004). In fact, black-and-white is now often used to give action a nostalgic, historic, anachronistic or fantastical feel, while many have emulated *The Wizard of Oz* (1939) and *A Matter of Life and Death* (1946) in using colour and monochrome to contrast different settings within a single film.

Yet while digitization has made it easier to produce hybrid pictures such as *Pleasantville* (1998), directors including Woody Allen (*Manhattan*, 1979), Aki Kaurismäki (*Juha*, 1999) and Michel Hazanavicius (*The Artist*, 2011) have regularly produced uniquely black-and-white features. However, it seems likely that budgetary constraints will compel those with monochrome visions to follow Michael Haneke (*The White Ribbon*, 2009) in shooting on standard stock – which is less expensive than black-and-white film – before digitally draining the colour in post-production. ∎

Pre-digital-era SFX

IDEA № 34
PROCESS SHOTS

ABOVE: *Fred Jackman's matte shots allowed Willis O'Brien's stop-motion dinosaurs to imperil Wallace Beery and Bessie Love in* The Lost World *(1925).*

BELOW: *The wave effects in* The Ten Commandments *(1956) were achieved by reversing footage of 300,000 gallons of water being poured into a tank.*

Such is the clamour for novelty and spectacle in cinema that little stays state-of-the-art for long. Yet several of the process techniques for combining different image elements first devised in the 1920s and '30s remained key to the creation of special effects until the advent of the digital age.

For much of film's first two decades, visual effects were simple in-camera illusions. Mattes, combining two elements into a single image, were achieved by covering the frame of the camera with shaped cards and rewinding the reel until Norman Dawn patented his glass process in 1911. However, such static mattes prevented intra-frame movement and travelling mattes were introduced in the mid-1920s to locate moving images within environments that were either impossible, impractical or too expensive to visit with a full cast and crew.

Frank Williams devised the first method of bipacking and contact printing to merge images on male and female mattes into a composite shot. The Williams Process was prone to leaving matte lines around the edges of foreground figures, but it enhanced silents like *The Lost World* and *Ben-Hur* (both 1925) and allowed John P. Fulton to create the still-impressive invisibility effects in *The Invisible Man* (1933). Generating colour mattes proved more problematic until Technicolor pioneered a blue-screen process (see **In-Camera Effects**) for *The Thief of Bagdad* (1940). Nonetheless, transparent, soft-edged and fast-moving objects invariably had a blue fringe, which detracted from epic sequences such as the Red Sea crossing in *The Ten Commandments* (1956).

Utilizing a yellow screen and a beam-splitting prism, Rank's sodium vapour process offered an alternative

in the 1950s. Yet, despite combining live and animated action in Disney's *Mary Poppins* (1964), the system couldn't be used with CinemaScope lenses – as they distorted the images – and it was superseded by Petro Vlahos's blue-screen colour-difference process. Intricate, laborious and time-consuming, this enduring technique nevertheless helped launch the blockbuster era and was only superseded by CGI.

Crucial to the working of all these processes was the optical printer, which linked one or more projectors to a camera to form composite images. In-camera tricks like fades, dissolves, wipes and superimpositions were now optically printed, with RKO's Linwood G. Dunn notably concocting extravagant scene transitions for *Flying Down to Rio* (1933). Dunn also worked on *Citizen Kane* (1941) and estimated that 50 per cent of its shots had been optically altered or upgraded. Indeed, printers could reframe images to remove imperfections or unwanted details (garbage mattes). They could turn long shots into close-ups; speed scenes up or down by removing or duplicating frames; feign pans, zooms and tilts; and even amend weather conditions and refine an image's lighting and texture.

By repeating the same shot, printers could also fashion freeze-frames, as in the iconic climax to François Truffaut's *The 400 Blows* (1959). They could also allow actors in dual roles, such as Danny Kaye in *Wonder Man* (1954), to play scenes opposite themselves, or they could divide the frame into split-screens, as in *The Thomas Crown Affair* (1968). Printers were also vital to the creation of opening titles and credit crawls at the end of the film, as were hand-drawn mattes. But all these tasks can now be performed with greater efficacy and efficiency by computers. ∎

Publicity shot for **Mary Poppins** *(1964), which won an Oscar for Peter Ellenshaw's matte paintings, Eustace Lycett's sodium travelling mattes and Hamilton Luske's animation.*

Fiat lux

ABOVE LEFT: *Classic chiaroscuro in a futuristic setting: Harrison Ford and Sean Young in* **Blade Runner** *(1982).*

ABOVE RIGHT: *Alfred Hitchcock put a light in the glass to make the milk seem more sinister in* **Suspicion** *(1941).*

IDEA № 35
ARTIFICIAL LIGHTING

Film lighting has always served three principal functions: to ensure visual clarity; to suggest a scene's authenticity; and to convey atmosphere in order to elicit an emotional response.

Despite the use of artificial lighting in photography, most early filming relied on diffuse daylight and took place on location or in studios that were either open to the elements or had glass walls and ceilings or retractable roofs. While Hollywood producers tended to shoot outdoors, their East Coast counterparts were using arc floodlights and mercury vapour lamps to supplement natural light by the mid-1900s. They also devised effects to show the source of lamp, fire and window light and made dramatic use of lighting to isolate characters within a scene, glamorize them with soft-edged close-ups and menace them with low-angle shots, silhouettes and shadows.

Along with single-source lighting, the latter techniques were imported from Europe after shaping Expressionism, Impressionism and **Poetic Realism** (which would all influence the chiaroscuro of film noir). But it was American cinematographers whose inventive use of spotlights, carbon arcs, reflectors and diffusing screens led to the abandonment of full-frontal and side lighting in favour of the three-point lighting system that provided sharper figure modelling and more distinct separation from the background. Flat lighting became bad form, as directors of photography (DPs) developed trademark methods of sculpting with light in order to reassure or disconcert audiences. Nevertheless, a classical Hollywood look for both interiors and exteriors did emerge around the coming of sound, with the introduction of panchromatic stocks and incandescent tungsten lights.

This mid- to high-key precision style, which avoids dark shadows, pertained until the post-World War II era, when faster films were employed on location sequences. Lighting designs were further simplified as sets grew smaller, colour took over from **monochrome** and DPs emulated both television's non-directional uniform brightness across the image and the bounce technique pioneered during the Nouvelle Vague. The European preoccupation with source light within the mise en scène also impacted upon 1970s America. But studio and independent features alike retained a characteristic aspect through the use of North (aka shadowless) or low-key lighting, which reflected the darker themes of New Hollywood and became pivotal to the sci-fi, fantasy and comic-book blockbuster, along with the increased incidence of coloured light.

In addition to consulting with the director, cinematographers also collaborate with production and costume designers to decide upon the positioning and concealment of lights around a set and advise on how their colour temperature will affect hues and textures. Modern lighting is notable for its diversity and soft-hard contrasts. But, even though digital cameras require less illumination than their celluloid counterparts, artificial lighting remains key to conveying a film's mood and meaning. ∎

'Modern lighting is notable for its diversity and soft-hard contrasts.'

DP Roger Deakins used car headlamps to backlight Ed Tom Bell (Tommy Lee Jones) as he enters a motel room in **No Country for Old Men** *(2007).*

Dr Caligari's long shadow

IDEA № 36

EXPRESSIONISM

Employing exterior or objective representation to convey interior or subjective states, the silent *Schauerfilme* (horror films), *Kammerspielfilme* (chamber dramas) and *Strassenfilme* (street films) produced in Weimar Germany between 1919 and 1929 continue to have a major influence on world cinema.

TOP: *Shot by émigré cinematographer Karl Freund, Tod Browning's* Dracula *(1931) launched the Universal horror cycle of the 1930s and '40s.*

ABOVE: *Gotham City Gothic: director Tim Burton and production designer Anton Furst pay homage to Fritz Lang's* Metropolis *(1926) in* Batman *(1989).*

OPPOSITE PAGE: *This poster for* The Cabinet of Dr Caligari *(1920) conveys the angularity of the stars and Walter Röhrig, Hermann Warm and Walter Reimann's sets.*

Expressionist films had their roots in the artist groups of Der Blaue Reiter and Die Brücke, the poetry, prose and plays of writers such as Georg Kaiser and August Stramm, and the theatrical stagings of Karlheinz Martin and Max Reinhardt. Easily the most significant of the resulting radical departures from cinematic bourgeois realism was Robert Wiene's *The Cabinet of Dr Caligari* (1920), which explored the themes of revolt, self-realization, insanity and primeval sexuality that reflected the mindset of a defeated nation beset by war reparations, political uncertainty and moral ambiguity. Moreover, it brought a fresh psychological and poetic complexity to what was essentially a narrative medium.

Determined to prove that high art could revive German cinema's commercial fortunes, *Caligari* producer Erich Pommer turned limited resources and an unreliable electricity supply to his creative advantage by having designers use canted angles, forced perspectives and painted backdrops to reinforce the mood of dislocation suggested by the stylized performances of Werner Krauss and Conrad Veidt. Yet, while it exhibited classical Expressionism, *Caligari* also drew inspiration from the atmospheric dramas of Swedes Mauritz Stiller and Victor Sjöström and Danes Benjamin Christensen and Carl Theodor Dreyer, as well as the sensationalist urban crime thrillers produced by Nordisk in the 1910s and gothic horrors such as Stellan Rye's *The Student of Prague* (1913) and Henrik Galeen's *Der Golem* (1915).

Indeed, these non-American cinematic influences also manifested themselves in Fritz Lang's *Destiny* (1921) and F.W. Murnau's *Nosferatu* (1922) which were hailed as Expressionist masterpieces (if not always box-office successes) long before Ernst Lubitsch's costume films, Murnau's invisibly edited chamber dramas and the realist street films of G.W. Pabst were added to the canon.

Ultimately, the high-key lighting (see **Artificial Lighting**), distorted two-dimensionality, subjective camera movements and macabre topics became part of an émigré cinema, as actors, directors, cinematographers and composers were lured to Hollywood or fled the Third Reich. Purists now insist that Expressionism cannot be used to define the films they produced outside Germany. But a term is required to validate the connection between the original works and such beneficiaries of their distinctive stylistic qualities and tone of angst and paranoia as the Universal horror series, film noir and the modern comic-book blockbuster, not to mention key works by acclaimed film-makers such as Alfred Hitchcock, Orson Welles, Carol Reed, Werner Herzog, Tim Burton, Terry Gilliam and Guy Maddin. Perhaps Caligarism, chiaroscurism or pseudo-Expressionism could serve instead? ■

ABOVE: *Production designer Lazare Meerson drolly contrasts Raymond Cordy's Art Deco phonograph factory with the prison in which he once served time in René Clairs musical comedy,* A Nous la Liberté *(1931).*

RIGHT: *Filmed in Brittany and combining documentary and avant-garde sensibilities, Jean Epstein's* Finis terrae *(1929) was a major influence on Neorealism.*

'French cinema must be cinema; French cinema must be French.'

Impressions of psychological realism

IDEA № 37

THE NARRATIVE AVANT-GARDE

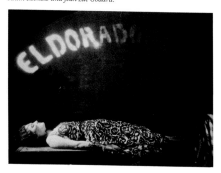

Marcel L'Herbier's Eldorado *(1921) was a masterclass in cinematic expression that influenced such* **Nouvelle Vagueurs** *as Alain Resnais and Jean-Luc Godard.*

In 1914, 90 per cent of films shown around the world were French. But the Great War halted this production, allowing Hollywood to assume hegemony and impose its preferred storytelling style. In the 1920s, however, a group of Gallic cineastes rebelled against this classical linearity and employed avant-garde techniques to imbue their narratives with greater emotional and visual complexity and veracity.

Postwar Paris bristled with modernist challenges to artistic convention. In keeping with this spirit, Louis Delluc called for film to sever its links with art, literature, theatre and music and develop a *photogénie* or photographic purity that was sufficiently free of commercial constrictions to allow personal expression and psychological exploration. His exhortation that 'French cinema must be cinema; French cinema must be French' led to two new waves: one was Surrealism and the other was a form of narrative avant-gardism that became known as Impressionism.

Critics dispute whether French Impressionism was a coherent movement or merely a coincidence of narrative avant-gardists. Delluc, Germaine Dulac, Jean Epstein, Marcel L'Herbier and Abel Gance were united in their admiration for German Expressionism and *Kammerspielfilme* and Hollywood features like Cecil B. DeMille's *The Cheat* (1915). Inspired by the use of editing to convey emotion, as well as to drive the drama, they made a character's inner life as important as his or her external deeds. Employing intimate narratives to suggest mood , they also manipulated plot, time and perspective to depict dreams, memories, ideas and fantasies.

Initially, these French film-makers adopted a pictorialist approach, using camera movement, mise en scène and **process shots** to present patterns of thought and feeling. But Gance's *The Wheel* (or *La Roue*) (1923) shifted the emphasis to rhythmic editing and audacious subjectivity that immersed audiences in the action and compelled them to seek meaning in technique rather than composition and performance. The other members of the loose cabal had likewise begun to exhibit more distinctive styles before the coming of sound ended the experiment altogether.

Operating within the mainstream industry, the Impressionists put theory into practice and exerted a sizeable influence on melodrama, horror and film noir, stirring film-makers as different as Maya Deren and Alfred Hitchcock. In addition to their collective achievement, they also attained individual significance.

Known as the 'father of French cinematic art', Delluc manipulated temporal and spatial unity to bring a sense of selective realism and lyrical interiority to fatalistic urban dramas that anticipated Poetic Realism. He also established the French tradition of aesthetic theory and founded the influential *ciné-clubs*. Germaine Dulac meanwhile devised an 'integral cinema', with *The Smiling Madame Beudet* (1923), demonstrating the subjective viewpoint ahead of F.W. Murnau's *The Last Laugh* (1924) and presaging many feminist themes.

Epstein anticipated Poetic Realism in *Faithful Heart* (1923), **Neorealism** in *Finis terrae* (1929) and Alain Resnais's experiments with structure, time and space in *The Three-Sided Mirror* (1927). L'Herbier was a master of Impressionistic evocation, whose 'plastic harmonies' in *The Inhuman Woman* (1924) and *Money* (or *L'Argent*) (1928) gave style a dramaturgic and formal function, while the self-reflexivity of *Eldorado* (1921) predated the Nouvelle Vague he further helped emerge by co-founding the **Cinémathèque Française** and the Institut des Hautes Études Cinématographiques (IDHEC).

Finally, Gance's metaphorical editing in *The Wheel* proved a major influence on Soviet montage, while its naturalism found echoes in Poetic Realism. He also pioneered handheld and widescreen techniques in *Napoleon* (1927), whose 1950s rediscovery saw him installed as one of the influential film journal *Cahiers du Cinéma's* few French auteurs (see **Auteur Theory**). ∎

Learning your craft

FILM SCHOOLS

Gong Li in Zhang Yimou's **Raise the Red Lantern** *(1991), which confirmed the status of the Beijing Film Academy's Fifth Generation graduates.*

All art forms spawn their own specialist training establishments. The world's first film school was the All-Union State Institute of Cinematography (VGIK), founded in Moscow in 1919. Many have since followed its model, although the content of courses has varied widely, with some schools encouraging conformity and others creativity.

A lack of equipment dictated the VGIK's first curriculum. With pro-tsarist producers hoarding film stock in the wake of the Russian Revolution, tutor Lev Kuleshov was forced to base workshops around simulated shoots with empty cameras and the re-editing of existing pictures, including D.W. Griffith's *Intolerance* (1916). He also taught students the Kuleshov Effect to demonstrate the associational power of montage and collaborated with them on features like *The Death Ray* (1925).

Alumni such as Sergei Eisenstein and Vsevolod Pudovkin became pivotal figures in the Soviet film industry and later returned to teach at the VGIK, alongside Mikhail Romm and Sergei Gerasimov (after whom the Institute was renamed in 1986). But while the VGIK nurtured homegrown talent like Andrei Tarkovsky, Sergei Paradjanov, Sergei Bondarchuk, Nikita Mikhalkov and Aleksandr Sokurov, it also accepted foreign students, including Ousmane Sembène and Souleymane Cissé, who proved key to the emergence of African cinema.

Ironically, the Communist-created VGIK inspired the foundation of the Centro Sperimentale di Cinematografia in Rome (1935) and the Deutsche Filmakademie in Berlin (1938), as the Fascist regimes sought to indoctrinate their own film-makers. But while the Universum Film Aktiengesellschaft (UFA), which dominated production in Germany throughout the Nazi era, assumed control of the Filmakademie

in 1940, the Centro produced graduates of the calibre of Michelangelo Antonioni, Pietro Germi, Marco Bellocchio, Dino De Laurentiis, Vittorio Storaro and Nestor Almendros.

FAMU in Prague and the Lódz Film School in Poland similarly reneged on their duty to produce artists to serve the state. Vera Chytilová, Jirí Menzel, Milos Forman and Jan Nemec became leading lights of the 1960s Czech Film Miracle (or New Wave), while Andrzej Wajda, Krzysztof Kieslowski and Krzysztof Zanussi were active alongside FAMU alumna Agnieszka Holland in the Cinema of Moral Anxiety, which captured the mood of civil unrest around the rise of Solidarity in the 1980s. The Institut des Hautes Études Cinématographiques (IDHEC) – the almer mater of Louis Malle, Alain Resnais, Costa-Gavras, Ruy Guerra, Volker Schlöndorff, Theo Angelopoulos and Claire Denis – played its part in the Parisian upheavals of 1968, by which time film schools had finally begun to make an impact in the United States.

When not poaching writers and directors from the theatre, the Hollywood studios (like the Japanese *zaibatsu*) preferred to train aspirants through apprenticeships. Thus, despite the founding of the University of Southern California School of Cinematic Arts, in 1929, few alums flourished. However, the decline of the studio system coincided with the opening of film centres at UCLA, NYU and Columbia, and this new generation

of 'movie brats' – which included Francis Ford Coppola, George Lucas, John Milius, Paul Schrader and Martin Scorsese – changed Hollywood forever.

Film schools continue to revitalize the moving image worldwide. The Beijing Film Academy, for example, produced Fifth Generation directors – Chinese film history is divided into generations – like Tian Zhuangzhuang, Chen Kaige and Zhang Yimou, who introduced Chinese cinema to a global audience in the 1980s. Yet there will always be those who, like one-time video-store clerk Quentin Tarantino, find their own way to make it. ∎

ABOVE: *Andrei Tarkovsky's feature debut,* Ivan's Childhood *(1962), had a poetic quality that confirmed the liberalisation of VGIK under director-tutors Mikhail Romm and Grigori Chukhrai.*

LEFT: *Old boy's network: Aleksandr Sokurov was mentored by Andrei Tarkovsky while at VGIK and* Mother and Son *(1997) bears the influence of the latter's* Mirror *(1974).*

Colliding images, compressed time

MONTAGE

Intellectual montage: Sergei Eisenstein juxtaposed three shots of lion statues in **Battleship Potemkin** *(1925) to suggest the rousing of the masses into action.*

Film movements and techniques are forever passing in and out of fashion. Some people, for instance, currently question montage's historical significance. But there seems little reason to doubt the great Soviet film-maker Sergei Eisenstein's contention that montage – the rapid putting together of miscellaneous imagery – is 'the nerve of cinema'.

Despite its Soviet associations, montage actually emerged outside Russia in the 1910s. D.W. Griffith instinctively understood that a shot's represented reality acquired additional meaning when juxtaposed with other images, while the Futurists, Formalists and Impressionists utilized metaphorical editing, accelerated montage and discontinuity in films like Anton Giulio Bragaglia's *Thais* (1917). However, it was the codification of these ideas by Lev Kuleshov at the VGIK and their exploitation by Dziga Vertov in his stylized documentary or 'kino eye' efforts to catch life unawares that prompted Eisenstein to devise a more aggressively expressive 'kino fist' method that drew on Japanese ideograms and the Marxist dialectic to force viewers into active engagement with the colliding images of montage.

Essentially, Eisenstein subverted Hollywood's continuity editing strategies as an act of anti-capitalist rebellion. Disregarding conventions of time and space, he broke the rules of screen geography and the axis of action and employed eyeline and graphic mismatches, ellipses and temporal expansion to forge metric, rhythmic, tonal, associational and intellectual montage sequences that were designed to arouse emotions and provoke ideas.

Yet while Eisenstein was refining this dramatic mode of editing in *Strike* (1925), *Battleship Potemkin* (1925) and *October* (1927), fellow Soviet Vsevolod Pudovkin was pioneering the epic

Constructivist principle of linkage (in which images were connected rather than impacted together) in *Mother* (1926) and *Storm over Asia* (1928). Elsewhere Alexander Dovzhenko was imbuing montage with lyricism in *Earth* (1930).

However, the coming of sound and the Kremlin's imposition of Socialist Realism saw montage denounced as decadent and debased. French critic André Bazin would further decry the technique's conflicts of scale, volume, rhythm and velocity as manipulative and undemocratic in proposing his theory of mise en scène. Yet montage continued to exert considerable influence worldwide.

Depicting meteoric rises, arduous journeys and training regimes in pictures like *Citizen Kane* (1941) and *Rocky* (1976), Hollywood montages condensed time, space and information in conjunction with fades, dissolves, split screens and double exposures. Such passages compress narrative rather than subvert it and have now become clichés. But, set to an evocative soundtrack, they remain surprisingly effective.

The British Documentary Movement of the 1930s employed montage, close-ups and **typage** to educate and inspire the masses, while Nouvelle Vagueurs François Truffaut and Jean-Luc Godard favoured such non-classical editorial gambits as jump cutting and multiple perspective montages to disrupt traditional forms of narrative linearity. Alfred Hitchcock, Francis Ford Coppola,

Brian De Palma and Oliver Stone also owed much to montage, as did the makers of Hong Kong martial-arts movies and Japanese *chambara* series.

Commercials and music videos also bear the montage imprint. But Eisenstein's legacy is most readily evident in the increasing rapidity of Hollywood editing. Two-hour pictures now contain upwards of 2,000 shots, compared to 300–500 over 90 minutes in the studio era. So, with average shot lengths halving from four to two seconds between *L.A. Confidential* (1997) and *The Bourne Supremacy* (2004), rumours of montage's demise seem greatly exaggerated. ∎

'Montage … is "the nerve of cinema".'

ABOVE: *Brian De Palma paid homage to the 'Odessa Steps' massacre in Battleship Potemkin with the runaway pram sequence in* **The Untouchables (1987).**

BELOW: *Unusually for a Hollywood picture, Sam Peckinpah's* **The Wild Bunch** *(1969) contained 2,721 edit points, with 325 coming in the infamous massacre montage.*

RIGHT: *In* Earth *(1930), Alexander Dovzhenko chose wife Yuliya Solntseva to embody the purity and fecundity of the Soviet countryside.*

BELOW: *Here playing a cop in Renny Harlin's* Cleaner *(2007), Puerto Rican Luis Guzmán is invariably cast as hard men on either side of the law.*

Looking the part

ABOVE: *Using a low angle to suggest the character's authority, director Vsevolod Pudovkin cast himself as the police officer in* Mother *(1926).*

ABOVE: *Hollywood's pernicious habit of making-up Caucasians to look Oriental limited opportunities for fine actors like Anna May Wong, seen here in* Shanghai Express *(1932).*

IDEA Nº 40

TYPAGE

Actors have long been chosen for their looks and demeanour as much as for their talent, in order to make a film's action more authentic and accessible. Indeed, typage (or typing or typecasting) is a crucial facet of cinematic shorthand.

Imported from the theatre, typage proved hugely useful to silent film-makers, as it enabled them to create readily recognizable characters without having to digress from the narrative. However, this identifiability didn't just apply to supporting players, character actors, bit-parters and extras. Stars also became known for taking particular roles, and this familiarity not only enhanced their commercial appeal but also reinforced the conventions of the genre they frequented, be it comedy, melodrama, crime, horror or the Western.

Sergei Eisenstein rejected many aspects of mainstream cinema, but he realized the value of typage to his formalist style – which placed as much emphasis on the visuals as the content – as it allowed audiences to understand instantly the status of each figure in a flurry of colliding images. Moreover, as *Strike* (1925), *Battleship Potemkin* (1925) and *October* (1927) were essentially propagandist works, it was vital that viewers saw themselves in the collective hero portrayed there as establishing a new order. Vsevolod Pudovkin and Alexander Dovzhenko also frequently cast unknowns and many of the types they depicted survived into the era of Socialist Realism.

Non-professionals cast for their suggestion of 'types' headlined Neorealist classics such as Roberto Rossellini's *Germany, Year Zero* (1948) and Luchino Visconti's *La terra trema* (1948). Indeed, Vittorio De Sica turned down Hollywood star Cary Grant to cast factory worker Lamberto Maggiorani in *Bicycle Thieves* (1948) opposite seven-year-old Enzo Staiola, who was selected to play the trusting son on the strength of his walk. French director Robert Bresson also prioritized qualities that would register on camera over photogenicity in choosing the 'models' he imbued with so-called 'automated naturalism'. The idea was that, in films such as *A Man Escaped* (1956) and *Pickpocket* (1959), viewers would project their own response onto a character's words and actions rather than share in a simulated emotion.

Frank Capra once described movies as tables with the stars on the shiny surface and the 'character people' as the legs. Hollywood certainly appreciated the need for a wide range of supporting actors and most studios had their own stock companies. This made both cinematic and economic sense, as many contractees were seasoned performers who knew their jobs, cost little and could keep the schedules moving by working on several projects at once. Moreover, unlike stars, these 'character actors' were rarely temperamental or miscast and audiences knew exactly what to expect each time C. Aubrey Smith, William Demarest, Margaret Dumont, George Zucco, Gabby Hayes or Gale Sondergaard appeared on the screen, even if they didn't always know their names. Racial stereotyping meanwhile severely limited the opportunities of stalwarts like Anna May Wong, Hattie McDaniel and Katy Jurado, as did the now discredited practice of 'white-washing', which saw characters of different races played by white actors.

Many of the old guard of supporting and character players drifted into television as the studio system wound down. However, they remain in demand with casting directors worldwide, with many ageing stars now settling for secondary roles alongside the dependables and versatiles who bring credibility, colour and conviction to scenes without stealing focus. ∎

Subversion and liberation

SURREALISM

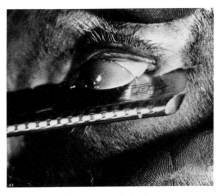

A calf's eyeball was used to give the impression Simone Mareuil was being sliced with a razor in Un Chien andalou (1928).

In order to liberate audiences from social, political and religious restriction, the Surrealists rejected accepted codes of cinematic representation and perception and embraced the logic of dreams, the psychological power of discordant juxtapositions of images and the innate truth of the absurd.

Luis Buñuel once claimed that he made films to 'disturb people and destroy the rules of a kind of conformism that wants everyone to think that they are living in the best of all possible worlds'. Despising the Impressionism that French producers had hoped would countermand Hollywood hegemony in the early 1920s, Buñuel and his fellow Surrealists took their cinematic cues from the trick films of Georges Méliès, slapstick, lowbrow serials and the exotic fantasies of German Expressionism. The influence of Soviet montage was also evident in the use of associative and abstract linkage to abjure narrative cogency in the likes of René Clair's Dadaist short *Entr'acte* (1924) and Germaine Dulac's *The Seashell and the Clergyman* (1928), which had been scripted as an exercise in 'raw cinema' by Antonin Artaud.

However, the Surrealists were less than impressed with Dulac's film, just as they had been with such Dadaist experiments as Man Ray's *Return to Reason* (1923), Fernand Léger's *Ballet mécanique* (1924) and Marcel Duchamp's *Anemic Cinema* (1926), which captured the rhythmic movement of geometric shapes. Even *Un Chien andalou* (1928), Salvador Dalí and Luis Buñuel's 'desperate and passionate appeal to murder', was viewed with suspicion, as its commercial success was interpreted as meaning that its cocktail of iconoclasm, lust, violence and blasphemy was insufficiently shocking. Yet André Breton, who had drafted the first Surrealist Manifesto in 1924, proclaimed the pair's follow-up, *L'Âge d'or* (1930), to be 'the only authentically Surrealist film ever made'.

Dalí only dabbled in cinema thereafter, most notably designing the dream sequence for Alfred Hitchcock's Hollywood film *Spellbound* (1945). But Buñuel continued 'raping clear consciences' with provocative assaults on Catholicism, the establishment and the bourgeoisie such as *The Young and the Damned* (or *Los Olvidados*) (1950), *The Exterminating Angel* (1962) and *That Obscure Object of Desire* (1977).

Despite Jean Cocteau's *Blood of a Poet* (1930), Jean Vigo's *Zero for Conduct* (1933) and the nature films of Jean Painlevé, Surrealist cinema lost its momentum with the coming of sound. Nevertheless, it impacted upon the anarchic comedy of the Marx Brothers, socko (see **Slapstick**) cartoons, the knowing sensuality of Mae West, and the mischievous malevolence of Hitchcock and James Whale. It might have been more influential still had it not been overshadowed by Sergei Eisenstein's writings on realism and the commercial dominance of the classical narrative style favoured by the Hollywood studios.

In 1946, Man Ray, Duchamp and Léger collaborated with Hans Richter on *Dreams That Money Can Buy* (1947), which is usually considered the last official Surrealist film. Screen Surrealism has never entirely disappeared, however. André Bazin reintroduced Surrealist notions of accidental significance in positing his theory of mise en scène and many European auteurs including Federico Fellini, Jan Svankmajer and Juraz Herz are indebted to the Surrealist aesthetic, as are numerous Japanimators and North American mavericks such as Terry Gilliam, Guy Maddin and David Lynch. ∎

'Surrealists rejected accepted codes ... and perception and embraced the logic of dreams.'

ABOVE: *Jean Vigo's* Zero for Conduct *(1933): the famous pillow fight culminates in a slow-motion parody of a religious procession.*

RIGHT: *Poster capturing the trippy nature of Terry Gilliam's adaptation of Hunter S. Thompson's* Fear and Loathing in Las Vegas *(1998).*

Maya Deren and Alexander Hammid's noirishly surreal masterpiece Meshes of the Afternoon *(1943) cost just $275 to produce.*

Beyond the mainstream

IDEA № 42

EXPERIMENTAL CINEMA

In Mothlight (1963), *Stan Brakhage affixed insect wings, leaves and grass to the celluloid to examine the projector beam's role in an animated life cycle.*

Experimental cinema – a term of convenience for the various avant-garde and underground attempts to coerce audiences into taking a more intellectually active part in viewing moving images – has emerged as an art form in its own right. It has also had a considerable influence on its commercial counterpart.

Conceiving, making and editing their low-budget works alone or with minimal collaboration, most experimentalists enjoy complete artistic freedom. But such independence has invariably led to marginalization, with screenings often being confined to galleries, museums, ciné-clubs and specialist venues. This alternative approach to exhibition reflects a resolute refusal to adopt industrial methods of production, with non-mainstream artists mostly opting for shorts over features and either making pioneering use of new technology or keeping faith with formats discarded by the studios. Thus, while many artists preferred to work with 16mm, 8mm or Super 8, Nam June Paik and Valie Export were switching to video in the 1960s, while John Whitney and Scott Bartlett were creating the first computer-generated items a full decade before mainstream cinema was.

Experimental film is characterized by a lack of linearity and the use of audiovisual distancing techniques. Although most experimentalists make contrapuntal or non-naturalistic use of sound, some embrace silence. Others eschew basic film-making methods altogether. Yet while the non-camera techniques – applying marks or materials directly on the celluloid surface – employed by Man Ray in *Return to Reason* (1923) and Stan Brakhage in *Mothlight* (1963) may have had a limited effect on popular cinema, the abstract images they generated showed that it was possible to use shape, texture, colour and tempo to express thought and to ignore, subvert or fragment narrative convention.

Crucial to the development of associational montage, the rhythmic juxtaposition of images in the city symphonies of the 1920s influenced the found footage collages of Stan Vanderbeek, which proved as significant as Bruce Conner's audiovisual synchronizations in the evolution of the music video. Contrasting with these exercises in rapid cutting, the time-lapse studies of Marie Menken and the dance-inspired dreamscapes of Maya Deren were more personal and accessible, hence their clash with structuralist titles using audiovisual distancing techniques like Michael Snow's *Wavelength* (1967) and Hollis Frampton's *Zorns Lemma* (1970), which were less concerned with content than the systems used to present it and the material nature of film itself.

Such self-reflexive, anti-illusionist tactics had their roots in Andy Warhol outings such as *Kiss* (1963), which also echoed the efforts of Kenneth Anger, Gregory Markopoulos and Jack Smith to explore the socio-political, erotic and gay themes that were proscribed by the Production Code. Such provocations not only encouraged '60s exploitation, but would also be taken to extremes two decades later by such exponents of transgressive cinema as the German horror auteur Jörg Buttgereit and Nick Zedd who emerged from New York's No Wave Cinema boom in the mid-1970s.

Besides inspiring the ironic kitsch of mavericks such as George and Mike Kuchar, radical auteurism also pushed the moving image in the direction of performance art, gallery installation and an expanded cinema dependent upon new technology. Moreover, it prompted the production of 'new talkies' like Laura Mulvey and Peter Wollen's *Riddles of the Sphinx* (1977), which deconstructed narrative codes by combining them with psychoanalysis and film theory. Fittingly, such invitations to see differently are now more widely available thanks to microcinemas and the internet. ∎

WARNER BROS. SUPREME TRIUMPH

AL JOLSON
"THE JAZZ SINGER"

WITH
MAY McAVOY
WARNER OLAND
Cantor Rosenblatt

Based upon the play by Samson Raphaelson as produced on the spoken stage by Lewis & Gordon... Sam H Harris
Scenario by Alfred A. Cohn

DIRECTED BY ALAN CROSLAND

ABOVE: *'You ain't heard nothin' yet!': Al Jolson and May McAvoy make history in* The Jazz Singer *(1927).*

BELOW: *The sound mix to Fredric March's transformations in* Dr Jekyll and Mr Hyde *(1931) included heartbeats and bells ringing in an echo chamber.*

Was silence golden?

IDEA № 43
SOUND

Nothing has had a greater transformational impact upon cinema than the coming of sound. Charlie Chaplin felt it destroyed 'the great beauty of silence'. To the contrary, it could be argued that dialogue, music, sound design and effects enhance a film's visuals by reinforcing their meaning and illusory realism.

Despite Thomas Edison's audiovisual ambitions, problems with synchronization and amplification retarded the development of practical sound apparatus until the 1920s. Even then, Hollywood resisted the overtures of the electronic companies AT&T and RCA, since the silent film had reached a level of sophistication that was commercially successful and aesthetically admired. Yet the lack of public demand and prohibitive cost failed to deter the cash-strapped Warner Bros, which released *The Jazz Singer* with a Vitaphone disc soundtrack in October 1927. Such was its reception that the other studios followed suit, with Vitaphone being discarded in favour of Western Electric's sound-on-film system which placed the sound track alongside the images on the celluloid strip.

The transition was actually rather slow, as studios and auditoria had to be wired for sound, and casts and crews had to learn new techniques. Unsurprisingly, with stage actors, playwrights, dialogue directors and composers now settling into Hollywood, the first talkies were often static and verbose. Performers congregated around microphones concealed about the set, while noisy cameras were confined in distant booths nicknamed 'ice-boxes'. Furthermore, synchronization difficulties limited intra-scene editing.

Such problems were eventually solved, however, by unidirectional boom mikes, camera blimps and Moviola sound readers, while **dubbing** and **subtitles** ended the practice of casting local stars in multiple-language remakes of prestige pictures for export. The universality of silent cinema was gone forever, as were the stars like Constance Talmadge whose voices didn't suit their image and the musicians who had provided live accompaniment in cinemas. Moreover,

David Lynch had the actors reverse their actions and invert the dialogue to achieve the sense of audiovisual dislocation in the Red Room sequences in Twin Peaks: Fire Walk With Me *(1992).*

'The universality of silent cinema was gone forever.'

the expense of conversion put the studios in hock to Wall Street, whose conservative backers were able to impose the Production Code in 1934 to restrict the talkies' ability to discuss contentious issues.

Once it was agreed that audio levels would remain constant regardless of camera distance from the actors and that dialogue would be prioritized over ambient sound and music (as audibility mattered more than authenticity), directors got the hang of sound reasonably quickly. Guns rattled and tyres screeched in gangster movies, melodramas echoed with **voice-overs** and interior monologues, and the musical emerged as a new genre. But while sound brought a fresh potency to silence and reinforced compositional hegemony by focusing the viewer's attention on specific details within the frame, it quickly became a necessary rather than an innovative component

of film-making, with the imaginative use of rhythmic and non-naturalistic sound being largely confined to experimental shorts and animation.

In the early 1930s, the Soviet film-makers Sergei Eisenstein and Vsevolod Pudovkin advocated the use of contrapuntal or asynchronous sound to contrast a film's audio and visual aspects rather than simply enhance naturalism. Subsequently, Jean Renoir and Orson Welles sought greater realism by employing off-screen noises, tonal shifts, aural bridges and overlapping dialogue, while Jacques Tati pioneered audio minimalism by dispensing with speech and placing comic emphasis on everyday sounds and Jean-Luc Godard subverted hierarchical convention by using sounds from both inside and outside the story world to disrupt the reality of the image. But such expressive use of sound has been rare, especially since

Hollywood introduced stereo in the 1950s, which presaged the noise-reduction, multi-track and digital techniques that increased the density of soundtracks that nowadays bombard audiences with sonic sensations that immerse them in the increasingly computer-generated action. ■

Zither player Anton Karas on a dubbing stage performing his famous 'Harry Lime Theme' for **The Third Man** *(1949).*

Storytelling on staves

IDEA № 44
MUSICAL SCORES

The modern compilation soundtrack has brought the screen score full circle by evoking the silent era, when accompanists included popular songs in their cue-sheet repertoires. The emphasis in the interim was on the symphonic. Yet while scores everywhere reflect individual films' particular origins, they also share some core principles.

Film music helps shape the meaning of an image and the viewer's identification with it. Remaining unobtrusive and subordinate to the dialogue, it establishes time, place and mood; defines character psychology; emphasizes dramatic themes; and delineates abstract ideas. Some scholars have claimed that music either parallels or counterpoints the action. But image and score often interact, with composers and arrangers varying melody, harmony, rhythm, tempo, volume, timbre and instrumentation to manipulate emotional response as John Williams did in Steven Spielberg's *Jaws* (1975). The repetition of leitmotifs is a very effective method of guiding reactions, although the suggestive nature of music can be misused to subliminally reinforce ideologically unsound notions about gender, sexuality and race, such as the use of tomtoms and chants in Hollywood Westerns.

Whether improvised or notated, the music played by pianists, organists and orchestras in the early cinema proved vital to the development of screen storytelling, as recurring motifs and associated conventions clarified both the plot and character motivation. Artists of the calibre of Camille Saint-Saëns (*The Assassination of the Duc de Guise*, 1908), Erik Satie (*Entr'acte*, 1924) and Dmitri Shostakovich (*The New Babylon*, 1929) composed for silent films. But scores seemed artificial in the early days of sound and music was limited to sources within the story world until Max Steiner's work on *King Kong* (1933) initiated the saturation style of scoring almost every scene that Hollywood exported around the world.

The influence of European romanticism on the Hollywood studio score was profound, with key composers such as Steiner, Erich Wolfgang Korngold, Dmitri Tiomkin, Miklós Rózsa, Bronislau Kaper, Hanns Eisler and Franz Waxman all being émigrés. However, a more distinctively American idiom became apparent in the 1940s and '50s, as Alfred Newman, Alex North, Leonard Rosenman, Elmer Bernstein and Henry Mancini introduced folk music, the blues and jazz.

Many film-makers and composers formed lasting partnerships, among them Sergei Eisenstein and Sergei Prokofiev, Alfred Hitchcock and Bernard Herrmann, Federico Fellini and Nino Rota, François Truffaut and Georges Delerue, and Sergio Leone and Ennio Morricone. Others directors composed their own scores, including Charlie Chaplin, Satyajit Ray, John Carpenter and Clint Eastwood.

In the 1950s, electronic music became more common, as did modernist concepts like dissonance, atonality, polytonality and serial music, most notably in cartoon and avant-garde scores. But rock'n'roll had the greatest impact on Hollywood music. The lyrics of songs were used to comment on a situation or reveal a character's feelings in pictures like Mike Nichols's *The Graduate* (1967), whose Paul Simon song score confirmed the trend for soundtrack albums.

ABOVE: *Riffing on the notes E and F, John Williams's 'shark' theme proved crucial to ratcheting up the suspense in* Jaws *(1975).*

BELOW: *Steven Spielberg with John Williams, who holds the Oscar record of 51 Best Score nominations, with five wins.*

The average feature contains around 40 minutes of music. However, some have none at all, while others follow the avant-garde Danish film-making group Dogme 95 in restricting themselves to the audio material recorded on set during filming. Many silent pictures have recently been revived with new scores, which are often played live. But whether it's classical or experimental, nostalgic or anachronistic, film music's primary function remains to sustain narrative unity and connect the audience to the action. ∎

Sound principles

IDEA № 45

DUBBING

Screen sound is often taken for granted. Yet the mix of speech, music and effects has to be as subtle and precise as a film's visuals. Modern audio effects are every bit as sophisticated as computer-generated imagery, and the bulk of this sound sculpting takes place during post-production.

Tolling bells, clashing swords and chirping crickets were among the sound effects recorded on a Vitaphone disc for Don Juan *(1926).*

Sound effects were initially generated in movie houses using machines like the Allefex, which could produce some 50 sounds ranging from storms to birdsong, while the first sound feature – rather than talkie – *Don Juan* (1926), contained effects and an orchestral score. The talkies then forced the focus onto dialogue, as the primitive microphones and mixing techniques didn't allow for the modulation of recording levels. Moreover, their sensitivity restricted movement by either the cast or the camera, while editorial difficulties with synchronization saw average shot lengths increase from 4 to 10 seconds, with pictures becoming more verbose and static.

However, techniques in dubbing or adding re-recorded sound improved immeasurably in the mid-1930s, especially once MGM technician Douglas Shearer established the Academy curve to standardize methods of reducing hiss during the recording, dubbing and theatrical playback of monaural sound. Equalizers enabled sound perspective and, even though engineers only had four channels at their disposal, they still achieved such memorable sounds as King Kong's roar, Fred Astaire's tapping feet and Orson Welles's overlapping dialogue.

The post-World War II development of magnetic tape and multi-track equipment gave mixers greater latitude. But with exhibitors reluctant to shoulder the cost of stereophonic

conversion after just installing wide screens, cinema sound only assumed a new dimension with the introduction of Ray Dolby's noise-reduction system in the mid-1970s, which greatly enhanced the quality of the sound in blockbusters like *Star Wars* and *Close Encounters of the Third Kind* (both 1977).

In many countries, dubbed dialogue is preferred to so-called live speech. But in Hollywood the original delivery is retained wherever possible, although looping, as re-recording dialogue is often called, does allow performers to rectify delivery or timing issues and make late script changes. The once-laborious task of dubbing has been expedited by the Automatic Dialogue Replacement process, which is also used to add the background chatter nicknamed 'walla'. ADR is also employed in restoration work, with Anthony Hopkins notably impersonating Laurence Olivier in the 1991 overhaul of *Spartacus* (1960).

Vocal substitution became a common practice in the early sound era, as *Singin' in the Rain* (1952) amusingly showed by having shrill Jean Hagen, a siren of the silent era, mime to Debbie Reynolds's mellifluous tones. Marni Nixon sang for Deborah Kerr in *The King and I* (1956) and Audrey Hepburn in *My Fair Lady* (1964). As a performer Nixon may have remained largely anonymous, but playback singers such as sisters Asha Bhosle and Lata Mangeshkar became as celebrated

as the Bollywood superstars who lip-sync to them. Nixon also guested in Disney's *Mulan* (1998) and the voice track for most animated features is pre-recorded to provide pacing and personality cues for the animators.

Sound effects, however, are dubbed after the shoot by either sound editors or Foley artists. Named after Jack Foley – an innovative but uncredited sound man at Universal between 1929 and 1960 – the latter create just about every movie sound that isn't ambient, spoken or musical. Using props to reproduce everything from footsteps to gunshots, they give fictional and documentary films alike the audio authenticity that reinforces three-time Oscar-winner Walter Murch's contention that 'the better the sound, the better the image'. Digitization may have transformed screen sound, but nothing beats a little human ingenuity. ∎

ABOVE: *The mighty ape's bellow in* **King Kong** *(1933) was achieved by effects mixer Murray Spivak playing a lion's roar backwards at half speed.*

RIGHT: *Marni Nixon dubbed much of Eliza Doolittle's singing in* **My Fair Lady** *(1964), but Audrey Hepburn performed the chorus of 'Just You Wait' herself.*

FAR RIGHT: *When* **Spartacus** *(1960) was restored, Anthony Hopkins dubbed Laurence Olivier's lines in the infamous 'snails and oysters' exchange with Tony Curtis.*

Overcoming the language barrier

IDEA № 46
SUBTITLES

Subtitles are often difficult to read, rarely provide verbatim translations and are actively disliked by a sizeable proportion of the world's viewing public. Despite their drawbacks, however, they have been helping audiences understand films for over a century.

No one's entirely sure when intertitles, the forerunners of modern subtitles, were first used, but captions linking the action appear in R.W. Paul's *Scrooge* (1901) and began occurring more frequently after multi-scene films became the norm. Most offered written expository outlines of the ensuing action, but spoken titles became increasingly common in American pictures from 1908, with the dialogue being intercut with shots of the speaker from around 1912.

D.W. Griffith resisted dialogue captions and the increasingly popular technique of cross-cutting between the speaker and the text. But, like many of his European counterparts, he continued to use narrative intertitles into the 1920s. Only the most significant parts of the dialogue were written out, and directors like Cecil B. De Mille and Ernst Lubitsch delighted in leaving the more risqué utterances to the viewer's imagination. However, many felt that intertitles slowed a picture's pace and distracted from the imagery and F.W. Murnau famously eschewed them altogether in *The Last Laugh* (1924).

Yet intertitles were crucial to cinema's successful export. Rather than simply being translated, they were creatively adapted for specific audiences, with names, settings and other cultural details being amended to increase accessibility. Indeed, by the end of the silent era, American captions were being reworked for 36 different language markets. Yet when the talkies arrived, Hollywood followed the example of its European rivals in producing foreign-language versions of its most prestigious pictures.

Filmed at Elstree in English, French and German, E.A. Dupont's *Atlantic* (1929) was the first multi-language release. But the hub of continental production was the studio Paramount built outside Paris, which employed a 24-hour shooting schedule to make movies in up to 14 languages. Joinville completed 100 features and 50 shorts in its first year, but language transfer dubbing and subtitling soon showed themselves more cost-effective, although that didn't stop later features such as Jean Renoir's *The Golden Coach* (1953) and Werner Herzog's *Nosferatu the Vampyre* (1979) from being issued in multi-language formats.

The European preference for dubbing was rooted in the refusal of the authoritarian regimes in Italy, Germany, Spain and the Soviet Union to screen films in their original

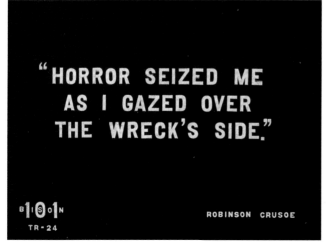

Intertitles conveyed Robert Z. Leonard's narration in Otis Turner's 30-minute adaptation of Daniel Defoe's Robinson Crusoe *(1913).*

language. However, nationalism also prompted France to adopt dubbing and this Gallicization became an art in itself: Gérard Depardieu thus revoiced Kenneth Branagh in *Henry V* (1989), although when *Cyrano de Bergerac* (1990) achieved an international release Depardieu's own performance remained intact courtesy of Anthony Burgess's English subtitles.

As this last example suggests, after long vacillation, Britain finally plumped for subtitling, along with Scandinavia, Japan and Brazil. But while subtitles preserve a picture's artistic integrity by retaining the original language and vocal performance, they can also obscure and deflect attention away from the visuals. Moreover, many consider them elitist in comparison with dubbing's greater

inclusivity. But problems with lip-synching and inflection and lapses in audio synchrony and ambient integration often reduce re-recording's effectiveness.

Clearly, neither technique is wholly satisfactory. Yet they enable cinema to be a truly global medium. Cost-conscious Hollywood has been keen to discard dubbing. But audience demand in key territories such as India, China and Mexico suggests there's no immediate end in sight to the sub-dub impasse. ∎

Scenes translated from Japanese into English, Danish and Finnish in Clint Eastwood's Letters From Iwo Jima *(2006).*

Keeping cinema-goers up to date

IDEA № 47
NEWSREELS

Newsreels proved crucial to several technological and stylistic developments in cinema, not to mention establishing the format of the TV news bulletin that would supplant them. First and foremost, though, they gave audiences around the world a better understanding of the tumultuous times in which they lived.

ABOVE: *Pathé News was a key part of British cinema shows from 1910–70.*

BELOW: *The Pathé News crew covers Elizabeth II's coronation in Westminster Abbey, June 1953.*

The first topicals or animated newspapers, as newsreels were initially known, allowed viewers with limited literacy skills to keep up with national and international events. Opening with a hard news story, the half-dozen pieces in a silent reel lasted between 40 and 90 seconds each. These rarely represented scoops and were often outdated by the time they were screened. But, with few papers printing photographs, the cine-gazettes launched by Pathé in France, Britain and the USA between 1908 and 1910 made the Great and the Good seem more familiar and fostered the new cult of celebrity.

Most newsreels adopted a neutral tone. However, Lenin recognized the propagandist value of cinema and supported Dziga Vertov's efforts to promulgate the Bolshevik message through the *Kino-Pravda* newsreels (1922–25) that afforded the first practical application of montage. Communist regimes in Eastern Europe, China and Cuba later followed suit, and the Allies and Axis powers alike sought to win hearts and minds with newsreels during World War II.

Sound significantly increased newsreel's potency after Fox Movietone added ambient noise, speech and music to its selections several months before the release of *The Jazz Singer* in 1927. Two years later, Fox attempted a widescreen version using the Grandeur

process, while a number of other newsreels experimented with colour. Whatever the format, the tone of the commentary allowed largely uncensored one-reelers to slip authoritatively but genially from weighty reportage to coverage of civic ceremonies, sporting events, novelty items and advertorial footage of the sponsoring studio's biggest stars attending the premieres of their latest pictures.

Such was the popularity of newsreels that they played in dedicated theatres as well as on standard cinema bills. Documentarist and critic Paul Rotha insisted that newsreels were descriptive rather than creative, yet they were frequently used as plot devices in the likes of Laurel and Hardy's *Sons of the Desert* (1933). The 'Voice of God' narrative style pioneered by Louis de Rochemont's *The March of Time* (1939–51) similarly influenced the opening segment of *Citizen Kane* (1941) and added authenticity to hard-hitting dramas such as *The House on 92nd Street* (1945), which de Rochemont produced for Fox. Roberto Rossellini's *Paisà* (1946) also reflected newsreels, while the lightweight cameras and portable sound equipment used to record them proved vital to the evolution of Cinéma Vérité, Direct Cinema, **Free Cinema** and the Nouvelle Vague.

Although editorial magazines like RKO's *This Is America* and Rank's *This Modern Age* enjoyed brief success,

growing public scepticism and the advent of television newscasts tipped the newsreel into a rapid postwar decline in the USA. Yet it remained the only form of indigenous film-making in many African and Latin American countries. Moreover, as Germaine Dulac, Esther Shub and Yuliya Solntseva had earlier demonstrated, it was also one of the few cinematic fields where women could thrive. ∎

ABOVE: *A Fox Movietone News van seeking out a story in 1931 in Culver City, the home of Hollywood's largest studio, Metro-Goldwyn-Mayer.*

RIGHT: *Between compiling the 23 editions of* **Kino-Pravda**, *Dziga Vertov applied his newsreel techniques to the Young Pioneers documentary,* **Kino Glaz** *(1924).*

'Debate rages ... about the justification for censorship.'

ABOVE: *Provocative shots of Jane Russell's bust in* **The Outlaw** *prompted a five-year stand-off between director Howard Hughes and the Production Code Administration.*

RIGHT: *While in prison, Yilmaz Güney wrote many screenplays like* **Yol** *(1982), which were directed according to his instructions by Serif Gören and Zeki Ökten.*

See no evil

Abbas Kiarostami's films, including Certified Copy *(2010), were banned in Iran during the later years of his life. The film was the first feature made outside his homeland.*

IDEA № 48

CENSORSHIP

Ever since Senator James A. Bradley objected to the sight of dancer Carmencita's ankles and petticoats in an 1894 Kinetoscope loop, moving pictures have been subject to censorship. The unique power of mass persuasion attributed to cinema has made it especially susceptible to proscription and classification.

Censorship is an instrument of control that has usually entailed the excision of unpalatable scenes, the banning of entire pictures or the silencing of contentious artists. Spaniard Luis Buñuel was among many film-makers who endured exile in the twentieth century to retain their freedom of expression. Sergei Paradjanov and Yilmaz Güney were imprisoned by the Soviet and Turkish authorities respectively for their refusal to conform, while Sadao Yamanaka and Herbert Selpin paid the ultimate price for resisting official policy in militarist Japan and Nazi Germany.

Countries with nationalized film industries tend to operate the strictest forms of censorship. But religious and ethical considerations often dictate what can be seen on screen as much as political expediency. Kissing was long prohibited in Indian features, while the depiction of women has often proved problematic for Muslim film-makers. For much of cinema's history, the portrayal of obscenity, profanity, blasphemy, criminality and violence was forbidden even in supposedly liberal states.

Hollywood has often been less concerned with the moral welfare of its audience than the profitability of its pictures. It grew increasingly daring following the Supreme Court's Mutual Decision (1915), which denied movies freedom of speech. But a series of scandals that tarnished the film community's reputation in the early 1920s persuaded the studios to demonstrate their contrition by adopting the list of 'Don'ts and Be Carefuls' drafted by Will H. Hays of the Motion Picture Producers and Distributors Association.

Talkies enabled a franker discussion of taboo topics than the silents and as a result Hollywood again incurred the wrath of conservative forces. But it took the Catholic Legion of Decency's threat of a nationwide boycott in 1934 for the moguls to accept the system of voluntary self-regulation known as the Production Code, which stipulated that a film's script and final edit had to be approved by the Hays Office in order to secure a release.

In addition to exerting moral control, the Code also promoted respect for the constitution, the law, religion, marriage and the family. Many blamed it for preventing Hollywood from tackling weighty issues in a realistic manner. It was only abandoned in favour of a ratings system in 1968, after movies had finally been granted First Amendment protection by the 1952 Miracle Decision and the market for family films had collapsed with the coming of television.

The home-entertainment boom of the 1980s precipitated several censorship crises, with the previously pragmatic British Board of Film Classification being coerced into slapping 18 certificates on so-called 'video nasties' by alarmist tabloids. Meanwhile, as debate rages elsewhere about the justification for censorship beyond issues relating to the protection of minors, the establishment continues to determine what can be screened in countries like Iran, China, Malaysia and Singapore. ∎

Beyond persuasion

IDEA № 49
PROPAGANDA

Whether consciously or not, all films contain an element of propaganda simply in the way they reflect the time and place in which they were made. However, the term is usually applied to features and documentaries that consciously strive to rally the committed, convert the sceptical or subvert the intransigent.

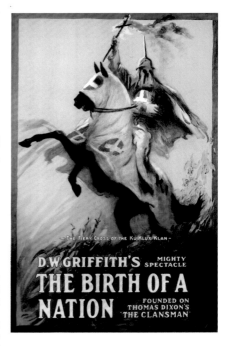

Once considered history written in lightning, D.W. Griffith's Civil War epic The Birth of a Nation *(1915) is now dismissed by many as racist propaganda.*

Propaganda succeeded for much of cinema's first century, since there was an innate trust in filmic truth. Yet early examples of films designed to arouse jingoistic sentiments like *Tearing Down the Spanish Flag* (1898) were actually reconstructions and not authentic records; much of the trench action screened during the Great War was similarly staged. The German High Command recognized the potential of film propaganda much more quickly than its British or French counterparts and, in 1917, it appropriated several commercial companies to form the state-controlled Universum Film Aktiengesellschaft to co-ordinate production (see **Film Schools**). UFA would continue to dominate the German film industry throughout the Weimar and Nazi eras.

Feigned footage of atrocities and savage denunciations such as Rupert Julian's *The Kaiser, the Beast of Berlin* (1918) confirmed[1] film's newfound potential for demonizing and demoralizing the enemy. Lenin similarly recognized its ability to inform and inspire and dispatched agit-prop trains across the Soviet Union to spread the Bolshevik message through Dziga Vertov's *Kino-Pravda* newsreels (1922–25) and the montage features of Sergei Eisenstein, Vsevolod Pudovkin and Alexander Dovzhenko. Stalin was more cautious about cinema and imposed a restrictive code of Socialist Realism designed to promote government policy. Yet front-line bulletins like the *Fighting Film Albums*

(1941–42) and allegories such as Eisenstein's *Ivan the Terrible* (1944) effectively sustained morale during World War II.

Escapism also played a significant part in propaganda material in the USSR, as it did in Germany. Following the failure of overtly propagandist pictures like *S.A.–Mann Brand* and *Hitler Youth Quex* (both 1933), Joseph Goebbels preferred to attempt to manipulate the masses through musicals, spectacles and biopics. Even Leni Riefenstahl's *Triumph of the Will* (1935) eschewed specific ideology to reinforce Hitler's cult of personality. On the other hand, no other warring nation produced films as pernicious as *Jew Süss* and *The Eternal Jew* (both 1940).

In Britain, the Ministry of Information encouraged a mix of firm paternalism and quirky humour in its newsreels and public information shots, while features such as *Went the Day Well?* (1942) and *Western Approaches* (1944) were notable for a documentary realism that was rarely employed in Hollywood's more gung-ho outings The US studios never really fathomed the mood of Occupied Europe, but the home-front dramas, service comedies, Good Neighbour musicals intended to bind Latin America to the Allied cause and combat adventures they churned out after Pearl Harbor proved as vital to the war effort as graver fare like Frank Capra's *Why We Fight* series (1942–45).

As a **Third Cinema** emerged, propaganda remained a key weapon throughout the Cold War. But while

state industries in Cuba and China and behind the Iron Curtain continued to toe the Party line, film-makers in the West were as likely to challenge government orthodoxy as support it. Consequently, John Ford's pro-war *Vietnam! Vietnam!* (1971) went unreleased as Peter Davis's *Hearts and Minds* (1974) won the Academy Award for Best Documentary; an oppositional tone has subsequently characterized most treatises on the wars in Iraq and Afghanistan. Many exposés of globalization, political chicanery and climate change have been similarly adversarial. But for all their postmodern irony and rhetorical irreverence, these films are every bit as propagandist as their forebears – and are often more sanctimonious, tendentious and unscrupulous. ∎

Eschewing political ideology, Leni Riefenstahl used spectacle, nature, religion and folklore to elicit a patriotic response to **Triumph of the Will** *(1935), her official record of the 1934 Nuremberg rally.*

„Triumph des Willens"

Foto: Reichsparteitagfilm

194

Tripping the social 'fantastique'

IDEA № 50
POETIC REALISM

TOP: *Dita Parlo and Jean Dasté: true love threatened by social reality in Jean Vigo's Parisian barge drama,* L'Atalante *(1934).*

ABOVE: *Terence Davies casts a Poetic-Realist glow over 11-year-old Liverpudlian Leigh McCormack in* The Long Day Closes *(1992).*

Focusing on shattered illusions, lost love and existential ennui, the French *cinéma du désenchantement* of the 1930s was characterized by a commitment to tackling the issues confronting the working poor with an elegiac naturalism that eschewed idealistic Hollywood conventions.

Rooted in the populist literature of Pierre Mac Orlan and Francis Carco and the sombre émigré silents made in Paris in the 1920s, Poetic Realism has exerted an influence that far exceeds its limited original output. It was foreshadowed by social-realist dramas like Jean Grémillon's *La Petite Lise* (1930) and Pierre Chenal's *La Rue sans nom* (1932), as well as René Clair's *Sous les toits de Paris* (1930), *À nous la liberté* and *Le Million* (both 1931), which sought to put ordinary people on screen. Marcel Pagnol's *Marius* trilogy (1931–36) similarly transcended its stage origins, and also anticipated Neorealism, through a use of Provençal locations. But it was the combination of French cinema's non-industrialization and the changing political climate caused by the rise and fall of the Front Populaire that allowed this form, which Mac Orlan referred to as the *fantastique social*, to flourish.

Jean Vigo uniquely depicted grinding urban poverty with an avant-garde sensibility in *L'Atalante* (1934), but the films of Marcel Carné, Jean Renoir and Julien Duvivier shared an everyday emotional veracity that was achieved through a mix of street authenticity and the studio stylization of designers Alexandre Trauner and Lazare Meerson.

The literate scripts of Jacques Prévert, Charles Spaak and Henri Jeanson prefigured the 'Tradition of Quality' that would so incense François Truffaut and prompt both the *politique des auteurs* (see **Auteur Theory**) and the Nouvelle Vague. But critic André Bazin detected in them a hard-boiled 'invisibly poetic' prose that not only influenced Hollywood noir, but also post-World War II outsider cinema, whose virile yet vulnerable anti-heroes recalled the everymen played by the great French actor Jean Gabin, whose fight for passion and happiness was doomed by their milieu, inherent flaws and fate. Indeed, as the communal optimism of Renoir's *Le Crime de Monsieur Lange* (1935) and *La vie est à nous* (1936) gave way to isolation and despair as Europe drifted inexorably towards war, Gabin served as a barometer of national self-esteem in Duvivier's *Pépé le Moko* (1937), Renoir's *La Grande Illusion* (1937) and *The Human Beast* (1938), and Carné's *Port of Shadows* (1938) and *Daybreak* (or *Le jour se lève*) (1939).

But it was Renoir's defeatist satire *The Rules of the Game* (1939) that extirpated Poetic Realism. Carné sought vainly to revive it in the 1950s, but audiences demanded coarser dramas about gangsters, rebellious youths and fallen women. Yet its legacy is much greater than the mise en scène technique it engendered. Jean-Luc Godard envisaged *Band of Outsiders* (1964) as 'a French film with a prewar atmosphere' and the Poetic-Realist spirit has since imbued works by directors as diverse as Robert Bresson, Agnès Varda, Jacques Demy, Olivier Assayas, Atom Egoyan, Terence Davies and Aki Kaurismäki. ∎

The epitome of poetic realism: Jean Gabin and Michèle Morgan face an uncertain future in Marcel Carné's Port of Shadows *(1938).*

'The first constructed sets were built for the Italian superspectacles.'

ABOVE: *Lazare Meerson's sets were key to achieving the romanticized working-class atmosphere in René Clair's* **Sous les toits de Paris** *(1930).*

RIGHT: *The sets used in Enrico Guazzoni's Roman epic* **Messalina** *(1922) were unrivalled in their day for size and historical accuracy.*

Designs for living

IDEA Nº 51

STUDIO REALISM

Designer Peter Grant created a 1930s American town with minimalist sets and lines on the studio floor for Lars von Trier's Dogville *(2003).*

Production design has come a long way in the past century, moving from painted backdrops to computer-generated scenery. But one thing has remained constant: the need to create credible environments to persuade the audience of the authenticity of the action on the screen.

Georges Méliès was the first production designer, with the atmospheric poetry of his fantasy settings influencing the series and serials of Victorin Jasset and Louis Feuillade. However, the first constructed sets were built for the Italian superspectacles of Enrico Guazzoni and Giovanni Pastrone, which inspired D.W. Griffith's *Intolerance* (1916) and instigated the American tradition of recreating reality on a studio stage or backlot.

Indoor shooting became more commonplace with improvements in artificial lighting. This not only enabled producers to keep costs down, but also gave directors complete control over every aspect of filming. Inspired by the work of Swedes Victor Sjöström and Mauritz Stiller, the German *Kammerspielfilm* and *Strassenfilm* (see **Expressionism**) used studio realism to reveal the psychology of their dramas by emphasizing symbolic elements within the mise en scène. Eschewing the stylization of Expressionism, G.W. Pabst's *Joyless Street* (1925) exploited optimum studio conditions to develop the subjective camera and invisible editing techniques

that had such an impact upon American cinema.

The industrial process allowed for less experimentation, however, and the Hollywood brand of studio realism was characterized by an impersonal technical perfection. Yet art directors Cedric Gibbons, Hans Dreier and Robert Day achieved recognizable styles of homely opulence, Continental elegance and urban grit at MGM, Paramount and Warner Bros respectively. Poverty Row also had its own realist aesthetic, whether it was re-imagining the look of a frontier town or fashioning the claustrophobic, chiaroscuro'd interiors of film noir.

But if Hollywood realism had a self-consciously generic feel, French realism was unique to a specific time and place. With milieu intrinsically linked to fate, designers like Lazare Meerson and Alexandre Trauner paid such meticulous attention to authentic detail that their studio sets had a profound influence upon Neorealism. Indeed, the mise en scène became so central to the action that the camera began to roam freely around it in long takes that challenged the

editorial strategies of the classical narrative style.

Yet the perfectionism of post-World War II designers was cited along with literate scripts for stifling French cinema and this 'Tradition of Quality' was swept away by the Nouvelle Vague, which advocated location shooting. The introduction of lighter cameras and faster colour stocks persuaded more directors to film in the real world, and this shift coincided with the decline of studio systems everywhere. Even Hollywood destroyed sets that had become too expensive to recondition and store.

Mainstream realism has been rare in the blockbuster age. But throughout film history, periods of stylization have usually been followed by returns to greater simplicity. So no matter how sophisticated CGI may become, there should always be a place for the intimacy and interactivity of a realistic studio set. ■

The buzz of the B-hive

BELOW: *Poster for* Cat People *(1942), the first of the nine superior horror Bs Russian-born Val Lewton produced at RKO.*

BOTTOM: *Shot in three weeks, Jean Rollin's* Lèvres de Sang *(1975) is an example of the erotic European horror Bs from the 1960s and '70s.*

IDEA № 52

B MOVIES

Produced on limited budgets by second-string casts and crews and frequently lacking in originality and technique, the B movies churned out by studios and independents alike were key to the aesthetic development and economic viability of film industries around the world.

Rooted in the low-budget featurettes released by Universal under Bluebird, Red Feather and Butterfly in the 1910s, the Hollywood B allowed executives to make the most cost-effective use of facilities and personnel, while also ensuring a steady supply of mainstream entertainment for neighbourhood venues whose regulars did not always appreciate the subtleties of more prestigious fare.

The B became a staple of American cinema shows during the Depression. The demise of ciné-variety, which offered live acts as a supplement to the movie bill, and the decline in weekly attendances from 110 to 60 million between 1930 and 1933 prompted the decision to add an hour-long attraction to the cartoons, newsreels and shorts already supporting the big picture in order to offer value for money to matinee patrons who often preferred quantity to quality. Costing $70–80,000, the average B picture was sold to exhibitors for a flat fee as part of a block-booked package and often made a $10,000 profit at a time when many theatres changed the bill twice a week.

With 75 per cent of Hollywood's 1930s output being second features, both majors and minors launched their own B units. These invariably adhered to the different studios' house styles in recycling old plots, sets and stock footage, while also providing gainful employment to contracted aspirants and veterans. The most popular items were Westerns, thrillers and comedies, with series evolving around such enduring characters as Hopalong Cassidy, Charlie Chan, the Falcon, Blondie and the Mexican Spitfire. But while MGM's Andy Hardy and Dr Kildare franchises were as polished as their rivals' A pictures, Poverty Row outfits like Monogram, Republic, Grand National and the Producers Releasing Corporation stuck to cheap-and-cheerful formulae in refining the horror, sci-fi and film noir genres.

Occasionally, the likes of RKO's Val Lewton produced a sleeper hit or cult classic. But while many stars and front-rank directors got their start in B movies, dependable artisans such as Edgar G. Ulmer, Phil Karlson, Sam Newfield, Lew Landers, William Beaudine and Joseph Kane spent much of their careers on Gower Gulch before moving into television after a combination of the Paramount Decrees, inflated costs, increased running times and the switch to colour shooting effectively ended traditional B production in the early 1950s.

Within a couple of years, however, a new wave of Bs was unleashed by Allied Artists and American Independent Pictures attracting a juvenile clientele who wanted the racier brand of counterculture movie that eventually became known as exploitation. Showmen like William Castle, Edward D. Wood, Jr and Roger Corman encouraged a vogue for teenpics, gory horrors, creature features, biker movies and nudie-cuties that played at drive-ins and grindhouses and eventually led to the collapse of the Production Code and the overdue emergence of free expression in US cinema.

Vincent Price in **The Masque of Red Death** *(1964), the penultimate entry in Roger Corman's eight-film Poe cycle for AIP.*

B movies weren't exclusively an American phenomenon, as they had long been produced worldwide, often to meet government-imposed quotas or to defy Hollywood. However, they were rarely exported before movie geeks like Quentin Tarantino referenced Asian and Latin American traditions during the 1990s indie boom that revived the B mentality. Subsequently, the greater affordability of film-making equipment has seen wannabe auteurs producing Z-grade fodder for specialist festivals and DVD labels, as well as for release online. Clearly, the spirit of the B-hive lives on. ∎

From Happy Hooligan to Harry Potter

IDEA № 53
SERIES

Few modern movie-goers will have heard of Bout-de-Zan, Joe Deebs, Philo Vance or Torchy Blane, let alone seen one of their films. Yet these characters headlined the series that preceded the mega-franchises that have dominated Hollywood thinking since the start of the blockbuster era.

Recurring characters had long been appearing in pulp fiction and the popular press before J. Stuart Blackton acquired comic-strip favourite Happy Hooligan for six films in 1900. Indeed, the emphasis was firmly on humour in many American and European series before the Great War, with the likes of Max Linder, Fatty Arbuckle and Charlie Chaplin adopting trademark traits in slapstick romps that often derived as much from character as situation.

Gilbert M. Anderson similarly devised the 'good bad man' persona for his Broncho Billy Westerns (1910–16) and their success inspired adventures like *The Hazards of Helen* (1914–17), which in turn affected the evolution of the serial. Yet action series had already become a fixture in France, thanks to Victorin Jasset's *Nick Carter* (1908) and *Zigomar* (1911).

Imitations featuring Dr Gar-el-Hama (Denmark, 1911–16), Stuart Webbs (Germany, 1914–26) and Za-la-Mort (Italy, 1915–24) followed, and genre franchises have since continued to flourish worldwide, whether they centre on sword'n'sandal strongmen like Maciste, masked wrestlers such as Santo, martial artists like Wong Fei-hung, master swordsmen such as Zatoichi, Native Americans like Winnetou or eccentric ghouls such as Coffin Joe. However, arthouse instances, such as François Truffaut's Antoine Doinel saga (1959–79), have been rarer, as there was less risk involved in producing populist fare that traded in either lowbrow comedy – like the *Carry On* films (UK, 1957–92) and *Le Gendarme de Saint-Tropez* (France, 1964–82) – or domestic scenarios constructed around cosy characters such as the Olsen Gang (Denmark, 1968–2001) and Tora-san (Japan, 1969–95).

Following the fortunes of an itinerant pedlar, the latter harked back to Hollywood's Golden Age, when cartoons, live-action shorts and second features were corralled into series to offer reassurance and value for money during the Depression and the war years. Majors, minors and B-hivers produced series pictures, with MGM's *The Thin Man* and Andy Hardy, Fox's Charlie Chan and Paramount's 'Road' movies devised for Bob Hope and Bing Crosby having considerably more polish than the low-budget comedies, thrillers, oaters (B Westerns) and jungle adventures churned out by Columbia, Universal, Monogram and Republic. Yet block booking ensured that audiences got to see the Mexican Spitfire, the Three Mesquiteers, Boston Blackie and Blondie as often as more iconic figures like Tarzan and Sherlock Holmes, which not only ensured that entire units were kept busy, but also that the studios could blood new talent in tried-and-trusted formats.

A number of series migrated to television, including *Perry Mason*, *Dr Kildare*, *The Saint* and *Lassie*, and small-screen staples such as the soap opera, the sitcom, the ranch Western and the police procedural all had their roots in

Between 1934 and 1947, William Powell and Myrna Loy played society sleuths Nick and Nora Charles in six MGM whodunits.

series features. However, *Star Trek*, *The Muppet Show* and *Mission: Impossible* subsequently made the opposite journey, as corporate Hollywood began placing increased reliance on strings of horror, sci-fi, action, cop, comic and **kidpic** sequels, as well as more consciously created series like *Star Wars* and *Harry Potter*. The latter now vies with *James Bond* for the most profitable franchise of them all. ∎

'Studios could blood new talent in tried-and-trusted formats.'

ABOVE: *Johnny Weissmuller with Maureen O'Sullivan and Cheeta while shooting of one of the 12 Tarzan movies he made between 1932 and 1948.*

LEFT: *Daniel Radcliffe asks for directions to Platform 9¾ at King's Cross Station in* Harry Potter and the Philosopher's Stone *(2001).*

Brevity is the soul of wit

Ben Turpin crosses Charlie
Chaplin in Essanay's two-reel
lampoon of showbiz types,
His New Job (1915).

IDEA № 54

SHORTS

The majority of moving pictures in cinema's first two decades ran for one or two reels of film. Yet even after features came to dominate, the so-called 'short' remained a versatile and popular form, with many of the medium's finest artists producing examples at various stages in their careers.

The first films were unedited and lasted no longer than 50 seconds. But even as content and form became more ambitious, film-makers continued to operate within one or two reels – running between 10 and 20 minutes – and industries worldwide were geared towards the production, distribution and exhibition of short subjects until the mid-1910s. However, the adaptability of the format enabled it to survive the switch to features, and shorts remained a mainstay of American cinema programmes until block booking was outlawed and the studios were divested of their theatre chains in 1948.

Short documentaries, travelogues and educationals were all produced during the silent era, along with slapstick comedies. Most countries had their own knockabout clowns, but

Charlie Chaplin found international fame and his success institutionalized the comic two-reeler, with Laurel and Hardy, W.C. Fields and the Three Stooges continuing the tradition through the transition to sound.

Animated shorts proved equally durable, with several studios having their own dedicated production units. Even after the cartoon migrated to television, short animation continued to thrive, both within the mainstream and the avant-garde. Indeed, the short provided the optimum form of expression for many **experimental** film-makers, as well as those specializing in nature, medical, instructional, sponsored, propaganda, sport and topical films.

The short also played a pivotal role in the development of sound. Thomas

Edison first matched sound and vision in the Kinetophone in 1895, but problems with synchronization and amplification confounded processes like the Cameraphone (1908) and Photokinema (1921).

In 1923, however, Lee De Forest began recording such vaudeville stars as Eddie Cantor on the Phonofilm sound-on-film system. Three years later, Warners used Vitaphone to showcase Al Jolson and Ruth Etting, and Fox followed suit in 1927 with its Movietone soundies and newsreel.

Bing Crosby, Judy Garland, Cary Grant, Ginger Rogers and Humphrey Bogart made their screen debut in such films, while directors from René Clair to Steven Spielberg started out making shorts. Indeed, the Hollywood studios used series like *Crime Does Not Pay*, the *Pete Smith Specialties* and *Joe McDoakes* as a proving ground for aspiring talent.

Film-making hopefuls still use shorts as calling cards. But the short is an art in itself, with its own international festivals and categories at the Academy Awards. The short also gained a new lease of life in the anthology film, which includes several self-contained stories within a single feature. Numerous horror movies followed in the wake of Ealing's *Dead of Night* (1945). But the omnibus also found an arthouse niche, with auteur anthologies like *The Seven Deadly Sins* (1962) and *RoGoPaG* (1963) inspiring recent outings such as *Paris, je t'aime* (2006) and *To Each His Own Cinema* (2007). ∎

'Directors from René Clair to Steven Spielberg started out making shorts.'

ABOVE: *Starring Stan Laurel and Oliver Hardy, James Parrott's* The Music Box *(1932) won the inaugural Academy Award for Best Live Action Short Film.*

BELOW: **Paris, je t'aime** *(2006), a portmanteau of vignettes by 20 different directors.*

BELOW: *Marjane Satrapi teamed with Vincent Paronnaud to adapt her graphic novel,* **Persepolis** *(2007), which recalled her experiences following the Iranian Revolution*

LEFT: *Chihiro and Haku in Hayao Miyazaki's Oscar-winning fantasy* **Spirited Away** *(2001), which confirmed Studio Ghibli's dominance of Japanimation.*

From pencils to pixels

IDEA № 55
ANIMATION

ABOVE: *Terrytoon stalwart Mighty Mouse was among the first big-screen cartoon characters to find a niche on television.*

BELOW: *Lotte Reiniger's exquisite silhouette masterpiece* **The Adventures of Prince Achmed** *(1926) is the oldest surviving animated feature.*

Much of cinema's prehistory was shaped by animated images produced by optical toys, while most cinema programmes included a cartoon until the 1970s. Today, animated features are key to children acquiring the movie-going habit.

Émile Reynaud projected the first animated films with his Théâtre Optique in 1892 (see **Persistence of Vision**). But the arrival of moving photographic pictures reduced animation to an expensive and time-consuming novelty. Nevertheless, Émile Cohl and Winsor McCay refined two-dimensional cartooning, while Arthur Melbourne Cooper and Ladislaw Starewicz mastered the stop-motion method of animating models one frame at a time. In the 1910s, Americans Earl Hurd and John Bray divided the drawing and colouring of characters and backgrounds between specialist artists and further streamlined the process by introducing cels.

This industrial approach was emulated by Walt Disney, whose success with characters like Mickey Mouse encouraged him to move into feature animation with *Snow White and the Seven Dwarfs* (1937) Although his stories emphasized conservative values, Disney was receptive to aesthetic and commercial innovation. Artists Ub Iwerks and Fred Moore convinced him to combine realism with anthropomorphism, earning the studio the loyalty of young fans who would purchase its merchandise, watch its TV shows and visit its theme parks. Disney also embraced new techniques such as multi-plane photography and rotoscoping, which allowed the tracing of live-action footage and paved the way for the digital mapping and tracing and image-capture processes now used in computer animation.

Such was the demand for cartoons that several Hollywood studios opened their own animation units. The Warner trio of Friz Freleng, Tex Avery and Chuck Jones, along with MGM's William Hanna and Joseph Barbera, channelled the old slapstick comedy style into socko vehicles for Bugs Bunny and Tom and Jerry, which hugely influenced television animation from the 1950s. However, some American graphics drew on the postwar European modernist aesthetic that had itself been inspired by avant-gardists such as Oscar Fischinger, Hans Richter, Lotte Reiniger, Len Lye and Norman McLaren, who had fashioned a non-linear, non-objective and often abstract style in experimenting with direct-application, pixelation, pin-screen and silhouette techniques

Iron Curtain animators like Jiri Trnka, Jan Svankmajer and the members of the Zagreb School often produced subversively satirical work, while Japanese artists like *Astro Boy* creator Osamu Tezuka and the Oscar-winning director of *Spirited Away* (2001) Hayao Miyazaki opted for an escapist approach that drew inspiration from manga comic books. Anime has since had a profound influence on adult animations like *Persepolis* (2007), as well as on the computer-game graphics and digitized effects that have become a staple of the Hollywood blockbuster.

However, it was Disney that revived the global popularity of feature animation, with the likes of *Beauty and the Beast* (1991) and *The Lion King* (1994) presaging computer-generated Pixar

hits such as *Toy Story* (1997) and *Up* (2009), as well as Nick Park's endearing Wallace and Gromit 'claymation' romps, which employ stop-motion techniques to animate Plasticine **models**. ∎

Realizing the impossible

IDEA № 56
MODELS

In 1898, J. Stuart Blackton used cardboard cut-outs for his naval re-enactment *Battle of Santiago Bay.* The ships in the *Pirates of the Caribbean* franchise may be more three-dimensional and convincing, but they also demonstrate cinema's continued reliance on artisanal models in the age of computer-generated imagery.

Created by Nick Park at Aardman Animations, Wallace and Gromit are plasticine figures modelled over metal armatures and filmed using the stop-motion technique.

Models enable film-makers to set scenes in environments that would otherwise be impossible, problematic or too expensive to visit or build. They also permit their destruction by earthquake, flood, fire, incendiaries, mutant creatures and invading aliens.

The earliest model shots were not integrated with the live action. But the introduction of foreground miniatures and the Schüfftan process facilitated the illusion of habitable spaces in historical and futuristic pictures like *Ben-Hur* (1925) and *Metropolis* (1926). Natural landscapes were also cast in model form, as were aircraft, spaceships, superheroes and monsters, with the ingenuity and authenticity of their design, decoration, lighting and operation eventually being seen in moving contexts thanks to the development of the motion-control camera that enabled the precise movements required to merge the different elements of an effects shot.

The artisanal aspect of model-making and its ancillary water, cloud and pyrotechnic effects has given the craft a romantic cachet among film buffs. Yet the best SFX are those that create spectacle while essentially remaining invisible.

Fascinated by the stop-motion magic that Willis O'Brien concocted for *The Lost World* (1925) and *King Kong* (1933), Ray Harryhausen turned the incremental movement of articulated armatures into an art form in sci-fi allegories such as *The Beast from 20,000 Fathoms* (1953) and mythical adventures like *The Seventh Voyage of Sinbad* (1958). Moreover, he inspired latter-day practitioners such as Phil Tippett, whose stop-motion experience on *Star Wars* (1977) prompted the invention of the Go motion technique employed on *RoboCop* (1987), which gave animated effects a more naturalistically blurred look.

Harryhausen served his apprenticeship with George Pal, who later directed the stop-motion fairytale *tom thumb* (1958). An exile from Nazi Germany, Pal perfected the replacement technique of progressing frame-by-frame movement by adding new pieces to his models rather than manipulating them. But while his Puppetoons failed to capture American imaginations besotted with Disney cartoons, they continued a European tradition that dates back to Arthur Melbourne Cooper's *Matches: An Appeal* (1899).

The doyen of stop-motion puppetry was the Russian-born Ladislaw Starewich, who followed intricate insect satires like *The Cameraman's Revenge* (1911) with wry fables such as *The Tale of the Fox* (1930), whose influence was evident in Wes Anderson's *Fantastic Mr Fox* (2009). Czech maestro Jiří Trnka also started with charming sagas like *A Midsummer Night's Dream* (1959), but a new political audacity emerged in *The Hand* (1965), which prompted fellow countryman Jan Svankmajer to take an even more subversive approach in shorts such as *Dimensions of Dialogue* (1982) and features like *Little Otik* (2000).

Svankmajer's disciples include the Brothers Quay, Kihachiro Kawamoto, Tim Burton and Henry Selick, who challenged the growing hegemony of CGI with the first all-stop-motion 3-D feature *Coraline* (2009). Like Nick Park claymations such as *Wallace and Gromit in The Curse of the Were-Rabbit* (2005), this championed a texturality and tactility that computer software still can't match. ■

Ernst Kunstmann, Konstantin Irmen-Tschet and Erich Kettelhut produced the state-of-the-art models and trick photographic effects for **Metropolis** *(1926).*

BELOW: *Model-makers Ian MacKinnon and Peter Saunders brought Nelson Lowry's designs to life for the Roald Dahl adaptation* **Fantastic Mr Fox** *(2009).*

In the gutter: Lamberto Maggiorani and Enzo Staiola as father and son Antonio and Bruno Ricci in the most influential Neorealist drama, **Bicycle Thieves** *(1948).*

The poetry of ordinary life

NEOREALISM

Variously labelled a movement and a genre, Neorealism was rooted in the social, political and economic turmoil of a traumatized nation as Italy threw off its Fascist shackles at the end of World War II. But its naturalistic, anti-classical Hollywood influence has been global and enduring.

'The ideal film,' wrote screenwriter Cesare Zavattini, 'would be 90 minutes of the life of a man to whom nothing happens.' Despite urging contemporaries to repudiate plot contrivance and studio artifice, the closest Zavattini came to realizing his ambition was Vittorio De Sica's *Umberto D* (1952), the last masterpiece of what critic Umberto Barbaro called 'Neorealism'.

The great myth of the genre was its newness, which was perpetuated by practitioners keen to obfuscate their connection to Mussolini's film industry. While it differed from the 'white telephone' comedies (see **Genre**), propagandizing **epics** and lavish melodramas of the Fascist era, Neorealism's origins lay not only in nineteenth-century *verismo* literature, as well as Soviet revolutionary realism and French Poetic Realism, but also in disparate features by Elvira Notari, Alessandro Blasetti and Francesco De Robertis who had all been prominent in Mussolini's film industry. However, the demise of Fascist censorship did allow Italian directors to address previously proscribed topics with increased freedom.

Several Neorealists were Marxists who wanted cinema to develop class consciousness and proletarian unity. Thus, they not only eschewed the individualism and optimism of Hollywood feature-making, but also its classical narrative techniques. Played by non-professionals, the new breed of anti-heroes spoke their own vernacular in episodic dramas that were often shot on location in natural light and in long, mobile takes that respected real time. Making innovative use of negative space like bare walls and open skies, as well as grainy stock and post-synchronized sound, features like Roberto Rossellini's *Rome, Open City* (1945), Luchino Visconti's *La terra trema* and De Sica's *Bicycle Thieves* (both 1948) presented an objective appreciation of other people's reality that approached moral poetry.

This hybrid style failed to find a domestic audience, but it has inspired and incited Italian film-makers ever since. It also influenced German rubble films, Free Cinema, British social realism, Cinéma Vérité, the Nouvelle Vague and the Czech New Wave. Subsequently, its legacy has also been evident in Dogme 95, the minimalism of the Dardenne brothers and the 'readjustment dramas' made in post-Communist Eastern Europe.

Neorealism also manifested itself in the work of Argentinian Fernando Birri, Brazilian Nelson Pereira dos Santos and Cuban Tomás Gutiérrez Alea, which prepared the ground for Third Cinema. In India, Satyajit Ray's *Apu Trilogy* (1955–59) instigated a parallel cinema to the Bollywood mainstream, while Youssef Chahine's *Cairo Central Station* (1958) did much the same in Egypt. Indeed, African film-makers from Senegal's Ousmane

TOP: *Shooting in long takes on the streets in available light: Anna Magnani in Roberto Rossellini's* Rome, Open City *(1945).*

ABOVE: *Giuseppe De Santis's* Bitter Rice *(1949) was accused of rose-tinting realism by emphasizing Silvana Mangano's sex appeal.*

Sembène to Chad's Mahamat Saleh Haroun have adapted Neorealism to explore local themes, as have Tadashi Imai, Lino Brocka, Fruit Chan and Abbas Kiarostami. Even American cinema has evinced Neorealism in postwar 'problem pictures' addressing issues such as alcoholism and racial prejudice, the working-class African-American dramas of the 1970s LA School and the so-called 'neo-Neorealism' of Kelly Reichardt and Ramin Bahrani. ∎

Confounding and enriching linearity

FLASHBACKS

'I didn't create the situation, I'm just dealin' with it!': Mr White (Harvey Keitel) and Mr Pink (Steve Buscemi) between flashbacks in Tarantino's Reservoir Dogs *(1992).*

Flashbacks allow the cinematic representation of history, memory and subjective truth. Signalled by intertitles, dissolves, fades and cuts, their use enabled early film-makers to introduce a structural and psychological complexity that was readily appreciated by the increasingly sophisticated audiences of the 1910s – and still is today.

Despite being in abeyance for much of the 1920s, the screen flashback returned in the following decade, as Hollywood writers borrowed from modernist literature and radio drama to break the stolid conventions established by the first talkies. The favoured styles were the external flashback, in which the action rewound from a momentous opening to delineate preceding events, and the personal flashback, in which a character remembered or related an experience or was prompted to reminisce by a chance occurrence.

Many courtroom dramas relied on flashback sequences: this testimonial mode has remained popular, reinforcing causality in pictures like *The Usual Suspects* (1995) and *Slumdog Millionaire* (2008). But flashbacks are much more than convenient framing devices or visual alternatives to verbosity. In addition to manipulating story and time, they can facilitate viewer identification and shape emotional response by providing insights into a character's inner life. By juxtaposing actions, they create parallels, as in *The Godfather, Part II* (1974). They can also reveal information that has previously been suppressed and generate suspense by delaying its consequences. Moreover, flashbacks can deliberately obfuscate and mislead.

Although the term 'narratage' never caught on, Preston Sturges's blend of narrative and montage in his screenplay for William K. Howard's *The Power and the Glory* (1933) proved hugely influential, not least upon Orson Welles's *Citizen Kane* (1941), which emulated the earlier picture's use of voice-over and multiple perspectives. Confessional and investigative flashbacks also became key components of film noir, after Billy Wilder's *Double Indemnity* (1944) and Robert Siodmak's *The Killers* (1946) respectively. But it was the technique's flexibility that made it so valuable, with Alfred Hitchcock and Salvador Dalí dabbling in psychoanalysis and Surrealism in *Spellbound* (1945) and John Brahm inserting a flashback within a flashback in *The Locket* (1946).

Also in 1946, Frank Capra experimented with hypothetical flashbacks in *It's a Wonderful Life*, while Gene Kelly and Stanley Donen demonstrated the comic potential of anterior visuals contradicting the audio content in *Singin' in the Rain* (1952), which also lampooned the still-rare concept of the flashforward. Meanwhile, Hitchcock's *Stage Fright* and Akira Kurosawa's *Rashomon* (both 1950) suggested that the camera could dissemble in presenting subjective reality, and this subversive approach prompted innovators such as Alain Resnais to rescue the flashback from its clichéd functions in his mesmerizing treatise on time and memory *Last Year at Marienbad* (1961).

Despite the current reluctance to use broken timelines in mainstream movies, they still recur in blockbusters like James Cameron's *Titanic* (1997) and Disney animations such as *Treasure Planet* (2002). However, flashbacks tend to be used most imaginatively in indie and arthouse features like Quentin Tarantino's *Pulp Fiction* (1994), Christopher Nolan's *Memento* (2000) and Michael Haneke's *Hidden* (2005). ∎

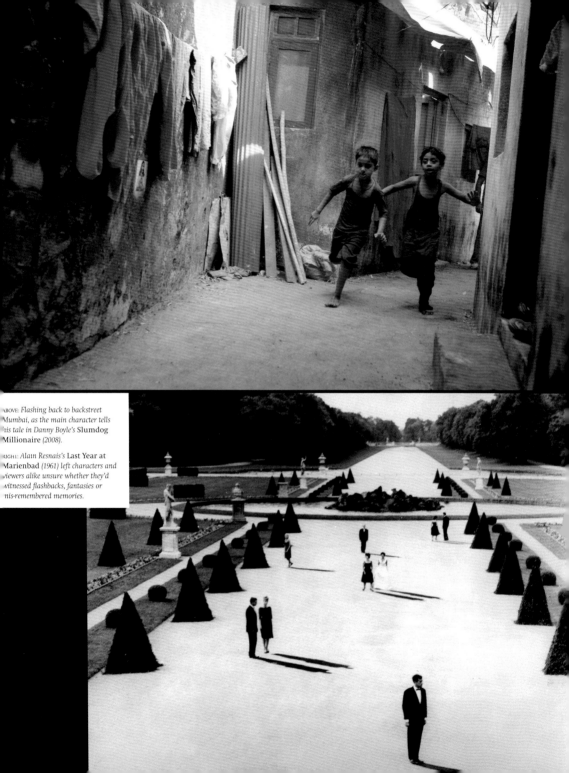

ABOVE: *Flashing back to backstreet Mumbai, as the main character tells his tale in Danny Boyle's* Slumdog Millionaire *(2008).*

RIGHT: *Alain Resnais's* Last Year at Marienbad *(1961) left characters and viewers alike unsure whether they'd witnessed flashbacks, fantasies or mis-remembered memories.*

*Borrowing from Bresson: Travis Bickle (Robert De Niro) writing the diaries that provide the voice-over for Martin Scorsese's **Taxi Driver** (1976).*

Telling it like it is?

ABOVE: *In adapting Georges Bernanos's* Diary of a Country Priest *(1951), Robert Bresson used voice-overs to emphasize its literary origins and filmic reality.*

BELOW: *Fred MacMurray's voice-over for* Double Indemnity *(1944) contains contrasting moments of naive optimism and wiser gloom.*

IDEA № 59
VOICE-OVER

Spoken narrative has often been dismissed by film theorists as the lazy last resort of writers unable to convey ideas audiovisually. Yet, for such a despised technique, the voice-over has proved invaluable across the generic range and been favoured by some of the world's best directors.

Despite most early films being accompanied by live lecturers (known as *benshi* in Japan), the popular attitude to voice-over can be summed up by Brian Cox's speech as screenwriting guru Robert McKee in Spike Jonze's *Adaptation* (2002): 'And God help you if you use voice-over in your work, my friends. God help you. That's flaccid, sloppy writing.' Partly inspired by Hollywood's preference for self-effacing craftsmanship and fears that talkies would reduce cinema to canned theatre, the technique was resisted outside documentaries and newsreels until the mid-1930s. However, the dynamism of radio narration prompted a volte-face and voice-overs have since been employed with distinction in melodramas (*The Magnificent Ambersons*, 1942), Westerns (*Red River*, 1948), musicals (*Singin' in the Rain*, 1952), epics (*King of Kings*, 1961), war films (*Apocalypse Now*, 1979), **teenpics** (*Stand By Me*, 1986) and comedies (*The Royal Tenenbaums*, 2001).

Regardless of time or setting, screen stories can be related from the viewpoint of a first person (*Fight Club*, 1999), third person (*The Shawshank Redemption*, 1994) or omniscient narrator (*Amélie*, 2001). In addition to providing basic exposition, such voice-overs can also clarify the action, offer character insights, enhance intimacy and introduce knowing irony. They can also replicate the tone of literary sources, as in *Tom Jones* (1963) and *Barry Lyndon* (1975), and can sometimes smooth awkward transitions in sprawling dramas like *Doctor Zhivago* (1965) or patch up pictures that have been heavily revised during editing, such as *Blade Runner* (1982). But, in the hands of masters like Orson Welles, Billy Wilder, Stanley Kubrick, Martin Scorsese and Woody Allen, voice-overs invariably complement the visuals rather than compensate for their shortcomings.

They were certainly central to the success of film noir, as on- and off-screen narration echoed around *Murder, My Sweet* (1944) and the Voice of God – as the style borrowed from newsreel was called – boomed in *The Naked City* (1948). Drawing on the acerbic argot of pulp fiction, saps confessed how they'd been duped by femmes fatales in *Double Indemnity* (1944) and *The Lady from Shanghai* (1947), while unreliable raconteurs dissembled in *Detour* (1945) and *Out of the Past* (1947). Noir also gave women a voice in *Mildred Pierce* (1945) and *Raw Deal* (1948), as well as in acclaimed melodramas such as *A Letter to Three Wives* (1949) and *All About Eve* (1950). However, female narrators have since mostly been confined to works by women directors like Jane Campion and Sally Potter.

Few European film-makers have emulated Sacha Guitry in preferring narration to dialogue in *The Story of a Cheat* (1936), but several have made exemplary use of voice-overs, including Robert Bresson, Ingmar Bergman, Alain Resnais, Jean-Luc Godard, François Truffaut and Eric Rohmer. Voice-overs also recurred in Third Cinema as a means of subverting Hollywood classicism, and they remain a valid narrative device in both arthouse and mainstream cinema. ∎

Low-key and hardboiled

IDEA № 60
FILM NOIR

An angel of doom lies in wait for Alain Delon's meticulous hitman in Jean-Pierre Melville's neo-noir masterpiece, Le Samouraï *(1967).*

Critically disdained, morally feared and industrially mistrusted, film noir subsisted on low budgets and B-movie status. Essentially an artistic ghetto for Hollywood's many European émigré directors in the 1940s and '50s, it used innovative shooting and lighting techniques to evoke the mood of anxiety and ambiguity sweeping postwar America.

Despite being named by the critic Nino Frank in 1946, film noir only became an acknowledged critical concept outside France in the 1960s. Subsequently, however, debate has raged about whether it's a genre, a movement, a style or a cycle. Few can even agree on what constitutes a 'noir'. Yet, regardless of canonical imprecision and terminological inexactitudes, film noir and neo-noir have had an incalculable impact on cinema worldwide.

Frank coined the phrase in noting the changed thematic and stylistic tone of five Hollywood features receiving a belated release in Paris: John Huston's *The Maltese Falcon* (1941), Edward Dmytryk's *Murder, My Sweet*, Billy Wilder's *Double Indemnity*, Otto Preminger's *Laura* (all 1944) and Wilder's *The Lost Weekend* (1945). Rooted in American hard-boiled fiction, German Expressionist and gothic horror films, radio dramas, French Poetic Realism and Italian Neorealism, these pessimistic studies of destructive urges and uncontrollable consequences reflected the changing social attitudes exacerbated by wartime events at home and abroad. Soon they were also conveying Cold War disillusion and paranoia, and earning their makers the censure of the House UnAmerican Activities Committee (see **The Blacklist**).

Many of noir's finest exponents were European émigrés who recognized the socio-aesthetic merits of location shooting with lighter cameras, portable wire recorders and faster monochrome film stocks, using chiaroscuro lighting, disorientating mise en scène, oblique angles and retrospective voice-overs to capture the mood of a nation inundated with frustrated veterans, susceptible bourgeois, cynical detectives, ruthless crooks, corrupt officials, opportunist drifters, fugitive couples and femmes fatales. Moreover, by challenging the Production Code, noir also demonstrated a determination to tackle topics like sex, class, identity, injustice, treachery, prejudice and violence with a new political and psychoanalytic maturity.

Without ever being a coherent category or achieving notable commercial success, noir helped change the landscape of American cinema. In addition to introducing contentious themes and iconic urban settings, it acquainted audiences with new scenarios and characters. Furthermore, it blooded newcomers such as Robert Mitchum, Gloria Grahame and Richard Widmark, while reinventing established stars like Humphrey Bogart, Barbara Stanwyck and Edward G. Robinson. Yet noir went out of vogue as the declining studios sought redemption with colour and widescreen, although its influence continued to be keenly felt in gritty British crime thrillers, Akira Kurosawa's 1950s pulp adaptations, Mexican *cabaretera* sagas, French Nouvelle Vague homages, Italian *giallo* thrillers and German Das Neue Kino melodramas.

Eventually the form resurfaced Stateside as 'après noir' or 'neo-noir', which imparted a modern, modernist or postmodernist spin to remakes such as *The Postman Always Rings Twice* (1981), original outings like *Chinatown* (1974), and even pastiches such as *Dead Men Don't Wear Plaid* (1982). Indeed, noir was becoming an increasingly cross-generic phenomenon, inspiring dystopian science fictions such as *Blade Runner* (1982) and amorally atmospheric Westerns such as *Unforgiven* (1992), as well as crime novels, video games and beyond. Indeed, with *Sin City* (2005) giving it a CGI makeover and the term being applied with ever more laxity to mainstream, indie and arthouse titles alike, it seems that film noir is destined to continue growing darker and more diverse and daring. ∎

*In Joseph H. Lewis's **The Big Combo** (1955), John Alton's low-key, high contrast lighting is key to creating the enveloping mood of mistrust and danger.*

'Soon they were also conveying Cold War disillusion and paranoia.'

Red panic

Going it alone: Marshal Will
Kane (Gary Cooper) doing what
a man's gotta do in Fred
Zinnemann's anti- HUAC
Western, High Noon (1952).

IDEA № 61
THE BLACKLIST

The impact of the House UnAmerican Activities
Committee's investigation into Communism in Hollywood
can never fully be assessed: after all, it's impossible to assess
the calibre of scripts never written and performances never
given. Nevertheless, the witch-hunt that took place between
1947 and 1952 represents the studio system's darkest hour.

Politicians had started delving into Hollywood ideology in 1938. However, the spate of 'problem pictures' and realist docudramas, together with the bleak portrait of postwar society presented in film noir, galvanized those seeking revenge on the studios for profiting from the New Deal and producing pro-Soviet propaganda for the Office of War Information. The House UnAmerican Activities Committee (HUAC) scarcely expected to find Marxist messages in movies that required the approval of both the conservative studio heads and the Production Code Authority. But, by inquiring about Communist affiliation, HUAC was able to use the arraignment of the so-called Hollywood Ten (a group of mostly screenwriters who refused to give information to the Committee) to coerce moguls like Louis B. Mayer, Jack Warner and Walt Disney into issuing the Waldorf Statement in December 1947, which effectively instigated a notional blacklisting of Left-leaning undesirables.

Faced with intransigent unions, falling attendances, rising costs and an anti-trust verdict on theatre ownership, Hollywood was willing to do whatever it took to keep Washington and Wall Street onside. With publications such as Counterattack and Red Channels identifying Communist Party members and fellow travellers, the studios must have been relieved when initial opposition from the stellar Committee for the First Amendment collapsed and the Screen Actors Guild under Ronald Reagan agreed to swear a loyalty oath.

But the depth of the divisions within the film community were made manifest by Carl Foreman denouncing betrayal in High Noon (1952) and Budd Schulberg condoning 'naming names' in On the Waterfront (1954); those films won four and eight **Oscars** respectively.

Blacklisted writer Dalton Trumbo pseudonymously won the Academy Award for The Brave One (1956) as Robert Rich, and numerous scripts credited to so-called 'fronts' have since been attributed to banned writers. Actors and directors couldn't assume such anonymity, however, and Charlie Chaplin, Paul Robeson, Kim Hunter, Joseph Losey and Jules Dassin were among those whose careers were affected. Less than 10 per cent of the 324 artists cited in the HUAC hearings

returned to pictures. Indeed, HUAC was largely responsible for the early deaths of John Garfield, Canada Lee and Mady Christians. It even accounted for the demise of a studio, as the scandal persuaded Floyd Odlum to sell his shares in RKO to Howard Hughes, whose regime proved calamitous.

Thwarted in its bid to avoid the Paramount Decrees and with the myth of the Dream Factory shattered, Hollywood entered an era of timidity and mediocrity, in which fear, suspicion and guilt ensured a self-censorship more draconian than anything HUAC could have hoped for. Doggedly peddling old-fashioned values and vacuous optimism long after the coming of rock'n'roll had undermined them, the studios turned to technology to combat television in the absence of the progressive artists who might have responded imaginatively to trends such as Neorealism and the Nouvelle Vague. Ironically, the blacklist hastened the end of the studio system by fragmenting the audience and encouraging independent production. But it also engendered the moral torpor and intellectual stagnation in which Hollywood wallowed until the mid-1960s. ∎

A protest supporting the Hollywood Ten – Alvah Bessie, Herbert Biberman, Lester Cole, Edward Dmytryk, Ring Lardner, Jr., John Howard Lawson, Albert Maltz, Samuel Ornitz, Adrian Scott and Dalton Trumbo.

Feeling the part

METHOD ACTING

TOP: *A classic clash of styles: Vivien Leigh and Marlon Brando in* A Streetcar Named Desire *(1951).*

ABOVE: *Silent mumming par excellence: Lillian Gish and Richard Barthelmess in D.W. Griffith's* Way Down East *(1920).*

Reacting to the seismic socio-cultural shift caused by World War II, Hollywood welcomed the immersive Method technique that brought an additional authenticity and realism to feature films striving to reflect the Cold War world.

Changes in screen-acting styles reflect a variety of factors: technological advances, commercial trends, generic conventions, national traditions and aesthetic upheavals. Silent acting had relied on pantomime and talkies witnessed a clash between screen veterans and those trained for the stage.

In the Golden Age of Hollywood, actors tended to opt for either impersonation or personification, with the director doing much to shape the tone of a performance through script analysis and rehearsal, camera placement and editing. However, 'the Method' gave its actor-disciples greater control over their work, as they were encouraged to draw on personal experience to discover the psychological truth about their character.

Method acting was developed at the Moscow Art Theatre by Konstantin Stanislavski, whose system of affective memory and physical expression was adopted by the Left-leaning Group Theatre in New York in the 1930s. But it wasn't until the end of the following decade that the Method began to impact upon Broadway, when Marlon Brando collaborated on a series of landmark theatre productions with director Elia Kazan. The pair was also largely responsible for introducing the Method into movies, most notably in *A Streetcar Named Desire* (1951) and *On the Waterfront* (1954), in which Brando mumbled his dialogue, toyed with props and exhibited a raw emotion previously unseen on screen.

Brando was soon followed by other graduates of Lee Strasberg's Actors Studio, including Montgomery Clift, James Dean and Paul Newman, as well as by students of such rival Method teachers as Sanford Meisner and Stella Adler. The studio heads recognized that this new breed of performer appealed to younger audiences, who were steadily becoming cinema's core demographic. Chiming in with the new rebellious attitude that accompanied rock'n'roll, the Method also brought an air of danger to movies. This continued into the 1960s, as the Production Code collapsed and filmmakers were finally able to tackle contentious topics with an unprecedented degree of realism, with some appropriating the radical Brechtian techniques employed by such European auteurs as Jean-Luc Godard and Rainer Werner Fassbinder.

Method acting peaked with Francis Ford Coppola's *The Godfather* (1972). Actors of the calibre of Dustin Hoffman, Jane Fonda, Robert De Niro, Al Pacino, Sean Penn and Daniel Day-Lewis have since continued to adhere to its tenets, but its long-term effect on screen acting has actually been rather limited. Many stars flirt with the process by immersing themselves in the lore and lifestyle of their character or by affecting drastic physical transformation. But the drift towards more casual speech patterns, as well as the vogue for green-screen acting and rapid editing, have mitigated against the Method and left it looking a little macho, mannered and self-indulgent, particularly in the hands of its less skilled practitioners. ∎

'Method … brought an air of danger to movies.'

Robert De Niro fought three amateur boxing bouts to prepare for **Raging Bull** *(1980), but then piled on 60lbs in four months to play the older Jake La Motta.*

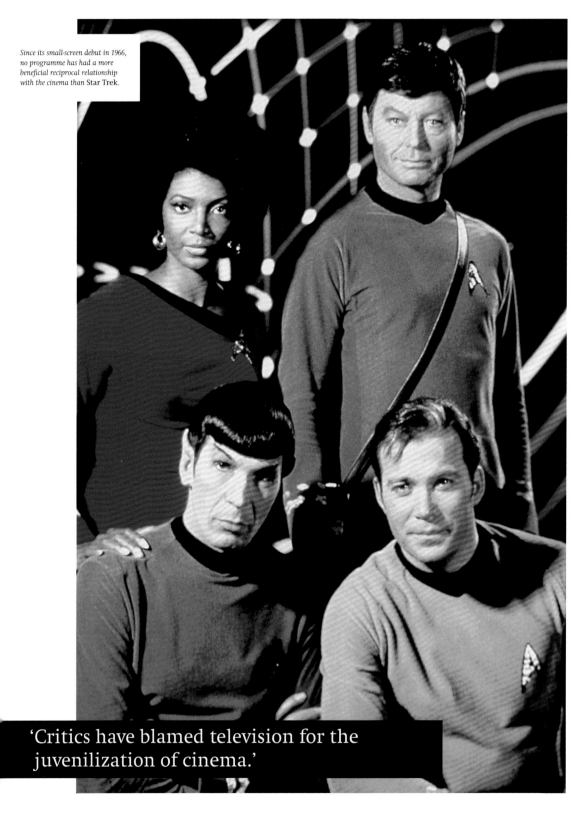

Since its small-screen debut in 1966, no programme has had a more beneficial reciprocal relationship with the cinema than Star Trek.

'Critics have blamed television for the juvenilization of cinema.'

Friend or foe?

IDEA № 63

TELEVISION

No medium has had a bigger impact upon cinema than television. Its emergence in the late 1940s exacerbated the economic crisis that threatened Hollywood's very existence. But, given more people now watch movies on TV than on big screens, television has become a major partner in film production worldwide.

After two decades of struggling in movies, 'Queen of the Bs' Lucille Ball became America's favourite sitcom star between 1951 and 1974.

Within two years of American attendances hitting a weekly record 100 million and box-office takings topping $1.75 billion, the studios were forced to impose cutbacks, sack staff and reduce output in the face of rising costs, foreign protectionism and the 1948 Paramount Decrees. But nothing hit harder than television, with cinemas closing across the country as the number of tuned-in households rose from one to 50 million between 1949 and 1959.

Frustrated by the Federal Communications Commission in its bid to launch subscription channels and theatrical broadcasting, Hollywood retaliated by refusing to sell movies to the networks and forbidding stars from appearing on their shows. It also invested heavily in new technologies like widescreen, colour, stereo and **3-D** to lure people back to cinemas. But this concentration on A pictures led to the abandoning of newsreels, cartoons and serials, which all found new homes on television, as did the Western. Moreover, NBC, CBS and ABC began making their own TV movies, while the takeover of the RKO studio by Lucille Ball's Desilu company in 1957 confirmed the shift in Hollywood's balance of power.

By the end of the 1950s, 80 per cent of prime-time programming was being produced in Hollywood. Furthermore, the studios had relented on leasing their back catalogues and films barely seen since their original release suddenly became family favourites. Yet, while viewers became increasingly cine-literate, they had to accede to features being cut to fit schedule slots, punctuated by commercial breaks and censored to appease sponsors and pressure groups. Audiences also tolerated the cropping of widescreen images to focus on the key action, although attempts in the 1980s to colourize black-and-white classics met with greater resistance.

Several ageing stars embarked upon new small-screen careers, with Groucho Marx and Loretta Young passing Charlton Heston and James Dean heading in the opposite direction. A new generation of writers and directors also emerged, with Delbert Mann's cinema adaptation of Paddy Chayefsky's *Marty* (1955) becoming the first tele-sourced winner of the Academy Award for Best Picture. Subsequently, shows like *Dragnet*, *Star Trek* and *The Simpsons* transferred to cinemas, while hit TV movies such as Steven Spielberg's *Duel* (1971) and John Dahl's *The Last Seduction* (1994) secured theatrical releases.

Many critics have blamed television for the juvenilization of cinema and the post-classical decline in plotting, characterization and narrative-spectacle balance, not to mention the increased use of close-ups, rapid focal shifts between subjects, flat lighting and fast cutting. Yet European directors of the calibre of Ingmar Bergman, Federico Fellini, Roberto Rossellini and Rainer Werner Fassbinder embraced television, and broadcasters like the BBC and Channel Four in Britain and France's Canal Plus led the way in co-producing features. Corporate synergy has recently strengthened the ties between Hollywood and America's 1,750 TV stations, with sell-through deals underpinning many budgets. But cinema's long-claimed cultural superiority over television is in jeopardy, with programmes such as *The West Wing* and *The Wire* often receiving better reviews than mainstream movies, although both formats face increasing competition from the original content produced by such online distributors as Netflix. ∎

Taking images to new dimensions

THE ACADEMY RATIO

Film-makers have never been able to settle on an optimum size and shape for their images, despite the difficulties such variety has caused the screening houses. When the Academy of Motion Picture Arts and Sciences imposed its ratio in 1932, uniformity was achieved – albeit only briefly...

In the 1890s, after abandoning experiments with square and round variations, Edison engineer William Kennedy Laurie Dickson (perhaps influenced by the Golden Section in Greek art) dictated that a moving picture frame's width-to-height ratio should be 1.33:1 or 4:3. His 35mm parameters were seized upon by the monopolistic Thomas Edison and Kodak boss George Eastman and readily accepted by the Lumière brothers in France for both aesthetic and economic reasons, as the rectangular shape was better suited to the sideways direction of the action, while the layout wasted less space between the frames.

The majority of silent films were shot in the 1.33:1 ratio. However, Soviet maestro Sergei Eisenstein proposed a square frame, in which compositions could be made along horizontal, vertical and diagonal lines, while French director Abel Gance employed the three-projector Polyvision system to present spectacular triptych sequences in his 1927 masterpiece, *Napoleon*.

In Hollywood, Paramount's widescreen technique, Magnascope, was used for action interludes in King Vidor's *The Big Parade* (1925) and William Wellman's *Wings* (1927). But, with audiences enthralled by the novelty of talkies, there was no great demand for its king-sized images. Consequently, heeding the call of the Society of Motion Picture Engineers for a proliferation ban after Fox introduced the 70mm Grandeur process – and

Paramount and Warners responded with 56mm and 65mm formats respectively – the Academy of Motion Picture Arts and Sciences decided that an industry dependent upon mass production, distribution and exhibition needed uniformity. So, in 1932, it imposed the Academy ratio of 1.37:1, even though the standard frame area was reduced by 31 per cent to accommodate the sound track on the film strip.

Hollywood's entire 35mm output over the next two decades was shot using the Academy aperture. Indeed, such was its ubiquity that television appropriated the configuration. But, in order to recover the audiences lost to domestic viewing, the studios soon turned to widescreen formats like Cinerama, CinemaScope, VistaVision and Todd-AO, which rendered the Academy style obsolete. Indeed, it is now primarily the preserve of iconoclasts like Jean-Luc Godard and Gus Van Sant.

Debuting with Henry Koster's *The Robe* (1953), CinemaScope used an anamorphic lens to squeeze a 2.55:1 image horizontally into a 35mm frame, while a compensating lens corrected the distortions during projection. As with the early days of sound, there were teething problems. The diminished focal lengths prevented staging in depth, while difficulties with close-ups, tracking shots, lateral movements and montages often led to static compositions. Yet CinemaScope changed the narrative form of cinema,

as directors developed the hugely influential mise en scène technique in response to it.

Yet, despite the emergence of similar processes worldwide, the 'Scope revolution proved short-lived after the introduction of Panavision in the early 1960s. The widescreen ratio has since been standardized to 1.85:1 in the United States and 1.66:1 in Europe. But while systems such as IMAX continue to strive for ever-more immersive imagery, the **digital video** boom has encouraged downsizing as more people watch films on portable DVD players, laptops and phones. ∎

The Polyvision process in all its triptych glory during a live orchestra screening of Abel Gance's **Napoleon** *(1927).*

'The studios soon turned to widescreen formats.'

BELOW LEFT: *A scene from Henry Koster's* The Robe *(1953) shown in the 1.33:1 Academy Ratio and the 2.35:1 widescreen CinemaScope version.*

BELOW: *The 20 × 26 metres screen at London's BFI IMAX colludes with digital surround-sound to immerse viewers and place them in the middle of the action.*

> 'Colour offered film-makers much more than naturalism and spectacle.'

ABOVE: *Cinematographer Christopher Doyle demonstrates the emotional rhetoric of colour in Wong Kar-wai's exquisite 1960s Hong Kong romance,* In the Mood for Love *(2000).*

LEFT: *Production designer Bernard Evein and cinematographer Jean Rabier made enchanting use of colour in Jacques Demy's* The Umbrellas of Cherbourg *(1964).*

A bolder, brighter world

IDEA № 65

COLOUR

Dorothy (Judy Garland) and Scarecrow (Ray Bolger) follow the famous Yellow Brick Road in Victor Fleming's The Wizard of Oz *(1939).*

Experiments with colour techniques started the moment images began to move. But it was only in the 1950s that the Hollywood studios decisively adopted colour in their bid to lure audiences away from the novelty of television.

The first film-makers were fully aware of the aesthetic and economic benefits of colour, which added realism to their imagery in the absence of sound. However, despite the failure to find a viable colour stock, moving pictures were far from limited to monochrome for their first four decades. The 1895 Kinetoscope record of Annabelle Moore's Serpentine Dance set the trend for hand-tinting. However, the painstaking and expensive colouring of longer items like George Méliès's *A Trip to the Moon* (1902) prompted the introduction of stencil systems such as Pathécolor and the Handschiegl Color Process, which was used to heighten the drama in pictures like Erich von Stroheim's *Greed* (1924).

Toning was a cheaper alternative, as it bathed scenes in a single evocative shade. It's estimated that over 80 per cent of features contained coloured elements by the 1920s, including the glowering masterpieces of German Expressionism. But, despite experiments with additive processes such as Kinemacolor (1908), subtractive alternatives like Prizma (1917) and even mosaic systems such as Dufaycolor (1932), the problems of colour registration and density loss on projection meant that full-colour films remained a novelty.

The solutions were finally provided by Herbert Kalmus and his partners at Technicolor, whose dye transfer process enabled them to produce prints of exceptional sharpness and richness from monochrome matrices. The two-colour additive process used on the Douglas Fairbanks swashbuckler *The Black Pirate* (1926) offered a pleasing if limited palette of colours. But its much-improved three colour panchromatic successor contributed hugely to the popularity of Disney animations and live-action favourites like *The Wizard of Oz* and *Gone with the Wind* (both 1939), as Technicolor didn't just reproduce natural hues, it made them bolder and more intense and, thus, reinforced the Neverland magic of the movie world.

Yet Technicolor's expense and restrictive usage policies meant that most Hollywood studios in the 1950s were glad to rely on the Eastmancolor monopack – which formed colours in the emulsion and could be used in any camera – in their battle with television. Only one film in ten was shot in colour in 1947. But that figure had risen to one in two by 1954 and 96 per cent of all American features were colour by 1979.

Colour offered film-makers much more than naturalism and spectacle. Reds, oranges and yellows suggested warmth and energy, while blues and greens were cooler and more relaxed. These contrasts could be exploited to enhance an image's apparent depth. They could also highlight items within the mise en scène or invest them with symbolic meaning, like James Dean's red jacket in Nicholas Ray's *Rebel without a Cause* (1955). Colour brought new vibrancy to genre films, most notably the musicals of Vincente Minnelli and Jacques Demy. But it also permitted greater artistic and psychological sophistication in the likes of Michelangelo Antonioni's *Red Desert* (1964), Ingmar Bergman's *Cries and Whispers* (1972) and Wong Kar-wai's *In the Mood for Love* (2000).

Colour is such a key component of the modern feature film that attempts were made in the 1980s to colourize black-and-white classics to enhance their commercial appeal. Moreover, the evolution of computer-generated imagery has seen colour become ever more crucial to the creation of fantasy landscapes and exotic creatures. But it could be argued that too many directors adopt a decorative attitude to colour so that its full cinematographic potential has yet to be realized. ∎

The depthie vogue

NOTHING THAT HAS GONE BEFORE CAN COMPARE WITH THIS!

Beauty and terror meet in your seat... as every thrill of its story comes off the screen right at you in NATURAL VISION

RIGHT AT YOU! The hand is at your throat...

RIGHT AT YOU! The kiss is on your lips...

RIGHT AT YOU! The horror that chills the spine!

3 DIMENSION

WARNER BROS. BRING YOU THE FIRST FEATURE PRODUCED BY A MAJOR STUDIO IN 3D!

"HOUSE OF WAX"
WARNERCOLOR

VINCENT PRICE · FRANK LOVEJOY · PHYLLIS KIRK CAROLYN JONES · PAUL PICERNI

Hungarian-born director André De Toth only had one eye and, therefore, couldn't appreciate the 3-D effects he created for **House of Wax** (1953).

IDEA № 66
3-D

No screen technology has been hailed as the future of cinema quite as frequently as 3-D. But its moment may finally have come in the first decades of the twenty-first century.

J.C. d'Almeida first projected three-dimensional images from twin magic lanterns in 1856. But, despite William Friese-Greene and W.K.L. Dickson's efforts in the 1890s, Louis Lumière's *L'Arrivée d'un train en Gare de La Ciotat* became the first 3-D film in 1903, although it remains unclear whether Lumière achieved this effect using a single anaglyphic duo-colour strip or two projectors synched through colour filters.

Various American processes were trialled over the next few years. In 1922, Harry K. Fairall completed the first 3-D feature, *The Power of Love*, while Pathé had some success with Stereoscopik shorts such as *Zowie* (1925). But sound and colour took precedent in Hollywood during this period and progress with three-dimensionality was limited to German outings like *You Can Almost Touch It*

(1937) and the Soviet feature *Robinson Crusoe* (1947), which used Semyon Ivanov's unique parallax stereogram system.

Avant-gardists such as Oskar Fischinger (*Stereo Film*, 1952) and Harry Smith (*Film #6*, 1950–51) were the first to be inspired by the state-of-the-art Telekinema cinema at the Festival of Britain in 1951, which was capable of screening 3-D films. Hollywood independent Arch Oboler was sufficiently impressed by it to release the jungle adventure *Bwana Devil* in the Natural Vision process in November 1952. Its box-office popularity persuaded the studios to produce 60 3-D features in 1953.

Most were generic items that used stereoscopy less to immerse viewers in the action than to bombard them with objects seemingly emanating from the screen. But André De Toth's *House of Wax*, MGM's Cole Porter musical *Kiss Me*

Kate (both 1953) and Alfred Hitchcock's *Dial M for Murder* (1954) succeeded better than most in integrating the effects into the narrative, while B movies such as *It Came from Outer Space* (1953), made grandstanding use of meteors, flaming arrows and subterranean monsters.

The depthie vogue proved short-lived, however. Critics dismissed its gimmickry, while viewers grew frustrated with the red-green polarized glasses they had to wear and problems with reduced brightness and synchronization. Moreover, 3-D features were expensive to produce and distribute and many had to be reissued in flat versions to recoup their costs. French, Dutch, German, Italian, Hungarian, Soviet, Japanese and Mexican initiatives similarly misfired. Consequently, 3-D was confined to sci-fi (*The Bubble*, 1966), sexploitation (*The Stewardesses*, 1969) and shlock (*Flesh for Frankenstein*, 1973), until *Friday the 13th Part III* (1982) and *Jaws 3-D* (1983) formed part of a fresh blockbusting mini-boom.

Digital systems like IMAX 3D, RealD and Sony's 4K transformed stereoscopy from the mid-2000s, however, as the studios invested in spectacles designed to beat both piracy and the recession. Indeed, many features underwent 3-D conversion to increase their appeal. But even though respected film-makers such as Martin Scorsese, Werner Herzog and Ridley Scott entered the field, critics were rarely as impressed as audiences. ∎

ABOVE: *Placing viewers at the heart of the action, the new generation of 3-D processes has brought the possibility of interactive cinema closer than ever.*

BELOW: *Having waited 15 years for technology to catch up with his vision of **Avatar** (2009), James Cameron devised the single-camera Fusion system to shoot live 3-D action.*

The (financial) attractions of cosmopolitanism

Ang Lee's **Crouching Tiger, Hidden Dragon** *(2000) was co-produced by companies from Taiwan, Hong Kong, China and the United States.*

IDEA № 67

CO-PRODUCTION

Although the term can be applied to any form of financial, creative or technical partnership, co-production is primarily reserved for pictures sponsored by two or more countries. In many cases, the alliance is forged in a bid to challenge American box-office supremacy, although Hollywood has itself been actively involved in co-production.

The history of film has largely been written around national traditions. Yet co-productions have played an increasingly significant role since the Austrian company Wiener Autorenfilm approached the French giant Pathé for help with *The Mystery of the Air* in 1913. Hollywood has actively encouraged co-production since the Parufamet Agreement of 1925 was contracted between Paramount and MGM to bale out UFA after the failure of Carl Laemmle's Film Europe initiative. Indeed, the early sound era saw several Hollywood studios open Continental facilities to make multi-lingual versions of prestige titles, with local stars being cast to enhance commercial prospects.

However, it wasn't until the 1948 Paramount Decrees exacerbated the crisis brought on by declining audiences and spiralling costs that Hollywood really embraced co-production, most notably with Italy. In addition to freeing up otherwise frozen assets, pictures filmed overseas like Mervyn LeRoy's *Quo Vadis* (1951) and William Wyler's *Roman Holiday* (1953) also allowed the studios to take advantage of local subsidies, exotic locations and cheap, non-unionized labour. Moreover, these runaways opened up Continental markets previously blocked by protective quotas and prompted the importation of new stars like Sophia Loren.

Yet, as fears were being raised back home about Hollywood's continued status as the world's movie capital, protests were being lodged in Europe about American cultural imperialism. Therefore, emboldened by the formation of the Common Market, states began signing co-production treaties, with the consequence that shared credits rose from 10 to 40 per cent between 1955 and 1965, by which time two-thirds of French films were to some extent co-produced.

The bulk of these features were dismissed as Europuddings. Designed to appeal to everybody, they were so cosmopolitan that they pleased no one, with too many scenes being shot in touristy locations to fulfil contractual obligations, while stars from participating countries took asinine cameos to entice local fans. Yet alongside the sword'n'sandal actioners, Spaghetti Westerns, war re-enactments, spy romps, comic capers and erotic horrors, arthouse cinema also became dependent upon foreign coin, with Fellini, Antonioni, Visconti, Bergman, Truffaut, Chabrol and Godard all directing a number of co-productions, with the latter even lampooning the whole sordid business in *Contempt* (or *Le Mépris*) (1963).

However, co-production didn't just sustain existing industries. It also bolstered nascent traditions in Africa, Asia and Latin America, both in the making of politically charged Third Cinema studies of the colonial experience and generic fare such as martial-arts movies. Since the 1980s, television companies like Canal Plus, RAI, Channel Four and HBO have proved a crucial source of co-production revenue. But while co-productions have accounted for half the major festival prizewinners over the last two decades, they are still regarded with suspicion by commentators who fear that the eradication of national identity from cinema will irrevocably reduce its aesthetic, cultural and commercial value. ∎

Director William Wyler refused to make Roman Holiday (1953) on the Paramount lot and it became the first American film shot entirely in Italy.

The chariot race in Ben-Hur
*(1959) was filmed on a replica
of the Circus Maximus that
occupied 18 acres of the
Cinecittà backlot, making it the
biggest outdoor set of that time.*

History writ large – very large

EPICS

Drawing on established literary traditions, while also offering unprecedented (audio)visual scope and scale, screen epics have been popular with audiences since the 1910s because – to paraphrase President Woodrow Wilson – they write history with lightning.

Produced in Italy, the earliest epics inspired rival film-makers and enticed the middle classes into becoming picture-goers. Furthermore, super-spectacles like Mario Caserini's *The Last Days of Pompeii* (1913) ushered in the feature film and forged the genre's enduring link with the ancient and biblical worlds. However, epics such as Raoul Walsh's *The Thief of Bagdad*, Erich von Stroheim's *Greed* (both 1924) and Cecil B. DeMille's *The King of Kings* (1927) were soon exploring a range of historical, fantastical and contemporary topics. Opening in a blaze of publicity and boasting specially commissioned scores, these weren't just event movies. They also helped refine storytelling techniques, engendered a new insistence on period accuracy and reinforced popular preconceptions of religion, nationhood, dynasty and empire.

Such 'destiny epics' also helped redefine the image of the male star and enabled Hollywood to dominate the global market, as few other national industries could match its lavish décor and costumes, casts of thousands or grandstanding set-pieces. However, the studios themselves allowed the epic to slip into abeyance during the two decades that followed the advent of sound, as they concentrated on prestigious literary adaptations, biopics and swashbuckling adventures. Yet, while they were notable for their increased intimacy and allegorical subtexts, these films still mythologized their subjects, as did European titles such as Sergei Eisenstein's *Ivan the Terrible* (1944), which was among the first epics to examine its protagonist's darker side.

Conflicting views of patriotism have informed national epics as diverse as Mehboob Khan's *Mother India* (1957), Sergei Bondarchuk's *War and Peace* (1967) and Edgar Reitz's *Heimat* (1984–2006), while Roberto Rossellini devised a meta-historical form of Neorealism for anti-epic teleplays such as *The Age of the Medici* (1973). But, apart from the odd indigenous outing like *How the West Was Won* (1962), Hollywood tended to borrow the heritage of others to showcase new techniques such as colour, widescreen and stereo sound in the runaways, remakes and co-productions that revived the epic for Cold War audiences seeking religious solace and superpower reassurance.

However, replicating the success of DeMille's *The Ten Commandments* (1956) and William Wyler's *Ben-Hur* (1959) proved difficult after the failure of Joseph L. Mankiewicz's *Cleopatra* (1963). Indeed, some four decades would pass before Ridley Scott's CGI-enhanced *Gladiator* (2000) restored antiquity's box-office credibility. ∎

TOP: *Poster for* Mother India *(1957), Mehboob Khan's Hindi epic about rural progress that earned India its first Oscar nomination.*

ABOVE: *Nikolai Cherkasov in Sergei Eisenstein's* Ivan the Terrible *(1944), an epic allegory on heroic leadership designed to inspire wartime audiences.*

The most amazing motion picture of our time!

I WAS A TEENAGE WEREWOLF

MICHAEL LANDON · YVONNE LIME · WHIT BISSELL · TONY MARSHALL
Produced by HERMAN COHEN · Directed by GENE FOWLER Jr. · Screenplay by RALPH THORNTON
A JAMES NICHOLSON-SAMUEL ARKOFF Production · AN AMERICAN INTERNATIONAL PICTURE

ABOVE: *Costing AIP just $82,000 to make,* I Was a Teenage Werewolf *(1957) grossed over $2 million and launched the vogue for camp horror.*

BELOW: *After four rejections, the British censor finally awarded a certificate to Roger Corman's 1967 LSD saga,* The Trip, *in 2004.*

Beyond the Production Code

IDEA № 69

EXPLOITATION

Originally denoting special-interest titles requiring additional promotion, exploitation came to define low-budget studies of risqué subjects made outside the mainstream. Though the term is now applied to sensationalist B–Z grade movies aimed at the fandom market, exploitation helped reinvent Hollywood and establish cult genres worldwide.

Despite the popularity of American features like *Traffic in Souls* (1913) and *Damaged Goods* (1914), and German *Aufklarungsfilme* or enlightenment films such as *Hyenas of Lust* (1919), early exploitation was strictly censored. Its typical subject matter of nudity, white slavery, sex hygiene and drug abuse was high on the lists of taboo topics drafted in Hollywood between 1921 and 1934. As a result, entrepreneurs with a carnival background stepped into the breach.

The most successful of these so-called 'Forty Thieves' were Samuel Cummins, Dwain Esper, J.D. Kendis, Willis Kent and Louis Sonney, who profited into the 1950s from pictures that broached anthropology, naturism, sexually transmitted diseases, narcotics, delinquency and vice, and were often screened with an accompanying lecture or book pitch. Despite their inept scripts, indifferent photography and inert performances, they attracted sizeable grindhouse attendances because of their 'educational' content.

Flicks like Edgar G. Ulmer's prison drama *Girls in Chains* (1943) and Kroger Babb's pregnant-schoolgirl shocker *Mom and Dad* (1945) – which reputedly grossed $100 million – were billed as being for 'adults only'. But the exploitation that plugged the gaps caused by the 1948 Paramount Decrees and television was aimed squarely at the new juvenile audience.

Recognizing the yen for novelty, William Castle became 'the king of the gimmicks' with theatrical **stunts** such as Percepto vibrating seats and Emergo

glow-in-the-dark skeletons floating over the audience. But it was James H. Nicholson and Samuel Z. Arkoff's American International Pictures that best caught the mood of the counterculture in the decade between Herman Cohen's *I Was a Teenage Werewolf* (1957) and Roger Corman's *The Trip* (1967). Pandering to the drive-in and midnite matinee crowds, AIP initiated the tactics of target marketing and saturation opening that the studios would eventually adopt for their blockbusters. Moreover, Corman gave directors of the calibre of Francis Ford Coppola, Martin Scorsese and John Sayles their first breaks, as well as blooding new stars like Jack Nicholson.

Exploitation also transformed the genre scene, as sci-fi, horror and macho action came to prominence and helped undermine the Production Code, along with the softcore sexploitation produced in imitation of Roger Vadim's *And God Created Woman* (1956) and the gore homages to Alfred Hitchcock's *Psycho* (1960) devised by David F. Friedman and Herschell Gordon Lewis.

With the Ozploitation of maverick Australian producers like Antony I. Ginnane mirroring the attitude of **blaxploitation** and with the erotic Euro horror of Jesus Franco and Jean Rollin finding an echo in the Latsploitation of Latin Americans José Mojica Marins and Alejandro Jodorowsky, exploitation erupted everywhere. Nuns, Nazis, bikers, samurai, martial artists, serial killers and vigilantes became the anti-heroes of the video age. Latterly, shocksploitation has defied political correctness to become increasingly graphic. Yet it's still seized upon by movie geeks united by fanzines, conventions and websites, and whose champion, Quentin Tarantino, finally gave exploitation the critical and commercial success it had always craved with hits like *Reservoir Dogs* (1992) and *Pulp Fiction* (1994). ∎

Such was the fandom buzz surrounding Snakes on a Plane *(2006) that New Line shot extra footage to incorporate online suggestions.*

Coming soon...

Trailer for Julien Duvivier's
Pépé le Moko (1937).

IDEA № 70
TRAILERS

Ballyhoo has long been central to screen success. The techniques may have become more sophisticated since cinema's fairground days, but publicity – particularly in the form of short trailers advertising forthcoming attractions – still plays on the public's obsessions with novelty, celebrity and familiarity.

Film-makers were slow to exploit the appeal of moving pictures. Apart from entries in distribution catalogues, the only promotion most releases received was concocted by nickelodeon owners, who used illuminated marquees, homemade posters, store displays, streetcar banners, stentorian barkers and blaring music to lure patrons into premises decorated to suit the latest release. However, the emergence of movie stars around 1910 prompted Mutual and Universal to establish their own publicity departments to devise lobby stunts and produce advertisements and pressbooks for America's voracious newspapers and fanzines.

But while the studio-owned theatre chains targeted family audiences, independent venues opted for more sensationalist promotional methods. Some even resorted to illegal cash games like Screeno and Bank Night to boost attendances during the Depression. The Advertising Code was instituted in 1930 to standardize practices following complaints from religious leaders.

Trailers were also strictly regulated. Despite the myth, these sneak previews of forthcoming attractions were not introduced to drive dream palace patrons out of continuous programmes. In fact, Georges Méliès ran the first promotional reel outside the Théâtre Robert-Houdin in Paris in 1898 and trailers caught on in the United States after Famous Players trailed clips from *The Quest of Life* in 1916. Three years later, Paramount established Hollywood's first dedicated trailer unit, only for the majority of the other studios to entrust production to the New York-based National Screen Service (NSS) the following year.

The NSS style was somewhat pedestrian and usually comprised a 'Voice of God' narrator good-naturedly linking visual snippets, graphic taglines and glamour shots of the stars. Directors like Cecil B. DeMille and Alfred Hitchcock were occasionally allowed to create their own trailers. But NSS packages satisfied producers and punters alike until the studio system began to unravel in the 1950s, when talent agents and publicists started dictating how their clients were presented in the media. Moreover, with the passing of block booking, individual pictures had to stand on their own merits and trailers became more crucial than ever to generating pre-release buzz.

In 1960, Columbia quit NSS to handle its own trailers. But specialist companies such as Kaleidoscope came to dominate the field, as trailers for *Dr Strangelove* (1963) and *The Night of the Iguana* (1964) pioneered a slicker style that placed a greater emphasis on mood than hyperbole (although many still relied on the trusted highlights-and-voice-over format). Now under the jurisdiction of the Motion Picture Association of America, trailers found a new outlet on television during the blockbuster era, with makers adopting the montage methods of the music video to appeal to cinema's increasingly youthful demographic. Indeed, this adaptability has enabled the trailer to remain effective into the digital age of DVDs, websites, downloads and apps. ∎

'Trailers became more crucial than ever to generating pre-release buzz.'

ABOVE: *Alfred Hitchcock fronted an amusing five-minute lecture with a shock ending to trail* **The Birds** *(1963).*

BELOW: *Cigarette cards were a cheap and effective way of promoting movie stars, with hundreds of sets being issued around the world in the 1920s and '30s.*

CLARK GABLE · JEANETTE MAC DONALD

CLAUDETTE COLBERT

ALICE FAYE

*Ingmar Bergman exploited
the fragility of celluloid for
metaphorical purposes, as
a frame freezes, burns and*

Preserving the most perishable art

SAFETY FILM

ABOVE: In Decasia (2002), Bill Morrison used nitrate film to explore material decay, the transience of life and the impermanence of memory.

BELOW: Mélanie Laurent uses flammable film stock to blow up her cinema in Quentin Tarantino's Inglourious Basterds (2009).

Only half of the 21,000 features produced in the United States before 1951 survive. These were shot on dangerously flammable and highly unstable cellulose nitrate. Eastman Kodak introduced a flame-resistant cellulose acetate alternative in 1909, but it was four decades before the industry finally made the transition to safety film.

Moving pictures only became feasible after the invention of a flexible strip that could pass intermittently through the camera mechanism at a speed of 16–20 frames per second. John Carbutt, Hannibal Goodwin and Henry Reichenbach all contributed to the evolution of celluloid, but it was George Eastman's Kodak company that profited from its launch in 1889.

The first orthochromatic films produced luminous images. But the base supporting the emulsion containing the light-sensitive silver salts was prone to ignition at temperatures as low as 40°C and released toxic fumes as it burned fiercely. Yet even though 180 people died at a charity bazaar in Paris in 1897 and 77 children perished in Montreal's Laurier Palace Cinema in 1927, film-makers continued to prefer to use nitrate as it was more pliable, easier to splice, less likely to shrink or curl, and more durable than acetate. Moreover, the new panchromatic stocks were capable of achieving rich, high-contrast monochrome imagery.

In 1948, however, Eastman Kodak converted to Improved Safety Base Motion Picture Film and, within four years, production worldwide had switched to the new format. But it soon became apparent that studio vaults everywhere were stacked with decomposing pictures. Initially, the nitrate stock started shrinking, with the diminution of the distance between the sprocket holes making projection impossible. However, such decay caused the emission of nitrogen dioxide, which reacted with the water in the gelatin to form nitrous and nitric acids, which corroded the emulsion salts and destroyed the images. The increased stickiness of the browning reels made them difficult to unfurl, while the formation of a brittle crust presaged their eventual degeneration into white powder.

Archive fires further depleted cinema's legacy over the next half-century. But while cellulose triacetate, cellulose propionate and cellulose butyrate reduced the risk of making, storing and screening films, they also brought problems of their own. With the exception of Technicolor, colours faded with alarming rapidity, while vinegar, rancid butter and pisces syndromes – named after their respective odours – betrayed their physical deterioration.

Polyester was introduced in the 1990s, but while its strength rendered it ideal for projection, the likelihood of it damaging the camera made it less suitable for shooting. Even digital preservation has its shortcomings, as not only is it expensive, but the various bits and bytes are also vulnerable to 'digital decay', while hardware and software alike are liable to rapid obsolescence. It's estimated that around 80 per cent of the films made between 1895 and 1930 have already been permanently lost. Yet even if sufficient

funding was available to save the surviving nitrate and acetate movies, the digital copies would still be several generations distant from the original negatives and only a fraction would ever be seen, such is the emphasis on the canonical classics of world cinema that even scholars rarely venture in search of the forgotten gems that could perhaps rewrite screen history. ∎

Creating a living tradition

THE CINÉMATHÈQUE FRANÇAISE

Directors Claude Chabrol and Jean-Luc Godard demanding Henri Langlois's reinstatement after Culture Minister André Malraux dismissed him from the Cinémathèque in February 1968.

While not the oldest film archive or repertory cinema in the world, the Cinémathèque Française in Paris has long enjoyed the highest profile. Without the efforts of its Falstaffian co-founder, Henri Langlois, and other like-minded cinephiles, we would know a lot less about the early days of cinema.

Louis Lumière is reported to have said, 'The cinema is an invention without a future.' It was a widely held view, moreover. Thus, though paper prints of motion pictures were sent to the Library of Congress to establish copyright, the vast majority of early films were destroyed, as they were deemed to have no long-term commercial or cultural value. However, critic Ricciotto Canudo not only argued that moving images had artistic merit, he also founded CASA (the Club for Friends of the Seventh Art) in Paris in 1920 and entered into acrimonious theoretical debates with Louis Delluc, whose *ciné-club* supplemented its screenings with lectures and publications.

It was this spirit of cinephilia that persuaded Langlois, Georges Franju, Paul-Auguste Harlé and Jean Mitry to establish the Cinémathèque Française in September 1936 and, two years later, form the Fédération Internationale des Archives du Film, with similar bodies being set up in New York, London and Berlin. Initially, Langlois sought works by screen pioneers, but the philistine cull of silents following the advent of sound convinced him to salvage works pell-mell and his collection grew during the war as he rescued outlawed prints from the occupying Nazis.

Nevertheless, preservation always mattered less to Langlois than presentation. At a time when films were available only on the big screen, he spurned the latest releases to revive forgotten gems and reacquaint audiences with neglected stars and directors. By showing fragile nitrate prints and hoarding them in less than ideal conditions, he enraged fellow archivists. Yet the classic screenings in the 50-seat auditorium at Avenue de Messines tutored some of the leading names in French cinema, from Jean Renoir and Robert Bresson to the cineastes of the Nouvelle Vague. Moreover, by opening his vaults to venues worldwide, Langlois helped popularize arthouse cinema and facilitated the emergence of film as an academic discipline.

Despite his brilliance as a programmer, Langlois was criticized for retarding the Cinémathèque's involvement in fighting nitrate decomposition by diverting scarce resources into his Musée du Cinéma at the Palais de Chaillot in Paris. The latter's exhibitions were emulated around the world, although its array of antique apparatus, sets, costumes, props, scripts, posters and documents remained quite unique. Moreover, since relocating to Bercy Park in 2005, the facility provides a valuable educational service to visitors and scholars alike.

A combination of industry indifference and a refusal to bear the prohibitive cost of storing items with limited commercial potential has meant that over 80 per cent of all motion pictures produced between 1895 and 1930 have perished, while only half of those photographed on nitrate stock before 1951 have survived. The Nitrate Won't Wait campaign saw much footage transferred to **safety film** in the 1980s, but those engaged in digitizing archives are now being faced with fading colours on acetate prints that are also prone to vinegar syndrome. It's sad that works by Lubitsch, Murnau, Hitchcock and Von Sternberg are lost forever. But without the 40,000-strong Cinémathèque collection, the toll might have been considerably worse. ∎

'Langlois spurned the latest releases to revive forgotten gems.'

After a peripatetic existence, the Cinémathèque Française found a permanent home at 51 rue de Bercy, designed by American architect Frank Gehry.

Festival fever

CANNES

Poster from the 1953 festival
showing the original Palais des
Festivals, which was inaugurated
on La Croisette in 1949 and
demolished in 1988.

It may not be the oldest film festival but Cannes is easily the most important. This annual event on France's Riviera has changed cinema by dint of the number of landmark pictures that have debuted there and the countless career-making deals that have been struck at Le Marché.

Festivals have their roots in the *ciné-clubs* and film societies that were formed outside America in the 1920s in response to Hollywood's growing dominance of the world market. In Europe, the emphasis was on foreign-language classics, documentaries and experimental works. In developing countries, on the other hand, such institutions were often the sole outlet for indigenous features. As many cineastes were also aspiring directors, they began to meet at international conferences for screenings and discussions. In this way, the latest technological, theoretical and stylistic innovations began to be disseminated.

The Italian dictator Benito Mussolini launched the Venice Film Festival in 1932 to propagate the achievements of the Fascist film industry. Cannes was founded shortly afterwards in reaction to Jean Renoir's pacifist masterpiece *La Grande Illusion* (1937) being overlooked by a politically motivated jury. The inaugural French event was abandoned after Germany invaded Poland in September 1939 and the postwar revival suffered a couple of false starts. But Cannes was established by 1951, and starlet Simone Silva's peekaboo flirtation with Robert Mitchum three years later imbued it with a scandalous glamour that has made it a paparazzo's paradise ever since. However, it was the introduction of the Palme d'Or (or Golden Palm) award for best film in 1955 that gave Cannes its unrivalled kudos among film-makers and critics.

The festival has grown considerably over the years, with the addition of sidebars like the Critics' Week and Un Certain Regard. Such diversification has enabled Cannes to celebrate film history through its retrospectives and encourage newcomers from movements like the Nouvelle Vague, as well as the previously neglected Asian and African traditions. Indeed, Cannes has helped globalize cinema by promoting arthouse pictures and allowing them to find their audience.

Even American independent features such as *Marty* (1955), *Easy Rider* (1969) and *Sex, Lies, and Videotape* (1989) have benefited from the Cannes effect. However, Hollywood has often been accused of attempting to hijack the festival by premiering blockbusters out of competition and importing stars for photo opportunities. But juries have tended to award prizes to less commercial items, even if choices like Maurice Pialat's *Under Satan's Sun* (1987) and Michael Moore's *Fahrenheit 9/11* (2004) have sparked controversy.

Away from the media spotlight, Cannes is a marketplace as well as a showcase, with some 10,000 buyers, sellers and hopefuls annually descending upon the Riviera. Only the Sundance Film Festival in America gets close to this amount of business activity. But, like Venice and Berlin, it can't match Cannes's prestige or its centrality in influencing the international screen agenda. Cannes's success has inspired a network of big city festivals and niche events for documentaries, animation, shorts, genre movies and the avant-garde. Yet, despite its size and significance, it remains committed to getting so-called smaller pictures seen, sold and appreciated. ∎

'Cannes has helped globalize cinema by promoting arthouse pictures.'

18-year-old Brigitte Bardot stole the show at the 1953 festival and photo opportunities on La Croisette have since become de rigueur.

CAHIERS
DU CINÉMA

Nº 31 • REVUE DU CINÉMA ET DU TÉLÉCINÉMA • Nº 31

The cover of the January 1954 edition
of **Cahiers du Cinéma**, *containing*
François Truffaut's famous article,
'A Certain Tendency in French Cinema',
which sparked the **Nouvelle Vague**.

Everyone's a critic

IDEA № 74
CRITICISM

Thanks to the arrival of specialist journals and the internet, the outlets for film criticism have grown and changed beyond recognition across the past century – with critics often determining a film's commercial prospects and the way it is interpreted either as art or entertainment.

Notwithstanding the critique of Edison's *The Kiss*, which appeared in *Chap Book* on 15 June 1896, cinema was initially seen as newsworthy rather than culturally significant. With trade publications reliant on advertising from film-makers, the first notices were essentially non-judgemental plot summaries. Producers and distributors have continued to use promotional largesse and access to talent to elicit positive responses to their latest releases ever since.

Many of the fanzines that emerged in the 1920s were happy to peddle a diet of glamour, gossip and gush. But the technical insights and aesthetic principles contained in Vachel Lindsay's book *The Art of the Moving Picture* (1915) encouraged a more informed brand of criticism that earned cinema greater social and intellectual respectability. Moreover, this new breed of critic-cum-theorist established the film societies that introduced urban audiences to international artists. They even translated treatises by the likes of Vsevolod Pudovkin and Sergei Eisenstein for their self-published periodicals.

Yet, despite the work of influential thinkers such as Rudolf Arnheim, Béla Balázs and Siegfried Kracauer, the majority of reviews remained more evaluative than analytical. Following the US film critic James Agee's example of fitting 'coherent language' into 'feasible space', many lambasted American movies for their unrealistic depiction of life. Critics worldwide were equally acerbic about domestic industries that duplicated Hollywood tropes rather than forging more culturally specific styles. Inspired by editor André Bazin, *Cahiers du Cinéma*'s cine-literate zealots were particularly ferocious in denouncing postwar French features and establishing the *politique des auteurs* (see **Auteur Theory**).

The feuds between the reviewers Andrew Sarris and Pauline Kael in the States and between the publications *Movie* and *Sight & Sound* in Britain typified the seismic shift in critical preoccupations that coincided with film studies becoming a university discipline and cinema being subjected to reappraisal according to the tenets of Marxism, feminism, gay activism, psychoanalysis, semiotics, post-modernism, structuralism and post-structuralism. Yet the best film polls and pantheon of auteurs inaugurated by *Cahiers du Cinéma*'s Young Turks before they began making their own films (like so many critics before and since), helped establish the canon that remains central to serious cinematic discussion and against which future generations will rebel.

The contemporary landscape is much changed, with the studios plastering posters with quotes from non-professional fanboys, print critics facing extinction and academics contesting subtexts and metaphysical minutiae online. It remains to be seen what lasting impact this so-called 'democratization' will have upon criticism and its role in the promotion and appreciation of film. ∎

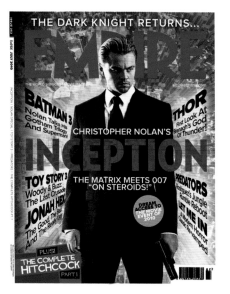

ABOVE: *The British magazine* Empire *typifies the polished, edgy and informed style of criticism popular with mainstream movie fans.*

BELOW: *Andrew Sarris's 1968 book* The American Cinema *proved contentiously influential by putting auteur theory at the centre of US critical debate.*

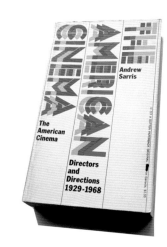

The camera goes deeper

IDEA № 75
MISE EN SCÈNE

The term 'mise en scène' can simply mean everything placed before the camera and its organization. But a more complex usage was coined by critic André Bazin to define the technique of using long takes with a deep-focused moving camera to unify character and environment and provide an alternative to Hollywood's classic cut-based narrative mode.

Various elements make up a film's basic mise en scène in the first, most general sense of the term: décor, space and props; costume and make-up; the blocking of the actors and the timbre of their performance; the score; the choice of lens, film stock and lighting design; and the placement and movement of the camera. Crucial to conveying meaning in fictional, documentary and avant-garde films, the mise en scène can establish mood, suggest motifs and reinforce themes. Moreover, a well-composed shot can reveal as much about a character and the world they inhabit as pages of dialogue.

Georges Méliès and the German Expressionists were among the earliest *metteurs en scène*. But shot duration shortened with the evolution of cross-cutting and the transition to sound saw image depth subordinated to narrative logic, psychological truth and spatial-temporal continuity. However, directors like William Wyler and Orson Welles rediscovered the technique and prompted Bazin to formulate the theory that inspired the *politique des auteurs*, the Nouvelle Vague and the emergence of an integral realism that would permit 'a recreation of the world in its own image'.

Improved lighting, smaller apertures and faster stocks enabled Gregg Toland to refine deep-focus cinematography and produce sharp images on close, intermediate and distant planes. Yet while Toland was shooting Wyler's *Wuthering Heights* (1939) and Welles's *Citizen Kane* (1941), Jean Renoir was revealing in films such as *La Grande Illusion* (1937) how a moving camera could alight upon details to guide the viewer, establish the characters within their locales, and draw parallels and contrasts between them. Post-World War II, Max Ophüls demonstrated his mastery of mise en scène with the sinuous camerawork in *La Ronde* (1950) and the 360-degree tracks and crane shots that redefine diegetic space in *Lola Montès* (1955).

Tracks, tilts, pans and crane shots also helped achieve longer takes, as they served as 'invisible cuts' that reframed the continuous action. Emphasizing the unity of time and space, long takes were hailed by Bazin as closer to life and more democratic than montage. Occasionally, they could be self-indulgent. But fluid sequence shots allowed directors as diverse as Kenji Mizoguchi, Roberto Rossellini, Miklós Jancsó, Theo Angelopoulos and

TOP: *Michelangelo Antonioni considered locale and character to be equally significant in films like* Red Desert *(1964).*

ABOVE: In **Play Time** *(1967), Jacques Tati used mise en scène and montage to allow viewers to discover the myriad gags for themselves.*

Hou Hsiao-hsien to create credible milieux, while also imposing their personality upon them.

Despite Hollywood resistance to a technique deemed self-reflexive, ostentatious and expensive, American directors such as Vincente Minnelli, Samuel Fuller, Robert Altman, David Fincher and Gus Van Sant have also favoured the mise en scène approach in a bid to capture a scene's spontaneity, specificity and equivocacy. A shot's length determines our understanding of it. However, the current vogue for rapid editing means that mise en scène remains more associated with indie and art-house cinema than the mainstream. ∎

Director William Wyler kept Lee Garmes's camera moving around Hal Pereira's sets to intensify the tension in The Desperate Hours (1955).

ABOVE: *Abbas Kiarostami exploited the 180-degree axis of action to maintain focus on the women watching an offscreen film in* Shirin *(2008).*

BELOW: *In* The Searchers *(1956), John Ford used offscreen space to sustain suspense and challenge both generic convention and racist attitudes to Native Americans.*

More than meets the eye

OFF-SCREEN SPACE

Mainstream cinema is so preoccupied with narrative that the focus inevitably falls on events occurring within the film frame. But off-screen space – those unseen areas beyond the camera's view – is often equally important in moving the story along, drawing attention to significant details and generating atmosphere or suspense.

Anna Massey is menaced by murderous off-screen cameraman Carl Boehm in Michael Powell's chilling exposé of cine-voyeurism, **Peeping Tom** *(1960).*

Few viewers will realize how much time they spend contemplating what they cannot see, but some critics insist that cinematic truth is almost entirely dependent upon off-screen space.

In order to render a three-dimensional world on a two-dimensional plane, film-makers adopted the concepts of space and depth that had pertained to painting since the Renaissance. Centrality and frontality were achieved by filming and cutting along a 180-degree axis of action, while pans, tilts and frame cuts maintained shot balance as the characters moved. Such movements were key to depicting spatial relationships, along with light and shade, overlapping contours, texture, colour and audiovisual perspective. However, in composing images to accommodate spaces that would be filled by new figures entering the shot, directors acknowledged the existence of off-screen space and soon began to exploit it for dramatic purposes.

Shot space, editing space and sonic space help viewers construct off-screen areas. According to theorist Noël Burch, six such zones exist, beyond the four edges of the frame, behind the set and behind the camera, and together they can convey both diegetic and non-diegetic space. Louis Lumière initially suggested the concept by having people appear from behind the camera in *L'Arrivée d'un train en Gare de La Ciotat* (1895) and film-makers quickly recognized the value of characters interacting with persons or props off screen or having objects suddenly enter the frame, such as the grasping hand in D.W. Griffith's *The Musketeers of Pig Alley* (1912).

Chase films relied heavily on the relationship between on- and off-screen space, as did quest pictures like John Ford's *The Searchers* (1956) and Michelangelo Antonioni's *L'Avventura* (1960). Off-screen space also became a staple of thrillers and horror films as protagonists ventured out of the frame and into potential danger. But it could also be subverted, such as when Oliver Hardy broke the fourth wall with one of his world-weary sighs or Michael Caine spoke directly to the camera in *Alfie* (1966).

The shifting line between on- and off-screen space was also crucial to the mise en scène style perfected by the likes of Max Ophüls and Kenji Mizoguchi. But the master of off-screen technique was Yasujiro Ozu, who used off-centre framing to exploit an image's centrifugal force to guide the viewer to the edges of the frame and the real world that existed beyond. In order to achieve this, he devised a fully circular film space around which he could construct alternative axes of action and thus create totally new spatial contexts throughout a scene.

Although requiring painstaking graphic matching and disallowing even the most basic pans, this method ensured the complete integration of action and location. Ozu also fashioned off-screen space through the 'pillow' shots or visual digressions that he used as scene transitions. Many film-makers have been influenced by his ideas, among them Abbas Kiarostami, who audaciously suggested off-screen space on a screen that was itself off screen in *Shirin* (2008). ∎

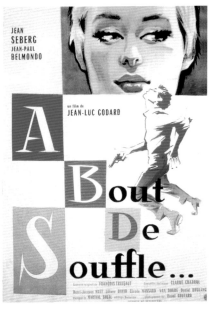

JEAN
SEBERG
JEAN-PAUL
BELMONDO

un film de
JEAN-LUC GODARD

A
Bout
De
Souffle...

FRANÇOIS TRUFFAUT

The director as superstar

ABOVE: *Scripted and directed by Jean-Luc Godard,* Breathless *(or* A bout de souffle) *(1960) was key to popularizing auteur theory.*

BELOW: *Godard and his muse Anna Karina on the set on* Alphaville *(1965).*

IDEA № 77
AUTEUR THEORY

Coined '*la politique des auteurs*', auteur theory was first proposed in the French journal *Cahiers du Cinéma* in the mid-1950s to identify film-makers whose consistency of theme and visual style made them to all intents and purposes the 'authors' of their pictures. Few concepts in screen history have proved as significant or contentious.

In addition to fostering the seismic cinematic shift known as the Nouvelle Vague, it also entirely revised the style of popular and scholastic **criticism**. Moreover, it weathered the scorn of vociferous detractors espousing the collaborative nature of film-making to reinvent the director as superstar. Yet perhaps its greatest achievement was to force a reassessment of the Hollywood studio system's ability to match the sophistication of European art cinema.

Film histories have always focused on innovative directors and distinctive stylistic traits. In the silent era, D.W. Griffith was very much the creative force behind his films, as were Erich von Stroheim, Victor Sjöström, Carl Dreyer and the principal German Expressionists and Soviet montagists. Into the sound era, Cecil B. DeMille and Josef von Sternberg defied the industrial nature of production to develop trademark traits, while John Ford and Frank Capra were among

those to make a bid for independence by pursuing more personal projects from the late 1940s.

But it was only during the postwar era, when French screens were saturated with long-withheld American imports, that cineastes began to equate Hollywood directors such as Alfred Hitchcock, Howard Hawks and Nicholas Ray with Europeans like Jean Renoir, Roberto Rossellini and Robert Bresson, who brought the same sense of personality and consistency to their work as writers by following critic-turned-director Alexandre Astruc's *caméra stylo* approach and using the camera as a writer would wield a pen. Indeed, it was the originality and audacity of their use of mise en scène that prompted François Truffaut to publish his article 'A Certain Tendency in French Cinema' in 1954 to denounce the old-fashioned *cinéma du papa* of conservative directors such as Jean Delannoy, Claude Autant-Lara, René Clément and Henri-Georges Clouzot,

François Truffaut as a director
encouraging neurotic actor
Jean-Pierre Léaud in the
Oscar-winning movie-making
satire, **Day for Night** (1973).

'Few concepts in screen history have proved as significant or contentious.'

who devoted more time to the script and the actors than to the visual aspect of their work.

However, it took Truffaut and fellow *Cahiers* alumni Jean-Luc Godard, Claude Chabrol and Jacques Rivette to begin actually making the radically innovative features that sparked new waves across the world before auteurism seized the Anglo-American imagination. The contribution of the British magazine *Movie* has often been overlooked, as the debate was hijacked by the feud between *New Yorker* reviewer Pauline Kael and Andrew Sarris, who had coined the term 'auteur theory' before compiling a pantheon of worthies for his book *The American*

Cinema: Directors and Directions 1929–1968. Positing a critical switch from theme and narrative content to style and aesthetic context, the book would become key to the evolution of university film studies. It remains hugely influential to this day, despite the rise of such competing notions as cine-structuralism and genre.

Sarris would later claim that 'auteur theory is not so much a theory as an attitude, a table of values that converts film history into directorial autobiography'. However, it was seized upon by the new generation of film-school graduates, who were no longer content simply to exercise hierarchical superiority on the set. These so-called

'movie brats' coveted authorship and their agents were quick to convince studio executives that director branding was as crucial to the marketing of a blockbuster as marquee stars. The credit 'A film by' has now been so abused that it has almost become meaningless (except, of course, where avant-garde film-makers are concerned). Nevertheless, even in an age in which post-production digitization is often more crucial than the live-action shoot, the unifying vision on most films remains that of the director. ∎

The rise of shakicam

Handheld camera was one of the Vows of Chastity in Lars von Trier's Dogme 95 Manifesto that challenged mainstream film-making styles.

IDEA № 78

HANDHELD CAMERA

Handheld images captured by portable cameras convey immediacy and pitch the viewer into the middle of the action. The Danes call the technique 'free camera'. Cinematographers in Hong Kong have their own saying: 'The handheld camera covers three mistakes: bad acting, bad set design and bad directing.'

The earliest hand-cranked cameras were too heavy to remove from their tripods but the need to balance compositions saw film-makers increasingly moving the camera to reframe the action as its focus shifted. The majority of mainstream directors tried to avoid drawing attention to their technique, but Karl Freund strapped the camera to his chest for the subjective shots in F.W. Murnau's *The Last Laugh* (1924), while Abel Gance attached cameras variously to a horse, a football and a pendulum for *Napoleon* (1927).

The invention of dollies and cranes permitted cameras to follow figures and objects, roam the mise en scène, highlight significant details, present character perspectives and reveal off-screen areas. By varying distance, angle and height, fluid camerawork could also establish patterns and rhythms and allow the long takes that critics such as André Bazin insisted unified time and space and were, therefore, more realistic than edited sequences. Alfred Hitchcock, Kenji Mizoguchi, Orson Welles, Max Ophüls and Miklós Jancsó demonstrated a mastery of the mobile frame. But film-makers sought a still-greater sense of freedom, vitality and authenticity.

The popularity of the portable 16mm cameras used for combat footage during World War II led to the development of the Auricon Cine-Voice, Arriflex 16BL and Eclair NPR, which enabled handheld shooting to become a signature technique of Cinéma Vérité, Direct Cinema and the Nouvelle Vague, as well as television news. Challenging staid orthodoxy, shaky and sometimes blurred handheld images adorned films as different as *Les Raquetteurs* (1958), *Breathless* (or *A bout de souffle*) (1960), *Jules et Jim* (1961), *A Hard Day's Night* (1964), *The Battle of Algiers* (1966) and *Medium Cool* (1969).

Notwithstanding the artistic and budgetary benefits of this inexpensive improvisational mode, there was a backlash among critics accustomed to Hollywood classicism. By way of response, in the early 1970s, cinematographer Garrett Brown combined handheld flexibility with the smoothness of a dolly when he invented the Steadicam rig, which was able to absorb sudden jolts as the operator followed the action. First employed on Hal Ashby's *Bound for Glory* (1976), Steadicam has since been memorably used by Stanley Kubrick, Brian De Palma and Martin Scorsese.

Making a virtue of jerky, pseudo-realistic imagery, so-called 'un-steadicam' reactions like Sam Raimi's *The Evil Dead* (1981) were quick in coming. Since Woody Allen's *Husbands and Wives* (1992) and Lars von Trier's *Dancer in the Dark* (2000), however, the vogue for 'shakicam' has shifted to the mainstream, as directors strive to make their pictures more kinetic and visceral. Juxtaposing jittery images with rapid, discontinuous cuts, directors like Oliver Stone, Tony Scott and Michael Mann developed the fast-moving run-and-gun style that originated in video games which some cite as demonstrating a decline in craftsmanship. Yet, despite denying a sense of space, limiting psychological insight and placing huge reliance on the score and sound effects to compensate for the lack of visual clarity and narrative coherence, pictures such as *The Bourne Ultimatum* (2007) and *Cloverfield* (2008) continue to thrill the gaming generation. ∎

ABOVE: *Lars von Trier experimented with dolly shots, handheld footage and computer-programmed motion control techniques in making* **Antichrist** *(2009).*

RIGHT: *Cinematograher Raoul Coutard mounted his camera on a bicycle to capture the exhilaration of the characters in François Truffaut's* **Jules et Jim** *(1961).*

In an attempt to heighten the drama of Nanook of the North *(1922), Robert Flaherty had Allakariallak enact long-abandoned Inuit hunting techniques.*

'The very process of framing and editing images diminishes their objectivity.'

Putting reality on screen

IDEA № 79
CINÉMA VÉRITÉ

ABOVE: *The documentarian as polemicist and provocateur: Michael Moore in* Fahrenheit 9/11 *(2004).*

BELOW: *Jackie Kennedy's cousin Edie Bouvier Beale dances with the American flag in the Maysles documentary,* Grey Gardens *(1975).*

Presenting their own versions of 'truthful cinema', Cinéma Vérité and Direct Cinema led a 1960s rebellion against the documentary tendency to manipulate reality for dramatic and propagandist purposes. However, they also sparked a debate about the ethics of actuality.

Made in the image of the first Lumière records of reality, the earliest documentaries were simple, static slices of life and views of faraway places. However, in striving for lyrical naturalism in *Nanook of the North* (1922), Robert Flaherty consciously shaped the action and thus romanticized his Inuit subject. The Soviet montagist Dziga Vertov took similar liberties with agit-prop constructs such as *Man with a Movie Camera* (1929), which forged the link between the documentary and the avant-garde. Yet John Grierson, who coined the term 'documentary', saw nothing wrong in exploiting this 'creative treatment of actuality' in the sponsored social-utility shorts he produced in the 1930s, which not only established the British documentary tradition, but also the blend of scripted narration, reconstructed incident and vox-pop opinion that has survived into the television age.

Indeed, poets and propagandists alike continued to manipulate reality (even in audiovisually and thematically innovative, but editorially neutral categorical pictures) until the end of World War II, when a decline in deference and the advent of Neorealism increased the clamour for greater transparency. However, Cinéma Vérité and Direct Cinema took markedly different routes to creating screen truth.

Taking their cue from journalistic photo-essays, both were keen to report from the heart of events and utilized the portable cameras that had been perfected for wartime newsreels and the latest stand-alone tape recorders. But whereas exponents of Direct Cinema were prepared to observe the unfolding scene, *vériteurs* actively sought to conduct it, either by appearing before the camera or interacting with the protagonists. Furthermore, there were differences within each tradition. Québecois pioneer Michel Brault devised the term *'cinéma direct'* to distance himself from Cinéma Vérité advocates like Jean Rouch and Chris Marker. Meanwhile, American counterparts such as Drew Associates alumni Robert Drew, D.A. Pennebaker, and Albert and David Maysles tended to focus on personalities, while the more rigorously detached Frederick Wiseman concentrated on institutions.

Some theorists lauded the purity of Direct Cinema's 'fly on the wall' technique, as it allowed viewers to reach their own conclusions. But the very process of framing and editing images diminishes their objectivity and, by making no attempt to disguise their hands-on methodology, the Cinéma Vérité provocateurs demonstrated that it was possible to entertain while also enlightening their audience. Moreover, their visceral handheld images proved a significant influence on the Nouvelle Vague, as well as the politicized Third Cinema that emerged in developing countries the 1960s. Their reflexive approach also informed the rhetorical films of star documentarists like Nick Broomfield and Michael Moore, who contributed to actuality's unexpected commercial success in the 1990s.

With camcorders and digital kit making it easier than ever to capture

what Albert Maysles called 'the drama of ordinary people in daily life', there has been a boom in politically engaged titles highlighting injustices, legitimizing subcultures, promoting causes and positing solutions. Reality television has also impinged upon the feature format. But, in order to snare an audience, the various exposés, confessionals, compilations, video diaries, docudramas, rockumentaries and mockumentaries have increasingly forsworn impartiality and become ever-more reliant on gimmickry. ∎

Gritty social realism

IDEA № 80
FREE CINEMA

Considering it was limited to six showcases at London's National Film Theatre between 1956 and 1959, Free Cinema had a remarkable impact, coinciding with the transition from a studio system to a new internationalism and inducing the social-realist style that remains a domestic staple in Britain.

The tenets of Free Cinema were developed by Lindsay Anderson, Tony Richardson and Karel Reisz while writing for the journals *Sequence* and *Sight & Sound*. They were rooted in Poetic Realism, Neorealism and the lyrical humanism of Robert Flaherty, John Ford and Humphrey Jennings, and firmly rejected the patronizing altruism of the documentary tradition established by John Grierson and the cosy good taste that producers had hoped would entrance transatlantic audiences. But it was primarily a desire to produce personal films that spurned commercial and propagandist pressure and did justice to the working class that united the low-budget shorts which were screened at the NFT, such as *Momma Don't Allow* (1955), *Every Day Except Christmas* (1957) and *We Are the Lambeth Boys* (1959).

The emphasis on ordinary people and the everyday echoed that of contemporary regional novels and plays by the likes of John Osborne, whose landmark *Look Back in Anger* was directed by Richardson on both stage (1956) and screen (1959). Indeed, such was the compatibility of the Free Cinema and 'kitchen sink' aesthetics that they combined to authentic effect in Reisz's *Saturday Night and Sunday Morning* (1960), Richardson's *A Taste of Honey* (1961) and Anderson's *This Sporting Life* (1963).

Always more of a tendency than a cogent movement, Free Cinema failed

in its bid to create the conditions for the continuing production and exhibition of independent shorts. But it did presage a new wave that repudiated the theatricality of coy sagas set in bourgeois suburbia, unleashing a generation of angry young men and liberated women, and unflinchingly tackling taboo social, political and sexual issues that subsequently recurred in everything from *Carry On* comedies to softcore smut and horror movies. Moreover, it inspired newcomers like Ken Russell and Ken Loach to refine small-screen docudrama and provided the impetus for the British Film Institute's Experimental Film Fund to encourage talents such as Ridley and Tony Scott, Peter Watkins, Sally Potter, Peter Greenaway, Derek Jarman and Terence Davies.

The Oscar success of Richardson's *Tom Jones* (1963) prompted major US investment in British pictures epitomizing Swinging Sixties chic. But the retreat to a rejuvenated Hollywood at the end of the decade plunged the UK industry into a slump from which it only recovered in the early 1980s. Some critics have complained that social realism hindered the thematic and stylistic development of British cinema by institutionalizing the gritty authenticity that is still espoused by filmmakers such as Lynne Ramsay, Shane Meadows and Andrea Arnold. However, Free Cinema also had an international

TOP: *Swiss-born Claude Goretta, one of the European contributors to Free Cinema, went on to direct such fine features as* The Lacemaker *(1977), starring Isabelle Huppert.*

ABOVE: *'I'm out for a good time – all the rest is propaganda!' Albert Finney in* Saturday Night and Sunday Morning *(1960).*

element and, with Roman Polanski, Claude Goretta and François Truffaut among its alumni, its overseas repercussions were more pronounced. Moreover, the influence of mission maxims like 'Perfection is not an aim' and 'An attitude means a style; a style means an attitude' was also evident in the Czech New Wave and both the 1962 Oberhausen Manifesto and 1995 Vow of Chastity, which initiated Das Neue Kino and Dogme 95 respectively. ∎

the Lambeth Boys *(1959)*.

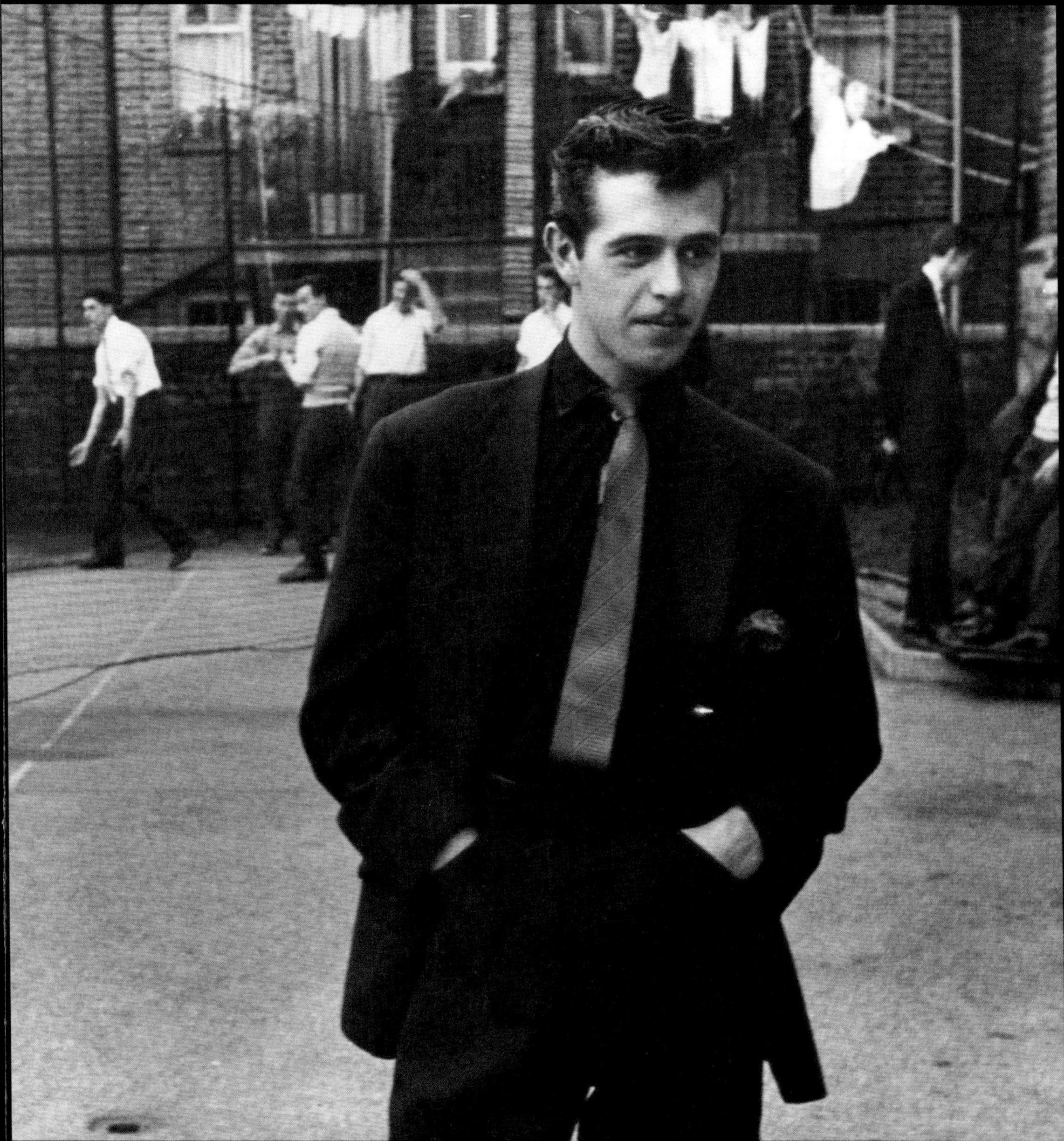

'Third Cinema sought to instill revolutionary ideals in audiences by subverting cinematic convention.'

ABOVE: *Tran Anh Hung, the France-based director of* Cyclo *(1995), was much criticised in his native Vietnam for his violent depiction of street life in Ho Chi Minh City.*

ABOVE: *Political protest via deadpan satire: Elia Suleiman's* The Time That Remains *(2009).*

RIGHT: *Hailed by Luis Buñuel for its 'savage poetry', Glauber Rocha's* Black God, White Devil *(1964) is a masterwork of Cinema Novo that spawned the equally imposing sequel* Antonio das Mortes *(1969).*

Towards a tri-continental revolution

Dariush Mehrjui's The Cow *(1969) established the tradition of subtle criticism and wry humanism that characterized Iranian cinema either side of the Islamic Revolution.*

IDEA № 81
THIRD CINEMA

Dismissing the Hollywood commercialism of so-called First Cinema and the auteurism of the European art film's Second Cinema, Third Cinema sought to instil revolutionary ideals in audiences by subverting cinematic convention and precluding passive reception. Originating in Latin America in the late 1960s, its influence soon spread to Africa and Asia.

Third Cinema was a cultural response to the anti-colonial struggle in Africa, the Cuban Revolution, the rise of black consciousness in the United States and the reconceptualization of Marxist and Maoist dialectics by intellectuals worldwide. Its filmic roots lay in the 1950s Neorealism of Brazilian Nelson Pereira dos Santos and Argentinian Fernando Birri, and in the 1960s Cinema Novo movement that had reinvigorated Brazilian film. Central to the latter's abrasively distanciated style was Glauber Rocha's 1965 essay 'An Aesthetic of Hunger', which became a key text alongside two 1969 manifestos, Cuban Julio García Espinosa's 'For an Imperfect Cinema' and 'Towards a Third Cinema: Notes and Experiences for the Development of a Cinema of Liberation in the Third World', in which Argentines Fernando Solanas and Octavio Getino codified the ideas and methods they had employed in their guerilla documentary *The Hour of the Furnaces* (1968).

Determined to depict life as it was lived, Solanas and Getino advocated an independent, oppositional cinema that rejected mainstream genres and arthouse existentialism in favour of socially relevant themes and techniques that challenged historical conceptions, exposed injustice and reclaimed national cultures. Moreover, in producing films that couldn't be appropriated by the establishment,

Third Cinema promoted a stylistic diversity that spawned newsreels, agit-prop documentaries, avant-garde shorts, realist epics and socio-political satires.

Yet the works of Cubans Tomás Gutiérrez Alea and Santiago Álvarez, Chileans Patricio Guzman and Miguel Littin, Brazilians Glauber Rocha and Ruy Guerra, and Bolivian Jorge Sanjinés failed to incite the anticipated tri-continental revolution. Indeed, Third Cinema came in for much criticism in the 1980s. Chilean maverick Raúl Ruiz complained that its objectives had been too narrow, while some lamented its neglect of feminist and ethnocentric issues and others questioned the involvement of European film-makers such as Joris Ivens, Chris Marker and Gillo Pontecorvo.

However, Third Cinema had become a global phenomenon that addressed problems like nation-building, post-colonial disillusion and newly emerging forms of racial, religious, social and sexual oppression. Its strongest base was in Africa, where the clash between tradition and progress was explored in allegories, satires and realist dramas by Youssef Chahine in Egypt, Merzak Allouache in Algeria, Ousmane Sembène in Senegal, Gaston Kaboré and Idrissa Ouédraogo in Burkino Faso, Souleymane Cissé in Mali, Jean-Marie Téno in Cameroon and Med Hondo in Mauritania.

In Asia, the cause of radical change was taken up by Lino Brocka in the Philippines, Mrinal Sen in India, Tran Anh Hung in Vietnam and Dariush Mehrjui in Iran, while seeds of solidarity were also sown by Wayne Wang in America, Isaac Julien in Britain and Tracey Moffat in Australia. Subsequently, Third Cinema has endorsed diasporic and exilic film-makers, while also providing the impetus for the Latin American renaissance led by Walter Salles, Fernando Meirelles, Alejandro González Iñárritu, Pablo Trapero and Lucrecia Martel. ■

The camera's different eyes

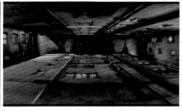

Alfred Hitchcock made disconcerting use of the 'trombone' or 'contra zoom' shot to emphasize James Stewart's terror in **Vertigo** (1958).

IDEA Nº 82

ZOOM

For the first third of cinema's history, most films were photographed with so-called normal lenses. But since the introduction of zooms and other forced-perspective techniques for making objects appear closer or farther away than they really are, movies have gone beyond ordinary human vision.

Perspective is key to the appreciation and understanding of moving pictures, as alterations to a lens's focal length affect the perceived depth and scale of an image, as well as its dramatic and expressive impact.

The standard lens in use between the 1910s and the early 1940s had a focal length of 35–50mm and sought to replicate human vision. The amount of light reaching the film stock was regulated by the width of the aperture and the speed of the shutter, while lens filters and gels were used to vary the quality of the light and these diffusion effects became a characteristic of French Impressionism and Josef von Sternberg's collaborations with Marlene Dietrich.

Longer-focus lenses were introduced in the mid-1910s, with cinematographer Henrik Sartov notably using them for the soft-focus close-ups of Lillian Gish in D.W. Griffith's *Broken Blossoms* (1919). Abel Gance and Marcel L'Herbier experimented with wide-angle, or short-focus, lenses in *Napoleon* (1927) and *Money* (1928) respectively, but it wasn't until Gregg Toland employed them on *Citizen Kane* (1941) that they became more common in Hollywood.

Emphasizing the illusion of depth and often distorting linear perception, wide-angle lenses initially proved more compatible with **Academy ratio** monochrome than widescreen colour processes. But, once the glitches had been ironed out, lenses with a focal length of less than 35mm became standard issue (especially for use in confined spaces), unlike fish-eye lenses affording angles of up to 180 degrees, which have been used primarily for depicting disorientation in trippy pictures such as *Easy Rider* (1969).

Telephoto lenses magnify distant action, while suppressing depth perception and narrowing the angle of view. Following their use in Claude Lelouch's *A Man and a Woman* (1966), telephotos were favoured by Robert Altman, Milos Forman and Akira Kurosawa, as well as by 'movie brats' such as Steven Spielberg, Francis Ford Coppola and Brian De Palma, who often mixed long-focus and wide-angle shots in the same sequence. But while they compressed distances, enhanced authenticity and were useful for location work and multi-camera studio set-ups, telephoto lenses were less versatile than zooms.

Paramount started using zoom lenses in features like *It* (1927) and *Love Me Tonight* (1932). But even after Zoomar lenses measuring 100–1,000mm were refined for aerial photography during the war and became a staple of early televisual and advertising techniques, they were rarely used in movies, despite Alfred Hitchcock's inspired combination of a track and a zoom for the celebrated and much-imitated 'trombone shot' in *Vertigo* (1958).

However, optical travelling shots that subverted impersonal, seamless classicism were eventually popularized by Europeans like John Schlesinger, Mario Bava, Roberto Rossellini and Michelangelo Antonioni, as well as Americans working in Britain such as Richard Lester and Stanley Kubrick. Offering a variable focal length from wide-angle to telephoto and allowing for controlled shifts during shots, zooms remain aesthetically and economically effective. Not only do the faster brands require less light, they also dispense with the need for dollies and tracks. Nevertheless, most viewers still struggle to differentiate between zooms shots taken with a stationary camera and slow dolly shots known as 'push-ins' filmed from a moving camera. ∎

Cinematographer László Kovács experimented with telephoto lenses and different film stocks to achieve the edgy visuals in Dennis Hopper's **Easy Rider** *(1969).*

'Zooms remain aesthetically and economically effective.'

BELOW: *Stanley Kubrick and cinematographer John Alcott not only used zooms for dramatic effect in* Barry Lyndon *(1976), but also to flatten images in imitation of eighteenth-century painting.*

ABOVE: *A revolutionary's education: Ernesto Guevara (Gael Garcia Bernal) and Alberto Granado (Rodrigo De la Serna) in Walter Salles's* **The Motorcycle Diaries** *(2004).*

BELOW: *'A place for dreams. A place for heartbreak.' Harry Dean Stanton in Wim Wenders's Palme d'Or-winning road movie,* **Paris, Texas** *(1984).*

From cattle driving to easy riding

IDEA № 83
ROAD MOVIES

Most films take their characters and viewers on metaphorical journeys. But road movies focus specifically on the travelling, with protagonists crossing geographical as well as moral boundaries in order to escape their problems, discover their true nature or attain a cherished goal.

Rooted in the mythical odyssey and the pastoral picaresque, American excursion fiction from Mark Twain to Jack Kerouac tapped into the pioneering spirit that drove a frontier society towards its Manifest Destiny. The dime Western also accentuated the perils of traversing a vast and often treacherous landscape, and its wagon-train treks, stagecoach rides and cattle drives inspired classic features such as *Stagecoach* (1939), *Red River* (1948) and *Bend of the River* (1952). However, the road movie proper relied on a very different kind of horsepower, with motor vehicles mirroring cinema's own obsession with movement and speed.

The itinerary of the Depression was captured in social dramas like *The Grapes of Wrath* (1940), but the road movie appeared in many other guises during Hollywood's Golden Age. In addition to screwballs such as *It Happened One Night* (1934) and *Sullivan's Travels* (1941), there were also homeward-bound musicals like *The Wizard of Oz* (1939), trucker tales such as *They Drive by Night* (1940) and battlefront epics like *A Walk in the Sun* (1945). But noirish fugitive sagas such as *Detour* (1945) and *Gun Crazy* (1949) had the biggest impact on the sub-genre, as they caught the burgeoning mood of youthful rebellion in postwar America and anticipated counter-culture landmarks like *Bonnie and Clyde* (1967) and *Easy Rider* (1969).

Though the road movie had long been a cinematic staple, the term itself was only first used in the New Hollywood era that started in the mid-1960s, when works reflected national disenchantment after Vietnam and Watergate. The format was subsequently exploited by mainstream, independent, documentary and experimental film-makers. Features such as *Two-Lane Blacktop* (1971), *Badlands* (1973), *Stranger Than Paradise* (1984), *Thelma and Louise* (1991) and *Little Miss Sunshine* (2006) centred on anti-heroic quests, outlaws and outsiders to offer acute socio-cultural critiques, while also revising generic convention. Indeed, the open-ended, modernist format proved sufficiently flexible to accommodate horror and sci-fi, as well as madcap and melodramatic takes on cross-country races, rock tours, student road trips and midlife crises. Lone drivers, parents and children, prisoners and escorts, buddies, hitchhikers, lost animals, yuppie couples, and busloads of losers and misfits have hit the cine-highway over the years, but not all have managed to find the road to redemption.

Despite its American associations, the road movie has also flourished worldwide. A typically European existentialism informed Federico Fellini's *La Strada* (1954) and Ingmar Bergman's *Wild Strawberries* (1957). But Jean-Luc Godard's *Pierrot le fou* (1965) revealed a debt to the US model that was also evident in Wim Wenders's *Alice in the Cities* (1974) and *Kings of the Road* (1976). Australian and Canadian outings like George Miller's *Mad Max* trilogy and Bruce McDonald's cult rock'n'road flicks similarly transported iconic tropes to distinctive environments, as did politicized Latin American pictures such as Walter Salles's *Central Station* (1998), Alfonso Cuarón's *Y tu mamá también* (2001) and Cary Fukunaga's *Sin nombre* (2009), which typified the form's latest variation: the migrant expedition. ■

ABOVE: *Reporter Clark Gable crosses America with runaway heiress Claudette Colbert in Frank Capra's multi-Oscar-winning* It Happened One Night *(1934).*

BELOW: *In Federico Fellini's Oscar-winning picaresque,* La Strada *(1954), waif Giulietta Masina is sold by her mother to itinerant strongman Anthony Quinn.*

From Sweetback to Spike Lee

IDEA № 84

BLAXPLOITATION

BELOW: *Pam Grier, the star of* Coffy *(1973) and* Foxy Brown *(1974), also headlined Quentin Tarantino's homage,* Jackie Brown *(1997).*

BOTTOM: *'Who's the cat that won't cop out when there's danger all about?': Richard Roundtree in* Shaft *(1971), which featured Isaac Hayes's score.*

After decades of marginalization, African-American cinema began to find a mainstream audience in the 1970s thanks to blaxploitation ('black' + 'exploitation') movies. Though often lacking in finesse, these gave a voice to ghetto life and opened Hollywood up to a whole new generation of radical black film-makers and actors.

Impervious to the Harlem Renaissance, Hollywood proved reluctant to depict everyday black experience. Isolated items like King Vidor's *Hallelujah!* (1929) reinforced the stereotypes later dubbed 'mammies', 'coons', 'Uncle Toms', 'mulattos' and 'bucks' by critic Donald Bogle. But while Hattie McDaniel could win a Best Supporting Oscar for playing a maid in *Gone with the Wind* (1939), black directors such as Oscar Micheaux and Spencer Williams were reduced to shooting shoestring 'race movies' for after-hours screenings known as 'midnight rambles'. The most prolific black auteur (making nearly 50 features between 1919 and 1948), Micheaux sought to encourage betterment by highlighting the aspiration and diversity of the African-American community. But distribution difficulties kept his tales of miscegenation and light-skinned women passing for white from being widely seen. It was only in the 1950s that black stars like Dorothy Dandridge and Sidney Poitier began to emerge.

Much scorn has been poured on the liberal melodramas Hollywood produced during the Civil Rights era, but they did much to challenge the Production Code's prohibition of mixed-race relationships and encourage independent black film-makers to make themselves heard. However, the cosiness of Gordon Parks's *The Learning Tree* (1969) soon gave way to the tougher urban realism of Ossie Davis's *Cotton Comes to Harlem* (1970) and Melvin Van Peebles's *Sweet Sweetback's Baadasssss Song* (1971), which broke with the bourgeois black film tradition to enter the ghetto and celebrate assertive masculinity and the separatist desire to stick it to the Man.

Impressed by *Sweetback*'s profitability, MGM backed Parks's *Shaft* (1971); others followed suit after it had saved the studio from bankruptcy. But while audiences revelled in the violent criminality and the consumerist superficiality of the pimps, pushers, gangsters and maverick cops in hits such as *Super Fly* (1972) and *The Mack* (1973) – which gained added kudos from their funky soundtracks – critics lamented the glamorization of ghetto life and the fact that the heroines of *Cleopatra Jones* (1973) and *Foxy Brown* (1974) were more male fantasies than female role models. Moreover, the majority of these increasingly cheap and formulaic pictures were being churned out by white directors devoid of socio-political insight.

However, many saw blaxploitation as a necessary stage in the evolution of genuinely revolutionary black cinema. It certainly prompted 1970s film school graduates like Charles Burnett, Larry Clark and Haile Gerima to launch their LA Rebellion, which in turn inspired the New Black Cinema of Spike Lee, John Singleton and Julie Dash in the early 1990s. Yet blaxploitation didn't simply reflect African-American despair at a corrupt, racist system. It also emboldened white film-makers to denounce the establishment and express the national sense of betrayal following Vietnam and Watergate in landmarks such as Sidney Lumet's *Dog Day Afternoon* (1975) and Martin Scorsese's *Taxi Driver* (1976).

Ultimately, blaxploitation led to Hollywood embracing African-American talent. But with many iconic actors and directors concentrating on mainstream fare, there was a danger that, apart from the odd gangsta saga, the black community could again lose its cinematic voice. Then came Oscar winners such as *Moonlight* (2016) and *Get Out* (2017). ∎

Never a dude like this one!
He's got a plan to stick it to The Man!

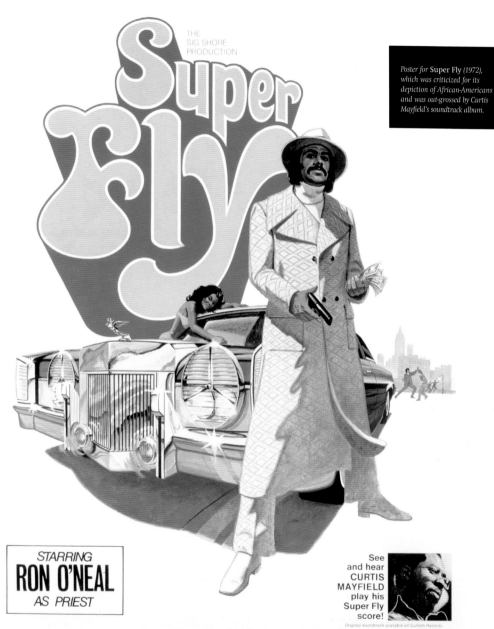

THE
SIG SHORE
PRODUCTION

Super Fly

Poster for **Super Fly** (1972), which was criticized for its depiction of African-Americans and was out-grossed by Curtis Mayfield's soundtrack album.

STARRING
RON O'NEAL
AS PRIEST

See
and hear
CURTIS
MAYFIELD
play his
Super Fly
score!

Original soundtrack available on Curtom Records

The SIG SHORE Production "SUPER FLY" Starring RON O'NEAL · CARL LEE · JULIUS W. HARRIS · SHEILA FRAZIER
CHARLES McGREGOR · Music Composed and Arranged by CURTIS MAYFIELD · Screenplay by PHILLIP FENTY · Produced
by SIG SHORE · Directed by GORDON PARKS, JR. · from Warner Bros., a Warner Communications company   **R**

72/319

Actress Maria Schneider always felt she had been violated by director Bernardo Bertolucci while filming **Last Tango in Paris** *(1972) with Marlon Brando.*

'Accessibility seems to have made porn more acceptable.'

What the Butler Saw and beyond

IDEA № 85
PORNOGRAPHY

ABOVE: *Images of an erection and unsimulated intercourse earned* The Idiots (1998) *the notoriety that boosted its critical and commercial profile.*

BELOW: **In the Realm of the** Senses *(1976) was the first arthouse-hardcore film. Director Nagisa Oshima fought a four-year court battle as the screenplay broke obscenity laws in Japan.*

Such is the enduring social stigma attached to pornography that it has largely been excluded from screen histories, even though it can trace an unbroken line of independent production from nineteenth-century magic-lantern slides to today's multi-billion-dollar industry, with its own star system, international festival circuit and awards.

Compared to the indecent images peddled by lanternists, the nude motion studies made by Eadweard Muybridge and the saucy antics viewed in the Mutoscope (known in Britain as the What the Butler Saw Machine) were decidedly tame. Yet Eugène Pirou's teasing collaborations with Louise Willy prompted Louis Lumière and Georges Méliès to make risqué one-reelers and companies in Central Europe and South America were soon churning out 'smokers', nicknamed after the smoking parlours of the gentlemen's clubs and brothels where they were shown.

Striptease and bathing scenes eventually gave way to the graphic depiction of sexual acts, which ranged from the perfunctory in A. Wise Guy's *A Free Ride* (1915) to the perverse in Gabriellino D'Annunzio's *Saffo and Priapo* (1922). But the imposition of censorship in Europe and America confined such stag films to private functions, educational screenings and coin-operated booths.

Blue movies remained amateurish and taboo for the next three decades. But a combination of World War II, the research of Alfred Kinsey and Masters and Johnson into human sexual behaviour, and the influx of erotic features like Roger Vadim's *And God Created Woman* (1956) did much to liberalize attitudes to sex in puritanical America.

Inspired by Russ Meyer's nudie-cutie *The Immoral Mr Teas* (1959), Radley Metzger, Doris Wishman and Joseph W.

Sarno produced dozens of titillatingly transgressive pictures for grindhouses (see **Exploitation**) nationwide. Titles such as *Sin in the Suburbs* (1964) and *Carmen, Baby* (1967) also sparked softcore booms in Denmark, Sweden and Japan, and, as the Production Code was replaced by a ratings system, the Stateside success of these increasingly hardcore imports paved the way for Artie and Jim Mitchell's *Behind the Green Door* and Gerard Damiano's *Deep Throat* (both 1972), which made stars of Marilyn Chambers and Linda Lovelace respectively. They also popularized porno chic with male and female viewers alike, and encouraged greater sexual frankness in commercial features like Bernardo Bertolucci's *Last Tango in Paris* (1972).

Yet porn's big-screen phase proved short-lived, as its generic scenarios and stock shots migrated to video, which enabled it to become increasingly explicit in catering for straight, gay and niche markets. Surviving a feminist backlash, the operation of the National Obscenity Enforcement Unit, the Traci Lords scandal and the onset of AIDS in the 1980s, the American porn business flourished to turn over $13 billion in 2007, with DVD sales being supplemented by on-demand television channels, internet sites and video-telephony.

Accessibility seems to have made porn more acceptable, with acclaimed features like Paul Thomas Anderson's *Boogie Nights* (1997) and Pablo Berger's

Torremolinos 73 (2003) satirizing the industry, while Lars von Trier's *The Idiots* (1998) and Catherine Breillat's *Romance* (1999) included uncensored images of erections and intercourse. Yet, even as the line blurs between mature representation and sex-ploitation, pornography continues to provoke controversy. ∎

Challenging the male gaze

FEMINIST FILM THEORY

The audience for Hollywood features was predominantly female into the 1950s, yet the studio front offices were exclusively occupied by men. Feminist film theory posed a radical challenge to this gender imbalance in the 1970s – but, despite the Bechdel Test, has anything really changed?

Despite their different personalities, silent stars like Lillian Gish, Gloria Swanson, Greta Garbo and Clara Bow all played independent characters, who were admired equally by women and men. Marlene Dietrich, Bette Davis, Joan Crawford and Katharine Hepburn continued this trend in the talkies. But while Frances Marion, Anita Loos and Dorothy Parker were respected screenwriters, and Hedda Hopper and Louella Parsons were the two most powerful columnists in Hollywood, few women emulated June Mathis in actually producing pictures. Indeed, following the pioneering efforts of Alice Guy Blaché and Lois Weber, only Dorothy Arzner and Ida Lupino directed sound features during the studio era.

The stereotyping of female characters and the docility they were forced to exhibit in order to conform to the roles assigned by a patriarchal hierarchy appalled the critics who emerged from the second feminist wave. In the vanguard, Marjorie Rosen's *Popcorn Venus* (1973) and Molly Haskell's *From Reverence to Rape* (1974) both adopted a sociological-empirical approach to denounce the situation. However, British counterparts such as Claire Johnston and Laura Mulvey drew on semiotics, Althusserian Marxism and Lacanian psychoanalysis to show that mainstream American cinema not only reflected societal attitudes, but also helped reinforce them.

In her seminal 1975 essay 'Visual Pleasure and Narrative Cinema', Mulvey stated that Hollywood pictures were about men pursuing, investigating and penalizing women because their differences threatened male characters,

Dorothy Arzner depicted strong, independent women in The Wild Party *(1929),* Christopher Strong *(1933) and* Dance, Girl, Dance *(1940).*

Isabelle Huppert in **White Material** *(2009), which adds race and colonialism to Claire Denis's trademark themes of the body, gender and sexuality.*

'Scholars began reclaiming the gaze ... forcing the abandonment of male identification. '

producers and viewers alike. Such codes and conventions, therefore, left women with only two spectating options: to accept the passivity of the female characters on screen, or to assume the male gaze for which such sensualized idealism had been concocted.

Stylistically influenced by Sergei Eisenstein, Bertolt Brecht and Jean-Luc Godard, a feminist counter-cinema evolved around this time. However, features like Chantal Akerman's *Jeanne Dielman, 23 Quai du Commerce, 1080 Bruxelles*, Marguerite Duras's *India Song* (both 1975), Laura Mulvey and Peter Wollen's *Riddles of the Sphinx* (1977) and Sally Potter's *The Golddiggers* (1980) had limited filmic influence. They did, however, spark an academic backlash that prompted Mulvey to address the question of female spectatorship by positing a notion of transsexual identification based on the pre-Oedipal and phallic fantasy of omnipotence.

In analyzing King Vidor's *Duel in the Sun* (1946), Mulvey suggested that women could identify with Jennifer Jones's put-upon character by either masochistically sharing in her suffering or assuming the male perspective and objectifying her. But as genres such as the Western, film noir and horror were decried by texts citing castration, fetishization and sadism, scholars began reclaiming the gaze through celebrations of vamps, femmes fatales and the slasher movie's Final Girl, whose survival feminizes the audience by forcing the abandonment of male identification. Moreover – as the emphasis on psychoanalytic theory was replaced by discussion of such previously neglected issues as class, race, age and sexual orientation – feminist film theory finally began to diversify and the results were reflected in the films of such global talents such as Margarethe von Trotta, Jane Campion, Kathryn Bigelow, Julie Dash, Ann Hui and Claire Denis. ∎

ABOVE: **Star Wars** (1977) launched a franchise that has taken over $8.55 billion at the box office and generated more than $32 billion in merchandising.

RIGHT: Despite being the first blockbuster, **The Godfather** (1972) is widely regarded as the finest American film of the post-studio era.

Big-budget, mass-market

IDEA № 87

BLOCKBUSTERS

Jennifer Jones in Duel in the Sun *(1946), which established new methods of marketing and distributing movies in the United States.*

The blockbuster era began in the 1970s and has now lasted longer than either the silent phase of film-making or the Golden Age of Hollywood. It has fostered several landmark features, yet many lament the mainstream's growing reliance on pre-sold properties, high-concept storylines, special effects, product placement, merchandising, remakes and sequels. Others blame the blockbuster for dumbing down cinema in the pursuit of a juvenile audience.

The nature of blockbusters is constantly evolving. Hollywood used to boost its most prestigious pictures by road-showing them at inflated ticket prices in big-city cinemas to create a buzz around them before consigning them to smaller local venues where the majority of viewers saw their movies. But when independent producer David O. Selznick released *Duel in the Sun* (1946) nationwide in a blaze of publicity, a trend was established that would be revived in the mid-1970s to counter the fiscal crisis provoked by the collapse of the studio system.

Francis Ford Coppola's *The Godfather* (1972) was the first modern blockbuster. But Steven Spielberg's *Jaws* (1975) and George Lucas's *Star Wars* (1977) captured the imagination of juvenile viewers, who would become New Hollywood's key demographic. Not only would they see these 'event movies' several times (often in the new shopping mall **multiplexes**), they would also buy into the tie-in novelizations, comic books, soundtrack albums, action figures, video games, fast food products and theme-park rides.

But blockbusters didn't just engender a new breed of fan. Since the outlawing of vertical integration in the late 1940s, movies were progressively being developed as packages, with casts and crews being provided by single talent agencies and the studios merely providing facilities, finance and marketing expertise. Initially, this gave stars capable of opening pictures tremendous power, with remuneration to match. But, as the increasingly fantastical action began to be driven more by plot than character, the emphasis fell on spectacular visuals that were predominantly computer-generated. Indeed, Hollywood became less of a production centre as more films were shot on location or in overseas studios promising reduced overheads.

The traditional release pattern was also revised. During the studio era, pictures had been given time to find an audience. However, by simultaneously releasing *Jaws* in 464 theatres on the back of countless stories leaked from the set, Universal devised the front-loading and saturation strategy that has since become the norm for making blockbusters all-but critic-proof. Furthermore, by selling 25 million tickets in 38 days, producers Richard Zanuck and David Brown demonstrated that summer launches could be just as profitable as end-of-year ones. Nowadays, the risk-averse studios put each big-budget feature through test screenings and focus groups to ensure it achieves its widest appeal. Yet they still invest heavily in glitzy premieres, multi-platform advertising campaigns, personal appearances, and profiles and interviews in the printed media.

Almost a genre in its own right, the blockbuster is not unique to Hollywood. However, few national industries can match the resources that enable it to continue creating the dazzling audiovisual entertainments that dominate the global market. In perpetuating the big-movie myth, the studios have often been guilty of small thinking. But even if blockbusters have contributed to the infantilization of cinema, they often have as much artistic integrity as more critically acclaimed films. ■

From greasepaint to prosthetic sculpting

IDEA № 88
EFFECTS MAKE-UP

The names of Cecil Holland, Jack Dawn and William Tuttle may not mean much to even the most fervent film fan. But these pioneers of movie make-up devised the techniques that refined classical Hollywood glamour and laid the foundations for the special effects that are so crucial to the modern blockbuster.

Jack Pierce spent four hours applying the cotton, collodion, gum and green greasepaint to transform Boris Karloff into Frankenstein's monster.

For much of cinema's first two decades, actors applied their own make-up and relied on trusted theatrical products and styles. Max Factor only introduced the first screen-specific greasepaint in 1912, and another five years elapsed before Selig opened the first studio make-up department. In this initial period, the primary purpose of make-up was to make Caucasian performers look natural on orthochromatic monochrome film stocks insensitive to reds and yellows. However, the switch to panchromatic stock and incandescent tungsten lighting prompted Factor to develop Pancake cosmetics, which so reinforced photo-realism that they became the industry standard before the advent of colour necessitated further modification.

Actor Lon Chaney, aka 'The Man of a Thousand Faces', was the undisputed master of silent make-up technique, using greasepaint, putty, mortician's wax, resin, liquid elastic and fish skin to metamorphose into the Hunchback of Notre Dame (1923) and the Phantom of the Opera (1925). Make-up artists

Bud Westmore and Jack Pierce continued the horror tradition at Universal in the 1930s, with the latter's look for Boris Karloff in James Whale's *Frankenstein* (1931) transforming the popular conception of Mary Shelley's monster.

However, a make-up artist's first duty was still to make a star seem naturally photogenic while in character. Many studied anatomy to ensure authenticity, among them Maurice Seiderman, who created 37 ageing designs for Orson Welles in *Citizen Kane* (1941). But effects were also required to attain physical accuracy in historical reconstructions and biopics. Moreover, at a time when non-white performers had limited opportunities in Hollywood, make-up also proved vital for ethnic characterizations. Eventually, however, the Oriental effects created for acclaimed features like Sidney Franklin's *The Good Earth* (1937) and B franchises such as Charlie Chan and Mr Moto were recognized as being as politically unacceptable as Al Jolson, Fred Astaire and Shirley

Temple's appearances in blackface and Alec Guinness's renditions of Fagin and Dr Godbole in David Lean's *Oliver Twist* (1948) and *A Passage to India* (1984).

As colour processes came to dominate cinematography worldwide, film make-up evolved to reflect everyday trends. Furthermore, the demise of the Production Code meant that everything from combat pictures to medical melodramas could become more graphic. Yet, even though techniques became increasingly sophisticated to produce convincing tones and textures, it took until 1981 for an Academy Award category to be inaugurated, as the boom in sci-fi and fantasy blockbusters and the vogue for gory horror led new talents like Dick Smith, Stan Winston, Rick Baker, Rob Bottin and Tom Savini to experiment with lifecasting, prosthetic sculpting and animatronics to create dynamic effects that could withstand close-up scrutiny.

Foam latex and gelatin are now complemented by CGI, so that Jim Carrey's face can morph in *The Mask*

(1994) and Ralph Fiennes can assume Lord Voldemort's evil countenance in the Harry Potter series. Indeed, with 3-D finally threatening to become an established facet of escapist film-making, the proficiency of effects make-up looks set to become more significant than ever before. ■

ABOVE: *Reiko Kruk based Klaus Kinski's make-up in Werner Herzog's* Nosferatu *(1979) (here) on Max Schreck's rodentine look in F.W. Murnau's 1922 original.*

BELOW: *Polish-born Max Factor created a heart-shaped pout for Clara Bow that reinforced her image as silent cinema's 'It Girl'.*

Director Albert Lamorisse's son Pascal in The Red Balloon *(1956), a delightful film for children that remains the only short to win an Oscar (for Best Original Screenplay) outside its category.*

Cinema for life's beginners

IDEA № 89
KIDPICS

BELOW: *Between 1922 and 1944, Our Gang (aka The Little Rascals) appeared in 220 slapstick shorts aimed at younger audiences.*

BOTTOM: *A birthday card produced by Rank for members of its Saturday matinee club.*

Films for children in the multimedia age have become cinematic commercials for spin-off DVDs, video games, toys, comics, fast foods and theme-park rides. But movie-makers were slow to tap into this kidpic market, only beginning to exploit it systematically after adults started staying at home to watch television in the 1950s.

With moral guardians concerned about the deleterious impact that flickers and nickelodeon patrons might have on impressionable minds, children played little part in cinema's first few decades. Indeed, even juvenile roles were taken by grown-up stars like Mary Pickford. In 1925, the Motion Picture Producers and Distributors Association circulated 52 programmes of re-edited child-friendly titles. But the initiative lasted only a year, and the standard matinee programme of cartoons, serials, B movies and slapstick shorts was established.

Things began to change in the early 1930s with Mickey Mouse, whose popularity was reinforced by a pact between Walt Disney and the Better Films Committee that led to the formation of the Mickey Mouse Club, with its oath, elected officials and charitable activities. However, Disney was quick to see the club's commercial as well as civic benefits and began sponsoring tie-in toys, dinnerware, watches and comestibles, which established a brand loyalty that somewhat reduced the risk of Disney's first venture into children's feature animation with *Snow White and the Seven Dwarfs* (1937).

Around the same time, the Moscow Children's Film Studio began producing fairytales that extolled the virtues of collaboration and hard work without being excessively propagandist. Soviet director Alexander Row's template was widely copied behind the Iron Curtain over the next 40 years. The Children's Film Foundation in Britain specialized in semi-comic adventures that saw plucky kids outfoxing dim-witted crooks, while Germany, the Netherlands and Scandinavia established kidpic traditions that continue to combine escapism with an unpatronizing exploration of the everyday problems of growing up.

Hollywood, on the other hand, has invariably opted to entertain rather than enlighten. Moreover, by churning out hundreds of B Westerns, action serials and sci fi blockbusters for children, it has tended to cater for boys rather than girls, who have had few screen role models since Shirley Temple grew out of her Curly Top phase and Judy Garland and Deanna Durbin started falling in love rather than putting on shows.

Recognizing that younger audiences were being neglected, as teenagers were lured away by sensationalist exploitation, Disney responded with a series of live-action features that ranged from true-life adventures such as *The Living Desert* (1953) and animal escapades such as *The Incredible Journey* (1963) to cosy but visually innovative musical adaptations like *Mary Poppins* (1964). Yet, despite the introduction of G-rated movies (for General Audiences) in 1968, few notable kidpics were made during the ensuing decade, as directors revelled in their newfound freedom to explore adult themes without Production Code constraint.

However, *Star Wars* (1977) revitalized the form and so decisively shifted the

emphasis onto spectacle, special effects and superheroes that many critics complained about the juvenilization of American film and the strengthening links between cinema and consumption. Deals with CGI pioneers Pixar and Japanimators Studio Ghibli have enabled Disney to retain its status. But with kidpics becoming increasingly lucrative, rival conglomerates are always looking for hit franchises such as Harry Potter to hook the next generation of movie-goers. ∎

Adolescent screen angst

IDEA № 90
TEENPICS

ABOVE: *Mickey Rooney looks unimpressed as* Love Finds Andy Hardy *(1938)*.

BELOW: *The Brat Pack came of age in John Hughes's* The Breakfast Club *(1985)*.

Teenagers saved Hollywood. When adult audiences began to decline from 1947, producers realized that adolescents had an appetite for sensation and spectacle, not to mention the leisure and disposable income to indulge it. Consequently, what had once been a mass medium suddenly became a teenpic production line.

Until the late 1930s, film-makers made little effort to discriminate between juvenile age groups. But, having invested so heavily in maturing **child stars** like Judy Garland, Deanna Durbin and Mickey Rooney, they began making features about school, family and dating that reflected the rising bobby sox culture. However, the Production Code limited their scope, so the innocent scrapes of the suburban middle-class hero Andy Hardy were only marginally less egregious than the miscreancy of the Dead End Kids, who initially appeared in gangster pictures.

Postwar ephebiphobia saw teenagers demonized in pictures such as *The Wild One* (1953). But *Rebel Without a Cause* and *Blackboard Jungle* (both 1955) made greater attempts at understanding the teen psyche, with the latter even depicting a cross-racial alliance against injustice. Yet while rock'n'roll brought a new edge to teenpics, it wasn't until the Production Code was revised in 1956 that Hollywood finally began tackling taboos like angst, alienation, sexual identity, underage pregnancy and domestic dysfunction.

Emulating American International Pictures, producers began churning out teenpics across the genres for the drive-ins and double-feature houses. As a result, they were accused of juvenilizing cinema, as most of the films were riddled with artifice, clichés and stereotypes, and provided conservative and shallow solutions to pressing problems. Yet, alongside the 1960s beach movies that sought to sanitize rock'n'roll attitudes, the glut of delinquency, hot-rod, biker and drug-trip pictures persuaded the studios to embrace the lucrative counterculture, with the result that the Code collapsed and a New Hollywood emerged.

This brief post-classical epoch was soon deluged by a second wave of teenpics that arrested another box-office slump by pandering to media-savvy and insatiably consumerist Generation Xers. Initially enticed by the nostalgia of films such as *American Graffiti* (1973) and the sex-quest antics of *Risky Business* (1983), they particularly identified with John Hughes's Brat Pack pictures, which provided cosy correctives to the punishments being meted out for teenage transgression in slasher movies such as *Halloween* (1978), which helped sustain the 1980s **video** boom.

Despite a more ironic approach in the *Scream* and *American Pie* series, the majority of teenpics centred on white suburbanites, who knew little of poverty, violence, peer pressure, substance abuse or family breakdown. New Black Cinema outings like *Boyz N the Hood* (1991) offered a more realistic vision of inner-city America, but they also adopted a largely male perspective. Indeed, Hollywood fell far behind the Dutch, Germans and Scandinavians in discussing gynocentric issues and, when it responded, it merely imported the mean-girl persona from TV shows such as *Beverly Hills, 90210*. Thus, while the studios continue to exploit teenagers as their core audience, they still struggle to speak to them on their own terms. ∎

'Rock'n'roll brought a new edge to teenpics.'

ABOVE: *Vampire Edward Cullen (Robert Pattinson) submits to the Volturi in* **New Moon** *(2009), the second of five films adapted from Stephenie Meyer's Twilight Saga.*

LEFT: *James Dean transformed the image of the American teenager in Nicholas Ray's* **Rebel without a Cause** *(1955).*

*James Acheson's costumes helped
director Sam Raimi and actor
Tobey Maguire re-invent the
Marvel Comics hero in*
Spider-Man *(2002) and its
2003 and 2007 sequels.*

Familiarity breeds content

IDEA № 91
SEQUELS

Sequels exist in many narrative forms, from novels to video games. Homer's great verse epic *The Odyssey* was a progression of *The Iliad*, and even Shakespeare was not averse to sequelizing his histories. In producing sequels, therefore, cinema has merely adhered to the artistic adage of 'same again, but different'.

The sequel has a bad name. Indeed, it has several bad names – prequel, threequel, midquel, interquel and sidequel. Then there's the parallel and the distant sequel, as well as the reboot, the stand-alone and the companion piece. Each summer, critics bemoan another outbreak of sequelitis and denounce Hollywood for its creative torpor and commercial timidity. Yet sequel isn't always a synonym for lazy repetition.

D.W. Griffith was one of the first to attempt a sequel when he concluded the narrative started in *His Trust* in *His Trust Fulfilled* (both 1911). But while Hollywood produced occasional studio era outings like *The Son of the Sheik* (1926) and *Edison, the Man* (1940), the sequel tended to coalesce into the film series, which featured recurring characters in self-contained storylines. It was only in the 1970s that the sequel became institutionalized. Francis Ford Coppola's *The Godfather Part II* (1974) was uniquely a sequel and a prequel, not only continuing the story begun in *The Godfather* (1972) but also filling in backstory to the earlier film; it also remains one of the few follow-ups to be as critically lauded as its predecessor. However, the *Jaws* spin-offs and the glut of slasher movies that spawned 1980s franchises established a trend for diminishing dramatic and box-office returns that inevitably prompted a backlash.

Many first-wave sequels were cheaply produced in the hope of making a quick buck. But the mega-franchise sequel became crucial to the media synergy strategy devised by corporate Hollywood, as the more successful sequels a blockbuster generated, the more opportunities there were for tie-in merchandising. Consequently, storylines became more open-ended to allow for continuations, while the studios started timing sequel releases to coincide with the launch of home-entertainment formats. Moreover, they also began pre-sequelizing pictures, with *Pirates of the Caribbean: At World's End* (2007) being in the pipeline before *Dead Man's Chest* (2006) had even opened.

The cynicism of such horizontal integration has led to accusations that effects-laden sequels are devoid of ideas and intelligence. But there's no reason why plots involving popular characters, situations and settings shouldn't be innovative and challenging. In revitalizing Spider-Man and Batman, for example, Sam Raimi and Christopher Nolan were able to play with audience expectations, while also exploring their own insights into the superhero psyche.

There's also an element of snobbishness involved in naysaying *Naked Gun 33⅓: The Final Insult* (1994) or *Shrek Forever After* (2010), while acclaiming such foreign-language sequels

TOP: *Romantic icon Rudolph Valentino made his final screen appearance in the silent sequel,* The Son of the Sheik *(1926).*

ABOVE: *Charlie Yeung in* Fallen Angels *(1995), Wong Kar-wai's sequel-cum-companion piece to* Chungking Express *(1994).*

as Fritz Lang's *The Testament of Dr Mabuse* (1933), Satyajit Ray's *Apu Trilogy* (1955–59), Akira Kurosawa's *Sanjuro* (1962) and Wong Kar-wai's *Fallen Angels* (1995). In fact, Hong Kong, Japan, Bollywood and the various European industries are as reliant on sequels as Hollywood. ∎

What's new?

Anne Heche and Janet Leigh perish in the shower in the Gus Van Sant (1998) and Alfred Hitchcock (1960) versions of Psycho.

IDEA № 92

REMAKES

As rights fees are rarely required for remakes, producers readily emend both classic and obscure movies in the hope of intriguing viewers already familiar with the original, as well as those who know it only by reputation or are completely oblivious of it. But risk aversion isn't the only motive for such makeovers.

Jean Renoir once suggested that directors often spend their entire career remaking the same film. Yet while exploring recurring themes in a recognizably personal style is supposedly the sole preserve of auteurs, artists and artisans alike have long produced remakes of their own works, among them Cecil B. DeMille, Yasujiro Ozu, Howard Hawks and Michael Haneke.

Critics have tended to look benignly upon such authorial repetition but the remaking of an existing film by a different director is invariably decried as evidence of creative indolence and commercial conservatism. Yet film-makers have been recycling successful storylines since cinema's first decade, when a lack of copyright legislation meant that remakes could abound. Literary works in the public domain were frequently revisited; even when studios began purchasing rights, they usually acquired them in perpetuity to enable future remakes at no additional cost. Such **pre-sold sources** were usually refurbished in the interests of fidelity or in a bid to update them for new generations. However, remakes have also been undertaken to pay homage to previous adaptations or to render them superfluous. Many remake directors seek to do justice to a promising premise that has initially been mishandled or undervalued. Some relish utilizing improved sound, colour or effects technology to enhance the action's audiovisual quality, while others are adept at translating foreign hits to novel settings to reach new and often wider audiences.

No remake is a shot-for-shot duplication, with even Gus Van Sant's infamously slavish 1998 *Psycho* remake differing in several regards from Alfred Hitchcock's 1960 original. However, essential remakes are produced with only minor variations of plot, characterization, dialogue, setting and form. By contrast, revisionist remakes strive to put an entirely new slant on the material, while unofficial or 'disguised' remakes relocate the core action and change the title to avoid direct overlap with the often uncredited original.

Cross-generic remakes are often equally audacious in allowing storylines to be reimagined. In Hollywood's Golden Age, for example, various film styles were musicalized. Bollywood has recently adopted this trend by inserting musical numbers into revamps of *Reservoir Dogs* (*Kaante*, 2002) and *E.T.: The Extra-Terrestrial* (*Koi... Mil Gaya*, 2003).

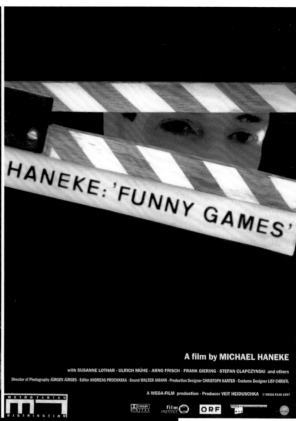

YOU MUST ADMIT, YOU BROUGHT THIS ON YOURSELF.

FUNNY GAMES NAOMI WATTS · TIM ROTH · MICHAEL PITT
BRADY CORBET · DEVON GEARHART

A FILM BY **MICHAEL HANEKE**

www.funnygames-themovie.com

HANEKE: 'FUNNY GAMES'

A film by **MICHAEL HANEKE**

with SUSANNE LOTHAR · ULRICH MÜHE · ARNO FRISCH · FRANK GIERING · STEFAN CLAPCZYNSKI and others

Director of Photography JÜRGEN JÜRGES · Editor ANDREAS PROCHASKA · Sound WALTER AMANN · Production Designer CHRISTOPH KANTER · Costume Designer LISY CHRISTL

A WEGA-FILM production · Producer VEIT HEIDUSCHKA © WEGA FILM 1997

'Film-makers have been recycling successful storylines since cinema's first decade.'

ABOVE: *Posters for Michael Haneke's American remake of* Funny Games *(left) and for his 1997 Austrian original (right) made a decade earlier.*

BELOW: *Rippling paranoia: Hitomi Kuroki in Hideo Nakata's J-horror gem* Dark Water *(2002) (right) and Jennifer Connelly in Walter Salles's 2005 Hollywood remake (left).*

The connection between small-screen spin-offs such as *Bewitched* (2005) and their source is often tenuous. Whether revering or parodying, few TV transfers have found box-office favour. But, along with video and DVD, television has contributed significantly to remake culture since it has helped familiarize viewers with cinema history. This cine-literacy has made remakes as diverse as *Scarface* (1983), *You've Got Mail* (1998) and *Let Me In* (2010) easier to finance and promote. Consequently, film industries worldwide will no doubt continue to plunder the archives for remakeable properties. ∎

Far from increasing choice, venues like this Warner multiplex in Preston, Lancashire, reinforced Hollywood's dominance of the world market.

Cinema's supermarkets

IDEA № 93

MULTIPLEXES

Opened in 1988 and boasting 25 screens, the Kinepolis in Brussels was the world's first megaplex.

If dream palaces were cinema's cathedrals, multi-screen venues are its superstores. It's no coincidence that they're located in shopping malls or out-of-town retail parks, as they also promise everything under one roof. But, whether with three, 13 or 30 screens, multiplexes rarely offer as much choice as patrons might expect.

The 1948 Paramount Decrees were intended to open up the exhibition market by breaking Hollywood's monopoly over America's movie theatres. However, they served only to disincentivize the increasingly impecunious studios and leave the new movie-theatre chains and independents with fewer films to screen. Consequently, the drift to suburbia and competing leisure activities like television saw ticket sales plunge by almost 50 per cent between 1946 and 1953. Despite the introduction of drive-ins, art cinemas, and revival and grindhouses (see **Exploitation**), the weekly attendance of 30 million in 1960 had dropped to 18 million by the end of the decade.

Multi-screen theatres had existed since the 1930s. But with so many downtown sites, as well as second-run and neighbourhood operations, disappearing, exhibitors in the 1970s made a concerted effort to twin and triple screens in a bid to extend the run of successful pictures. The practice coincided with the emergence of the blockbuster and the Reaganite deregulation policies that allowed the conglomerates now controlling the studios to restore circuits to their portfolios. Consequently, a multiplex building boom followed that prompted audience figures to rise to 20 million in 1980, 25 million in 1995 and 30 million in 2002.

However, rather than creating spaces in which indies and imports could find their niche, the new venues simply enabled greater numbers to see ubiquitous 'event movies', as the studios adopted the strategy of mass-media advertising and saturation booking. Thus, instead of allowing publicity, reviews and word of mouth to accrue an audience, the emphasis shifted to making a splash on opening weekend and exploiting box-office data to sustain grosses until the release of the video or DVD.

In order to maximize returns, the studios began taking fewer risks with content. The reliance on enticing younger viewers with sequels, remakes and pre-sold spin-offs from TV shows, bestsellers, comic books and video games prioritized spectacle over story. This resulted in more effects-laden blockbusters being released at inflated prices in 3-D and such large-screen formats as 70mm and IMAX. In order to combat piracy, home-entertainment lead times were also reduced and even bigger 'megaplex' venues were constructed with stadium seating, convenient parking and state-of-the-art projection and sound systems to pack in as many people as possible before the arrival of the next must-see – which was often bundled with lesser titles from the same producer or distributor in a cynical return to block booking.

Slashing transportation and staffing costs and raking in 40 per cent of their profits from concession stands, megaplexes made economic sense. But they also put many smaller multiplexes out of business, as well as the more traditional city-centre venues. Multi-screen theatres continue to spring up at a rapid rate across every continent, with many being wired for digital projection. The majority reinforce Hollywood's commercial dominance. However, their capacity, comfort and convenience contributed significantly to the rise in cinema attendances during the most recent global economic downturn. ∎

The VT revolution

VIDEO

Even in an industry of rapidly changing technology, video's moment came and went with remarkable speed. But, for two decades at the end of the last century, videotape (VT) and the videocassette recorder (VCR) transformed the production, reception and study of commercial and art film.

Introduced in 1956, video was used primarily in television until Sony and Matsushita developed the Betamax and Video Home System (VHS) cassettes respectively in the 1970s. Having thwarted Disney and Universal's challenge that video contravened copyright law, Sony lost the format battle and, by 1988, 60 per cent of American households owned a VHS machine. Around the same time, combined video rental and sales figures doubled theatrical takings to $7.2 billion annually.

Independent production burgeoned to meet the demand for 'straight-to-video' titles, although the resulting boom in **pornography** and splatter horror sparked controversy about underage viewers being exposed to excessive sex and violence. Aesthetic debates also flared, as purists complained that images captured on magnetically coated tape lacked the density, detail, dimensionality and dynamic range of those on celluloid. They also denounced the panning and scanning of pictures to fit television screens (see **Television**), and the fact that spectatorship was less controllable and concentrated in domestic environments than in darkened auditoria.

Nevertheless, video significantly facilitated scholarly study and it soon proved equally valuable on film sets. Several directors used video for storyboards and rough cuts, while video assist monitors and instant playback – made possible because video did not need processing like film – reduced the need for expensive retakes. Steven Spielberg even used video conferencing to assess the special effects for *Jurassic Park* while he was on location making *Schindler's List* (both 1993).

But video didn't just impact on Hollywood. Documentarists could shoot for longer using tape, with Jean-Luc Godard and Anne-Marie Miéville adopting stylized actuality techniques for personal projects such as *France/tour/detour/deux/enfants* (1977). In 1980, Wim Wenders incorporated Tom Farrell's video footage in his Nicholas Ray profile, *Lightning over Water*, while Michelangelo Antonioni experimented with video colour tones in *The Oberwald Mystery* (1981). More recently, video also enabled the meteoric rise of Nollywood in Nigeria.

Video also featured prominently in Steven Soderbergh's *Sex, Lies, and Videotape* (1987), Oliver Stone's *Natural Born Killers* and Atom Egoyan's *Exotica* (both 1994), while the 'music video' influenced the production numbers in *Flashdance* (1983) and *Dirty Dancing* (1987). Yet, as the video revolution prompted Hollywood to start producing high-concept spectacles like *Top Gun* (1986) in order to rebrand the big-screen blockbuster, a new breed of video artist was finding an appreciative audience in the world's art galleries and museums

Having emerged in the 1960s, Nam June Paik, Peter Campus, Joan Jonas, and Steina and Woody Vasulka were among the first to exploit loops, surveillance techniques, multiple monitors, and the electronic distortion of sound and image to create videos and installations that weren't always designed to be watched in their entirety. Subsequently, Bruce Nauman, Bill Viola, Sadie Benning, Matthew Barney, Matthias Müller, Pascal Auger, Pipilotti Rist and Douglas Gordon melded video with performance, conceptual art and experimental film.

Digital video prompted videotape's gradual obsolescence from the mid-1990s. But many critics are concerned that the malleability of digital imagery will foster a cinema that no longer presents recorded reality, but a cosmeticized idealization. ∎

Art installation as feature film: video artists Douglas Gordon and Philippe Pareno used 17 cameras to shoot Zidane: A 21st Century Portrait *(2006).*

BELOW LEFT: *Having shot* **The Oberwald Mystery** *(1981) on videotape to conduct colour experiments, Michelangelo Antonioni transferred the results to a standard 35mm release print.*

BELOW: *Steven Soderbergh incorporated handheld camcorder footage in his Palme d'Or-winning study of voyeurism,* **Sex, Lies, and Videotape** *(1989)*

Ingmar Bergman swapped a set of tin soldiers for his brother's magic lantern and he recalls his childhood enchantment as Bertil Guve gives a slide show in Fanny and Alexander *(1982).*

Bringing it all back home

Jacques Demy made animated and live-actions films as a boy, as widow Agnès Varda recalls in the affectionate biopic, Jacquot de Nantes *(1991).*

IDEA № 95
HOME ENTERTAINMENT

Far from being a modern phenomenon, home entertainment has been provided by moving images since cinema's prehistory. However, what was once a niche novelty is now a crucial component of the global cine-economy, providing among other things a welcome new outlet for forgotten classics.

Optical toys like the thaumatrope, phenakistoscope and zoetrope (see **Persistence of Vision**) were the first to find a home market in the mid-nineteenth century. Scale versions of public entertainments such as the diorama were also produced, although Émile Reynaud reversed that trend by converting the praxinoscope (a variation on the zoetrope) to project animated images before larger audiences at his Théâtre Optique.

None of these devices proved as popular domestically as the magic lantern, which Ingmar Bergman recalled so fondly in *Fanny and Alexander* (1982). Even so, it was rapidly surpassed by the projector, as home movies became a craze after the introduction of safety film (1923) and 8mm (1932). Jacques Demy, Bernardo Bertolucci, Francis Ford Coppola and Steven Spielberg were among the many aspiring directors who crafted juvenilia for family and friends. But domestic cinema could never match the impact of television.

Despite sharing the culpability for the slump in American box-office takings from 1947, television quickly became a Hollywood lifeline. In the mid-1950s, the studios began selling their back catalogues for broadcast. Martin Scorsese cites shows like *Million Dollar Movie* for acquainting him with classic films that had been barely seen since their original release.

This new availability was expanded two decades later by the advent of videocassettes, which permitted the rental or purchase of films from all periods and places. Initially, the industry opposed video on copyright grounds, but by 1995 the home market accounted for over half of Hollywood's worldwide revenue.

Moreover, video enabled film-makers outside the mainstream to find an audience. In particular, the exploitation genres acquired cult followings, with Quentin Tarantino famously furthering his screen education as a video-store clerk. The boom had its controversies, however, with the graphic horrors nicknamed 'video nasties' sparking a censorship debate in 1980s Britain, while purists decried the techniques employed to transfer widescreen pictures to tape.

Image quality was also a concern, as was perishability. But both issues were ameliorated by the launch of laser disc, DVD and Blu-ray. Outstripping VHS rentals for the first time in 2003, DVD has markedly altered home presentation, with extras packages containing commentaries, 'making of' documentaries, alternative versions, deleted scenes, **trailers**, bonus shorts, galleries and biographical information. The disc for Greg Marcks's *11:14* (2003) also had an interactive element: the link between films and games is growing increasingly strong.

The same is true of the relationship between films and the internet. A website hyped *The Blair Witch Project* (1999) to a $240.5 million return on its makers' $22,000 outlay, while the script for *Snakes on a Plane* (2006) was shaped by forum feedback. Broadband has allowed animators and experimental film-makers to exhibit online, while sites such as YouTube afford showcases for amateur talents. However, file-sharing has seen an increase in illegal downloading and the window between theatrical presentation and release on disc has consequently been drastically reduced. Investment in 3-D spectaculars has increased in a bid to combat piracy, with the result that, in 2009, theatrical takings ($9.87 billion) exceeded DVD sales ($8.73 billion) for the first time in almost a decade. Supplemented by downloading and streaming, home entertainment may be big business, but nothing beats the big-screen experience.∎

Challenging the studio system

US INDEPENDENT CINEMA

Independent production has always played a vital role in America. But whereas such independence once served to introduce innovation and iconoclasm to the mainstream, in the blockbuster era it is increasingly marginalized.

TOP: *Monochrome indie chic: John Lurie, Eszter Balint and Richard Edson in Jim Jarmusch's* **Stranger Than Paradise** *(1984).*

ABOVE: *Strike up the band: Jan Nowina-Przybylski and Joseph Green's Yiddish cinema gem,* **Yiddle With His Fiddle** *(1936)*

It's one of the great ironies of screen history that the mavericks whose Motion Picture Distributing and Sales Company broke the cartel operated by the Motion Picture Patents Company established the infinitely more restrictive system of vertical integration that enabled Hollywood to dominate world cinema. Indeed, as early as 1919, D.W. Griffith, Mary Pickford, Douglas Fairbanks and Charlie Chaplin felt compelled to form United Artists to protect their creative and commercial interests. Metro chief Richard A. Rowland scornfully opined that 'the lunatics have taken over the asylum', but both the majors and the minors not only accommodated independent producers such as Samuel Goldwyn, Joseph M. Schenck and David O. Selznick during their heyday, but they also allowed Poverty Row to copycat their product for the lower half of double bills.

However, the emphasis shifted firmly in favour of independent production following the Paramount Decrees of 1948. United Artists flourished, with producers Walter Wanger, Sam Spiegel and Walter Mirisch, directors Stanley Kramer and Otto Preminger, and actors such as Burt Lancaster and Kirk Douglas cutting their own distribution deals. By 1958, 65 per cent of Hollywood features were being independently produced, with the numbers being significantly increased by prolific newcomers like Allied Artists and American International Pictures.

Exploitation helped American cinema survive the onset of television but the blockbusters that Hollywood devised to appeal to the new juvenile market – which were rooted in indie genre flicks – came to dominate the industry and a backlash against corporate gigantism in the late 1980s saw the emergence of new talents such as Jim Jarmusch, Hal Hartley, Steven Soderbergh and the Coen brothers, who were sponsored by fledgling companies like New Line, Orion and Miramax, promoted by the Sundance Film Festival and lauded at the Independent Spirit Awards.

However, while many film-makers managed to debut successfully with shoestring pictures that prioritized character and plot over spectacle, few succeeded in sustaining a career. Despite critical support, breakout hits like *Reservoir Dogs* (1992) and *The Blair Witch Project* (1999) proved rare, and most indie features were restricted to arthouse venues, specialist festivals and cult video labels. Moreover, just as the 'race' films of Noble Johnson, Oscar Micheaux and Spencer Williams and the Yiddish features of Sidney M. Goldin, Joseph Green and Edgar G. Ulmer were once consigned to the indie fringes, so now are the vast majority of pictures made by women, queer, African-American, diasporic and exilic film-makers.

Independence has always been a relative term but the gap between US mainstream and independent production is wider than it has ever been and it seems destined to grow wider still. ■

‘A backlash against corporate gigantism in the late 1980s saw the emergence of new talents.’

Heather Donohue in **The Blair Witch Project** *(1999), which started an indie trend for 'found footage' horror films.*

> 'Queer cinema now sustains its own festival circuit and porn industry.'

ABOVE: *Gael García Bernal in* **Bad Education** *(2004), Pedro Almodóvar's* **noirish** *exposé of Franco-era religious schools.*

RIGHT: *Alessandro Gassman on a journey of self-discovery with Mehmet Günsür in Ferzen Ozpetek's* **Hammam** *(1997).*

Out of the closet

IDEA № 97
QUEER CINEMA

Written by Christa Winsloe and directed by Leontine Sagan, Girls in Uniform (1931) also had an all-female cast.

Homosexuality was illegal in many countries for much of cinema's first century. Consequently, the representation of openly gay or lesbian characters in mainstream films was nigh-on impossible until the late 1960s launched a revolution in the West not just in the way films were made but also how they were interpreted.

The Production Code introduced in Hollywood in the 1930s forbade the depiction of any kind of 'sex perversion' and, even when the rubric was amended in 1961, same-sex situations were only permissible if handled with 'care, discretion and restraint'. Features like *Girls in Uniform* (or *Mädchen in Uniform*) (1931) and *Victim* (1961) were consequently rare during the decades of persecution and prosecution. Indeed, gay and lesbian themes were mostly confined to non-commercial outings such as Kenneth Anger's *Fireworks* (1947) and Jack Smith's *Flaming Creatures* (1963). However, the collapse of the Code in 1968 and the following year's Stonewall riot saw Hollywood tentatively promote naturalness and shared humanity in films like *Midnight Cowboy* (1969) and *The Boys in the Band* (1970).

Yet in urging acceptance and upgrading gays and lesbians from supports to leads, many of these pictures succeeded only in reinforcing platitudes. These became more entrenched in the well-meaning but often patronizing AIDS dramas that began to appear in the mid-1980s. It was a reaction against such political correctness and aggressive activism that provoked what critic B. Ruby Rich dubbed 'New Queer Cinema'.

Disavowing positive images, but politically assertive and committed to revising and reappropriating stereotypes, Todd Haynes's *Poison* (1991),

Gregg Araki's *The Living End* and Tom Kalin's *Swoon* (both 1992) were accused of producing elitist, postmodern 'Homo Porno' around white, middle-class gay men. However, by eschewing a single aesthetic and encouraging multiplicity, New Queer Cinema reflected the growing confidence of established and emerging film-makers worldwide, including Chantal Akerman, Barbara Hammer, Su Friedrich, Monika Treut, Sadie Benning, Gus Van Sant, Derek Jarman, Pedro Almodóvar, John Greyson and Bruce LaBruce.

New Queer Cinema also sparked an academic revolution. Accommodating a wide range of political and ideological positions, queer theory became an umbrella term for any 'non-straight' perspective. Consequently, theorists were able to re-examine Hollywood history and acclaim the camp of so-called pansies like comedic actor Franklin Pangborn, while also questioning the derangement of sissy psychos like Jame 'Buffalo Bill' Gumb in *The Silence of the Lambs* (1991) and killer dykes like Beth Garner in *Basic Instinct* (1992). They reassessed generic convention and found queer subtexts in vampire and monster movies, in Hitchcock thrillers, and in all manner of musicals, screwballs and romcoms.

Queer theorists challenged the feminist theory of the gaze (see **Feminist Film Theory**) and declared it to be reciprocal rather than repressive

in highlighting the androgynous appeal of Greta Garbo and Marlene Dietrich and the homoerotic charm of Marlon Brando and Tom Cruise. They celebrated the excess and suffering of Judy Garland and Carmen Miranda, proclaimed early female film director Dorothy Arzner an auteur, and accepted that, for all their faults, mainstream representations of gay, lesbian, bisexual and transgender characters were often as worthy of inclusion in the canon as those in independent, avant-garde, underground or documentary films.

Queer cinema now sustains its own festival circuit and porn industry, while also enjoying crossover hits such as *The Adventures of Priscilla, Queen of the Desert* (1994), *Boys Don't Cry* (1999), *Far from Heaven* (2002) and *Brokeback Mountain* (2005). Films aimed at audiences identifying as lesbian, gay, bisexual, trans, queer/questioning and other orientations (LGBTQ+) are far from universally accepted.∎

Middlebrow nostalgia?

Julian Sands and Helena Bonham Carter in Merchant Ivory's A Room With a View (1985), which typified British heritage cinema in the 1980s.

IDEA № 98
HERITAGE FILMS

Heritage film is a divisive and often derisive term. Although scholars reserve it for the lavish costume dramas released since the mid-1980s, it can be applied with equal validity to cinema's first attempts at literary adaptation, historical reconstruction and biography, as they share a superficial sophistication designed to achieve a degree of socio-cultural respectability.

The most immediate preoccupation of the earliest film-makers was recording the present. But once Alfred Clark made *The Execution of Mary, Queen of Scots* (1895), they quickly sought to emulate art, literature, theatre and waxworks by recreating the past. **Film d'Art**, the Italian superspectacle, and D.W. Griffith's *The Birth of a Nation* (1915) and *Intolerance* (1916) all tackled literary or historical topics and helped transform the scale and ambition of cinema, as well as earning it a new, more educated audience.

Such titles set the template for period re-enactment. But whether celebrating or subverting the social, cultural or political heritage they depicted, features as different as Ernst Lubitsch's silent 1920s German *Kostümfilme* (costume films), the 1930s Hollywood biopics starring George Arliss and Paul Muni, and the Gainsborough bodice-rippers of the 1940s in the UK reflected the sensibilities of the place and time in which they were made. Indeed, subsequent critical

debates have turned around the extent to which heritage pictures shape popular understanding of the past by promoting national myths, eulogizing heroes and drawing allegorical parallels with contemporary events.

Whether adapting ancient texts, literary masterpieces or penny dreadfuls, post-World War II costume films exhibited a greater complexity and scope and were often used to showcase new technologies. In biopics, the subject's flaws became as important as his or her achievements, and the growing emphasis on psychological realism in widescreen epics like David Lean's *Lawrence of Arabia* (1962) anticipated the naturalism of New Hollywood, as well as the meta-historical reportage of Roberto Rossellini's *The Rise to Power of Louis XIV* (1966) and the anachronistic iconoclasm of Hans-Jürgen Syberberg's *Hitler: A Film from Germany* (1978).

ABOVE: Jean de Florette (1986) won French film an international audience by contrasting its period trappings with the slick visuals of the contemporary cinéma du look style.

BELOW: Gabriel Axel's Karen Blixen adaptation Babette's Feast (1987) is one of many heritage titles to win the Oscar for Best Foreign Film.

In many ways, 1980s-and-later heritage cinema was a reaction against such departures from narrative classicism. Yet it also shifted the storytelling focus from technique to mise en scène, as meticulously researched costumes, props, décor, manners and rituals imbued adaptations of Austen, Dickens, Dumas, Zola, James, Forster and others with enhanced levels of coded significance.

Handsome international outings such as *Jean de Florette* (1986), *Like Water for Chocolate* (1992), *The Age of Innocence*, *The Piano* and *Farewell My Concubine* (all 1993) found appreciative audiences, who were otherwise alienated by the muscular antics of the mainstream's action heroes. But, despite saving the domestic industry by using authentic locations to chronicle the rites of passage of independent women, gay men and lower-class aspirants, British heritage cinema was widely ridiculed for its elitist Laura Ashley pictorialism and for sanitizing the satirical intentions of its source material. Merchant Ivory's output was particularly castigated for supposedly peddling uncritical nostalgia to middle-aged, middle-class middlebrows at the height of Thatcherite social upheaval.

The period picture is no longer so contentious or ubiquitous. But, with CGI offering it a chance to further reinvent itself, it enters the post-heritage era as knowing and self-reflexive as ever. ■

'Cinematographers have had to relearn lighting strategies.'

*As **Collateral** (2002) takes place at night and Michael Mann wanted to shoot mainly in natural light, he became the first director to use high-definition video cameras in a major movie.*

Cheaper, more versatile, better?

IDEA № 99

DIGITAL VIDEO

A Steadicam rig and a high-definition digital camera captured the sweep of history in one 96-minute take in Aleksandr Sokurov's Russian Ark (2002).

Digital video encodes images electronically rather than photochemically. Despite storing information in binary units on tapes, discs, hard drives or flash memory cards, digital cameras rely on roughly the same optical principles as their analogue forebears. Thus, with new software packages constantly improving the efficacy of applications from storyboarding to viewing, digitization represents one of the most radical technical transformations in cinema history.

Initially employed in the computer generation of animated images and special effects, digital technology became an on-set option with the introduction of Sony's HDCAM in 1998. George Lucas's *Star Wars: Episode II – Attack of the Clones* (2002) became the first blockbuster to be shot on 24-frame high definition digital video (DV) and sealed the revolution that Lucas had first predicted in the mid-1970s. The critical acclaim for Aleksandr Sokurov's one-take *Russian Ark* (2002) and the Oscar success of Danny Boyle's *Slumdog Millionaire* (2008) confirmed DV's aesthetic acceptance.

Numerous different kinds of camera have been employed on mainstream features, including the Panavision Genesis, Arriflex D-20, Silicon Imaging SI-2K and the Red One. Their portability has seen an increase in handheld imagery and rapid action, tendencies which haven't always met with critical approval. But their ease of use has enabled directors to speed up production and keep down costs.

Revealing enough of an image's brightness and resolution to determine its quality, instant playback facilities have proved similarly beneficial. But cinematographers have had to relearn lighting strategies, as the limited dynamic range of most high-end digital formats means that they either emphasize shadow or diminish brighter lights. Thus, whereas they once selected film stock to achieve a certain look, directors of photography now choose a camera according to the light-sensitivity of its CMOS or CCD sensor and the graininess created by its electronic noise levels.

Some people dislike the plasticity of digital imagery and blame non-linear editing systems that allow instant access to any frame for the increased incidence of cuts and close-ups. Yet random-access systems such as Avid, Lightworks and Final Cut Pro give editors greater control over the selection and assembly of images, and thus, save time and money. Digital formats are also used for sound editing and colour timing. Moreover, as they are non-degrading, they also play a part in the restoration and storage of classic pictures.

Hollywood has been accused of converting to digital primarily for economic reasons. However, arthouse movements like Dogme 95 and Mumblecore have also exploited its potential to produce stylistically innovative features on tight budgets. Indeed, more independents than ever are making films and getting them viewed, either online or through a variety of home-entertainment formats. Moreover, the fact that it is cheaper to share files than strike prints enables them to show their work at domestic cinemas and international festivals.

Exhibitors are increasingly willing to screen digital movies, which can either be dispatched as a disc or computer file or be delivered via an internet or satellite link. In 2005, the major US studios launched the Digital Cinema Initiatives to encourage a theatrical switchover. The majority of cinemas utilizing 2K, 4K or 6K projectors are still in North America. Yet, while directors acclimatize to new technology and techniques to make iPhone features such as *Tangerine* (2015), such venues have added live broadcasts to their digital repertoires. ∎

From screen to screen

LEFT: **Star Wars** *fans were divided over the switch from the original puppet Yoda to the CGI version of the prequels.*

ABOVE: *Even auteurs dabble with CGI: Revolutionary France was digitally recreated for Eric Rohmer's* **The Lady and the Duke** *(2001).*

IDEA № 100
COMPUTER-GENERATED IMAGERY

Computers allowed Yoda to impart wisdom in the *Star Wars* prequels and a rogues' gallery to inhabit Sin City. With technologies rapidly becoming more sophisticated, there's no predicting where the digital revolution will lead next. But, though computer-generated imagery (CGI) has fundamentally changed Hollywood, most features produced worldwide are still effects-free.

John Whitney pioneered the use of computers in film-making with abstract animations such as *Lapis* (1963–66); his son, John Jr, helped devise the landmark effects in Michael Crichton's *Westworld* (1973). However, computers were still insufficiently powerful to create cine-credible images, and Hollywood took stock after the critical and commercial failure of *Tron* (1982) and *The Last Starfighter* (1984), which contained the first CGI character and photorealistic effects respectively. But the attendance slump of the late 1980s persuaded the studios to commit to computerized techniques to prise younger viewers away from their PCs and games consoles, and the success of James Cameron's *Terminator 2: Judgment Day* and Disney's *Beauty and the Beast* (both 1991) heralded a momentous aesthetic and economic shift that some compared to the coming of sound.

No aspect of film-making has been more radically altered by the CGI revolution than animation, which has undergone a dimensional transformation since Pixar's *Toy Story* (1995), although the standard graphic style has also benefited from computer embellishment. Moreover, digitization forced Hollywood to rethink its blockbuster strategy in order to exploit CGI to the full in sci-fi, fantasy and comic-book narratives.

The switch also made fiscal sense, as it was much cheaper for a single operator to create an alternative reality than to pay for expensive sets or unpredictable location shoots. The cost of hiring and costuming extras could also be reduced by swelling crowd scenes with 'artificially intelligent' bystanders programmed to repeat appropriate actions in random sequences. Stunts could also be made safer by utilizing digitized stand-ins, while set-pieces like the rooftop shootout in *The Matrix* (1999) could be enhanced by the temporal and spatial manipulation of a technique dubbed 'bullet time'. CGI could also lend greater authenticity to models and miniatures, and even enabled a body double to complete the late Oliver Reed's scenes in Ridley Scott's *Gladiator* (2000).

Despite the advances made in films like *Tron Legacy* (2010), the creation of realistic virtual humans, or synthespians, has yet to be perfected. But, in the meantime, CGI has had a marked effect on film acting. Performers often work before blank green screens while others don motion-capture suits that enable artists to fashion mythical beings such as Gollum in the *Lord of the Rings* trilogy. Many critics lament the prioritizing of spectacle over character and plot. But SFX can now open pictures as effectively as marquee names and the studios are happy to save on superstar salaries by casting unknowns in their event movies.

With technicians supplanting auteurs, the prospect of an interactive form of virtual entertainment replacing the traditional contemplative form becomes increasingly likely. Novelty sells tickets and tie-in merchandise. Thus, while cinema has always adopted a cautious approach to new technology, a box-office crisis may well prompt Hollywood to take what could prove to be an irrevocable step. ∎

In addition to building a nine-tenths scale model of the liner, James Cameron also spent $50 million on 500 effects shots for **Titanic** (1997).

Glossary

Actualités
French term for early topical shorts, which quickly came to refer to any factual film.

Anamorphic lens
A lens that 'squeezes' a magnified image into a 35mm frame. The image is 'unsqueezed' during projection to achieve a 2.35:1 aspect ratio.

Animatronics
Remote controlled or computer-programmed models used in the creation of special effects.

Anime
A style of Japanese animation inspired by manga comics. Pioneered by Osamu Tezuka in the 1960s, 'Japanimation' went global in the mid-1980s.

Backlot
The area behind a studio complex where full-size or scale exteriors are struck and stored. Most Hollywood majors had a variety of sets that could be re-dressed to suit any time or place.

Big Five
Nickname for MGM, Paramount, Warner Bros, Twentieth Century-Fox and RKO – the Hollywood studios that were vertically integrated until 1948.

Bipacking
A colour process in which two celluloid strips sensitive to different colours pass in direct contact through a camera or optical printer to achieve simultaneous exposure.

Blue- and green-screens
These neutral colour screens are used as a backdrop for performers illuminated by white light acting out scenes that will be composited in post-production with computer-generated characters and environments.

Bounce lighting
The technique of using off-set reflectors or surfaces within the mise en scène to direct light precisely on to a subject.

Breakaways
Stunt props made from lightweight materials like balsa wood that break convincingly on impact

without harming the performer.

Bullet time
The technique of shooting with a ring of synchronized cameras to allow footage to be manipulated in post-production to create the illusion of three-dimensionality.

Cel
A transparent celluloid sheet used by animators to overlay the moving elements of a shot upon static backdrops. Each cel contained an individual stage of an action and saved the time and expense of redrawing frames in full. Several cels could be layered to give the impression of image depth.

Cheat shots
A shot that imperceptibly mismatches a figure or prop's position within the mise en scène between cuts. This breach of continuity enables directors to shift visual emphasis.

CinemaScope
Trade name for the anamorphic process developed by Henri Chrétien. With an aspect ratio of 2.35:1, it was used in *The Robe* (1953) and was key to the evolution of widescreen cinema.

City symphonies
Avant-garde actualités like Walter Ruttmann's *Berlin: Symphony of a Great City* (1927) that sought to combine the sights (and ultimately sounds) of a metropolis with the rhythms of everyday life.

Crane
A large mobile camera mount fitted with a long arm or boom that accommodates the camera and crew on a platform that can be raised above the action or swooped down towards it.

Credit crawl
The closing or end credits identifying the contributions of the cast and crew, as well as any acknowledgements and copyright details.

Cut-ins
A brief shot (usually a close-up) that emphasizes a specific detail within the

mise en scène, such as an expression, gesture or prop.

Czech Film Miracle
An alternative name for the Czech New Wave (1962–68) that saw directors challenge the Soviet-imposed tenets of Socialist Realism.

Digital tracing
A computerized variation on the animation technique of rotoscoping.

Diorama
An optical entertainment premiered in Paris in 1822 that used magic lanterns and shutters to illuminate scenes within a vast translucent painting enveloping a revolving viewing dais.

Distanciation
Also known as alienation, this is a dramatic technique devised by Bertolt Brecht to distance the audience from the action and prevent easy association with the characters.

Dolly
A mobile platform supporting the camera and operator during a travelling or dolly shot. A 'dolly in' glides towards a subject, while a 'dolly out' retreats from it.

Double exposures
The superimposition of one image upon another by exposing a piece of film twice, in either a camera or an optical printer. In addition to suggesting spectres and interiority, double exposures were also key to dissolving between scenes.

Dutch angles
A camera angle devised by the German Expressionists that assumes a diagonal axis to suggest physical or psychological dislocation, as in Carol Reed's *The Third Man* (1949).

Edit point
The point at which a film's action cuts from one shot to another.

Establishing shot
A shot at the start of a sequence that sets the scene by establishing location, time and ambience, as well as sometimes the spatial relationships between the characters.

Event movie
A big-budget blockbuster that has been hyped as a

major socio-cultural, cinematic event.

Eyeline matches
A match shot crucial to continuity editing that cross-cuts from a medium or close-up shot of a character to the subject of their off-screen gaze.

Flat lighting
The even, front lighting of subjects to produce low contrasts and no shadows or key lit areas so that multiple moving cameras can be used without modifying the lighting design between shots.

Freeze frame
The repetition of a single frame to give the impression of 'frozen' action.

Glass shot
This process used in the 1920s and '30s spared the expense of constructing scale sets by shooting scenes through glass sheets on which scenery had been painted.

Go motion
A computer technique introduced in the late 1970s to move models slightly during the shooting of stop-motion animation sequences to create more authentic movements by blurring the staccato effect of frame-by-frame photography.

Graphic matching
A technique used in continuity editing to contrast compositional elements between juxtaposed shots, either to highlight similarities between the images or to make metaphorical comparisons between them.

Green-screen See **Blue- and green-screens**.

Grindhouses
Slang term for American cinemas specializing in exploitation movies, many of which were converted burlesque theatres.

Ice-box
Nickname given to the soundproofed booths in which cameras were confined during the early sound era to prevent the whirr of the motor from being picked up by the primitive microphones.

Image capture
The technique of uploading

images from a digital camera or scanner so they can be computer-modified.

IMAX
A giant screen process, which was developed in Canada in the 1960s to project images up to ten times the size of 35mm and three times that of 70mm systems with peerless definition.

Indie
Abbreviation for independent films.

Intermittent movement
The stop-go action that ensures each frame of film is momentarily held stationary before a camera or projector lens to allow light to pass through it. The movement is achieved through a Maltese cross gear connected to a series of sprocket wheels, which pull the celluloid strip through the mechanism, while a Latham loop relieves tension and prevents tearing.

Intertitles
A printed caption inserted into the action of usually silent films.

Jump cut
A consciously abrupt breach of temporal and/or spatial continuity that defies narrative logic and draws attention to a film's constructed nature.

Kino Eye
Term coined by the Soviet film-maker Dziga Vertov to define both his attitude to the camera as an observational and intellectual tool and his use of montage to create filmic truth in his *Kino Pravda* newsreels.

Lifecasting
The use of casting or moulding techniques to create three-dimensional copies of living forms.

Looping
Term for the process of dubbing or automated dialogue replacement (ADR), which sees performers re-record lines in post-production.

Matte
A masking device used to obscure part of a film frame during shooting or optical printing so that foreground and background images can be accurately composited

into a single image or matte shot.

Medium shot
The most widely used shot in cinema, it usually depicts a human figure from the waist up.

Midnite matinees
Late-night screenings of usually genre, exploitation or cult films.

Midnight rambles
Late-night screenings exclusively for black audiences at a time when segregation dictated American movie-going habits.

Motion capture
The process of recording movement with sensors attached to a performer's body and using the captured data to animate 2-D or 3-D digital models.

Motion Picture Association of America (MPAA)
Founded in 1922 as the Motion Picture Producers and Distributors of America, this non-profit body has overseen the US ratings system since 1968.

Multi-plane photography
A technique used in animation to increase shot depth and perspective. Glass sheets are positioned at different distances from the camera's lens so that cels bearing moving elements can be photographed against static backdrops.

Negative space
The space around and between subjects in an artistic composition.

New Hollywood
Name given to the post-classical period of studio film-making that lasted from the mid-1960s to the 1980s and constituted an American new wave.

New talkies
Produced in the 1970s by avant-gardists, these independent features drew on critical theory and political art cinema to deconstruct the conventions of traditional screen narrative.

Nouvelle Vague
The new wave in French film that occurred between 1959 and 1963 and promoted auteur theory in

seeking to regenerate screen storytelling.

Nudie cutie
Nickname for the softcore 'sexploitation' pictures produced in the 1960s for grindhouses.

Oater
Also known as a horse opera and a sagebrush saga, this was a B-movie Western.

One-reeler
A film lasting for one reel that ran for 10-12 minutes depending upon the projection speed.

Optical printer
A special effects device comprising one or more projectors locked in sync with a camera to re-photograph film to make composite images.

Over-the-shoulder shot
A camera angle used in shot-reverse-shot dialogue passages to present one character from over the shoulder of the other interlocutor.

Panning and scanning
The method of cropping the sides of widescreen images so that the key action can fit into the 'safe area' of a standard television screen.

Paramount Decrees
A decision passed in 1948 by the US Supreme Court that barred studios from owning their own movie theatres and ended the monopolistic Hollywood practice of vertical integration.

Patent and Trust Wars
Disputes that arose in 1897 and 1908 respectively, as Thomas Edison sought to coerce rivals into accepting his ownership of the principal film-making patents and the hegemony of his Motion Picture Patents Company over the nascent American film industry.

Pillow shot
A poetic digression (usually a still life) that was employed by the Japanese director Yasujiro Ozu to allow viewers to contemplate the significance of the preceding scene.

Post-production
The phase in the film-making process that follows principal photography and

usually involves editing, scoring, sound mixing and the creation of non-physical special effects.

Poverty Row
Nickname for the minor Hollywood studios located around Gower Street that churned out B movies, serials and shorts during the golden age of the studio system.

Prestige picture
Trade term for a feature with lavish production values and serious content that was designed less to storm the box office than assuage the critics.

Problem pictures
A cycle of social realist dramas produced in postwar Hollywood that tackled such previously taboo topics as poverty, racism, marginalization, delinquency, corruption and injustice.

Programmers
Another name for second features or B movies.

Prosthetic sculpting
The technique of shaping silicon rubber moulds to create special make-up effects.

Push-in
A slow travelling shot that moves the camera towards the subject on a dolly.

Rack focus
The technique of abruptly shifting focus during a shot to draw the audience's attention to a new element within the mise en scène.

Roadshowing
The strategy used to create pre-release buzz for prestige pictures by screening them with reserved seating and inflated prices at big theatres.

Rotoscoping
The technique of tracing live-action images to render them in animated form.

Safe area
The area of an image that can be seen on a standard television set with an aspect ratio of 1.33:1 or 4:3.

Saturation style
The practice of accompanying each scene in a film with background music.

Screwball comedy
A fast-talking form of

romantic comedy devised in the 1930s that usually involved a free-spirited female and a hapless male.

Shot-reverse-shot
A continuity editing technique often employed in dialogue sequences that relies on eyeline matches to alternate the perspective of the speakers.

Slow motion
Achieved by filming faster than the standard rate of 24 frames per second, this is the trick effect of slowing down the action for comic, dramatic or analytical purpose.

Socko
Name given to the frantic style of physical knockabout in slapstick comedy and animation.

Soundstage
A large soundproofed room on a studio lot used for the filming of motion pictures.

Squibs
A miniature explosive device, often fitted with a remote electronic trigger, used in the creation of pyrotechnic effects.

Stop-motion
The frame-by-frame animation technique of making incremental changes to a puppet, model or clay figure to create the illusion of movement.

Storyboard
A series of sketches created in consultation with the director to illustrate the angle, distance and content of the various shots in an action sequence.

Substitution splicing
The technique used in early film-making of stopping shooting so that objects could be manipulated or removed to complete an illusion when the camera started rolling again.

Synthespian
A computer-generated character that can either be an original creation or resemble a real person.

Technicolor
Trade name for the colour film process patented in 1915. Two-colour Technicolor was used on silent features like *The Ten Commandments* (1923), but the three-colour process introduced in 1932

produced much richer hues. However, it was expensive and was initially only used on prestige pictures like *The Wizard of Oz* (1939).

Topicals
The name given to the earliest newsreels, which were also known as 'animated newspapers'.

Tradition of Quality
Term coined by François Truffaut to denounce the verbose style of scriptwriting prevalent in postwar French film.

Treatment
A short story that comes in the screenwriting process between the outline and the first draft.

Two-shot
A shot that contains two characters in the same frame so their reactions to an event or statement can be directly contrasted.

Undercranking
Operating a hand-cranked camera at a slower-than-normal speed.

Vertical integration
The practice of uniting the means of production, distribution and exhibition in a single company that was adopted by the Big Five Hollywood studios before being deemed contrary to anti-trust laws by the US Supreme Court in 1948.

White telephone films
Nickname given to glossy comedies and dramas produced in Italy in the 1930s, characterized by their chic production design and resolute refusal to comment on the realities of life.

Widescreen
A film format that exceeds the Academy aspect ratio of 1.33:1 or 4:3

Wipe
A scene transition like a fade, dissolve or iris, in which an image is replaced by another gradually moving across the frame.

Wire fu
A technique employed in Hong Kong martial arts movies that uses wires and pulleys to enhance the athletic spectacle of kung fu sequences.

Index

Page numbers in **bold** refer to pictures

Further reading

Abel, Richard (editor). *The Encyclopedia of Early Cinema* (Routledge, 2004)

Altman, Rick. *Silent Film Sound* (2/e, Columbia University Press, 2007)

Andrew, J.D. *The Major Film Theories: An Introduction* (Oxford University Press, 1976)

Barnouw, Eric. *Documentary: A History of the Non-Fiction Film* (3/e, Oxford University Press, 1993)

Bendazzi, Giannalberto. *Cartoons: One Hundred Years of Cinema Animation* (John Libbey, 1994)

Bogle, Donald. *Toms, Coons, Mulattoes, Mammies and Bucks: An Interpretive History of Blacks in American Films* (4/e, Continuum, 2001)

Bordwell, David. *On the History of Film Style* (Harvard, 1997)

Bordwell, David. *Narration in the Fiction Film* (Routledge, 1985)

Bordwell, David, Janet Staiger and Kristin Thompson. *The Classical Hollywood Cinema: Film Style and Mode of Production to 1960* (Routledge, 1988)

Bordwell, David and Kristin Thompson. *Film Art: An Introduction* (9/e, McGraw-Hill, 2010)

Bordwell, David and Kristin Thompson. *Film History: An Introduction* (McGraw-Hill, 2009)

Braudy, Leo and Marshall Cohen (editors). *Film Theory and Criticism* (9/e, Oxford University Press, 2009)

Brownlow, Kevin. *The Parade's Gone By* (Knopf, 1968)

Burch, Noël. *Life to Those Shadows* (University of California Press, 1992)

Coe, Brian. *The History of Movie Photography* (Ash & Grant, 1981)

Cook, David A. *A Narrative History of Film* (4/e, Norton, 2004)

Cook, Pam (editor). *The Cinema Book* (3/e, BFI, 2007)

Cousins, Mark and Kevin Macdonald (editors)

Imagining Reality (Faber, 2006)

Dyer, Richard. *Now You See It: Studies on Lesbian and Gay Film* (2/e, Routledge, 2002)

Furniss, Maureen. *The Animation Bible: A Guide to Everything from Flipbooks to Flash* (Laurence King, 2008)

Gomery, Douglas. *The Hollywood Studio System* (BFI, 2005)

Gomery, Douglas. *Shared Pleasures: A History of Movie Presentation in the United States* (University of Wisconsin Press, 1992)

Hall, Ben M. *The Best Remaining Seats* (C.N. Potter, 1961)

Hill, John and Pamela Church Gibson (editors). *The Oxford Guide to Film Studies* (Oxford University Press, 1998)

Katz, Ephraim. *The Film Encyclopedia: The Complete Guide to Film and the Film Industry* (6/e, Collins, 2008)

King, Geoff. *American Independent Cinema* (I.B. Tauris, 2005)

Klinger, Barbara. *Beyond the Multiplex: Cinema, New Technologies, and the Home* (University of California Press, 2006)

Leyda, Jay. *Kino* (3/e, Princeton University Press, 1983)

Mannoni, Laurent. *The Great Art of Light and Shadow: Archaeology of the Cinema* (University of Exeter Press, 2000)

Mast, Gerald and Bruce Kawin. *A Short History of the Movies* (10/e, Longman, 2010)

Monaco, James. *How to Read a Film: Movies, Media, and Beyond* (4/e, Oxford University Press, 2009)

Pramaggiore, Maria and Tom Wallis. *Film: A Critical Introduction* (3/e, Laurence King, 2011)

Nelmes, Jill. *An Introduction to Film Studies* (3/e, Routledge, 2003)

Nowell-Smith, Geoffrey (editor). *The Oxford History of World Cinema* (Oxford University Press, 1997)

Rickitt, Richard. *Special Effects: The History and Technique* (Aurum, 2006)

Salt, Barry. *Film Style and Technology* (2/e, Starword, 2009)

Schatz, Thomas. *The Genius of the System: Hollywood Filmmaking in the Studio Era* (2/e, Faber, 1998)

Sitney, P. Adams. *Visionary Film: The American Avant-Garde, 1943–2000* (3/e, Oxford University Press, 2002)

Thornham, Sue. *Passionate Detachments: An Introduction to Feminist Film Theory* (Hodder, 1997)

Usai, Paolo Cherchi. *Silent Cinema: An Introduction* (2/e, BFI, 2000)

Wakeman, John (editor). *World Film Directors: Vol. 1 1890–1945, Vol. 2 1945–1985* (H.W. Wilson, 1988)

Film Institutes and Museums

American Film Institute, Los Angeles
www.afi.com

British Film Institute, London
www.bfi.org.uk

Cinémathèque Française, Paris
www.cinematheque.fr

Museo Nazionale del Cinema, Turin
www.museonazionaledelcinema.it

Deutsche Kinemathek, Berlin
www.filmmuseum-berlin.de

Nederlands Filmmuseum, Amsterdam
www.filmmuseum.nl

Film Museum, Vienna
www.filmmuseum.at

London Film Museum, London
www.londonfilmmuseum.com

National Media Museum, Bradford
www.nationalmediamuseum.org.uk

Museum of the Moving Image, New York
www.movingimage.us

The Hollywood Museum, Los Angeles
www.thehollywoodmuseum.com

Australian Centre for the Moving Image, Melbourne
www.acmi.net.au

Picture credits

Grateful acknowledgement is extended for the use of the following images. Every effort has been made to trace any copyright holders The publisher apologizes for any unintentional omission or error and will be pleased to insert the appropriate acknowledgement in any subsequent edition of the book.

Courtesy of The Kobal Collection: p13 Kinetoscope parlour; p16 *L'Arrivée d'un train en Gare de la Ciotat*, Lumière; p17 *The Sound of Music*, Paramount; p20 *Once Upon a Time in the West*, Paramount/Rafran; p21 *Grandma's Reading Glass*; p25 *Lady in the Lake*, MGM; p27 *The Ghost*, RP Films; *42nd Street*, Warner Bros.; p28 *Keystone Kops*, Keystone Film Company; p29 *The Italian Job*, Paramount; *Raiders of the Lost Ark*, Lucasfilm Ltd/ Paramount; p34 Nickelodeon; p35 Hale's Tours; p38 *The Story of the Kelly Gang*, J&N Tait/Johnson and Gibson; p43 Boris Karloff, Universal; p44 *The Third Man*, London Films; *The Lord of the Rings: The Fellowship of the Ring*, New Line/Saul Zaentz/Wing Nut; p47

Fantômas, Gaumont; p48 *The Finishing Touch*, Hal Roach/MGM; p49 *Duck Soup* poster, Paramount; *Austin Powers: International Man of Mystery*, New Line; p50 *Hero*, Beijing New Picture/Elite Group; p52 *Movie Stars Parade*; p53 *Devdas*, Damfx; p54 *Gone with the Wind*, Selznick/MGM; p57 *The Last Tycoon* poster, Paramount; p58 *Cleopatra*, Twentieth Century-Fox; p61 Paramount Pictures Bronson Gate, Paramount; p62 *Once Upon a Time in the West*, Paramount/Rafran; p63 *All That Heaven Allows* poster, Universal; p66 *The Wizard of Oz*, MGM; p72 *Pleasantville*, New Line; p73 *Seventh Heaven*, Fox Films; p74 *The Lost World*, First National; *The Ten Commandments*, Paramount; p75 *Mary Poppins*, Walt Disney Pictures; p77 *No Country for Old Men*, Paramount/Miramax; p78 *Batman*, Warner Bros./DC Comics; p80 *L'Inhumaine*, Cinégraphic-Paris; p80 *Finis terrae*, Société Générale de Films; p81 *Eldorado*, Gaumont Serie Pax; *Mother and Son*, Sverny Fond/O-Film; p85 *The Wild Bunch*, Warner 7 Arts; p86 *Earth*, Vufku-Kino-Ukrain/Amkino; p86 *Cleaner*, Nu Image/Anonymous Content; p87 *Mother*, Mehzrabpom, Moscow; p87

Shanghai Express, Paramount; p89 *Zéro de Conduite*, Jacques-Louis Nounez/Gaumont; p92 *The Jazz Singer* poster, Warner Bros.; p93 *Twin Peaks: Fire Walk with Me*, Lynch-Frost/CIBY 2000; p94 Anton Karas scoring *The Third Man*, London Films; p95 *Jaws* poster, Universal; Steven Spielberg and John Williams, Universal; p96 *Don Juan*, Warner Bros; p97 *My Fair Lady*, Warner Bros.; *Spartacus*, Bryna/Universal; p100 Pathé news crew, Pathé; p101 Fox Movietone news van; *Kino Glaz* poster; p102 *Yol*, Guney Film/Cactus Film; p105 *Triumph of the Will*, NSDAP; p106 *L'Atalante*, Nounez/ Gaumont; p108 *Sous les toits de Paris*, Tobis; *Messalina*; p109 *Dogville*, Zentropa Entertainment; p110 *Lèvres de Sang* poster, Nordia Film; p111 *The Masque of the Red Death*, A.I.P.; p112 *The Thin Man* poster, MGM; p113 *Tarzan Escapes*, MGM; p114 *His New Job*, Essanay; p115 *Persepolis*, 2.4.7. Films; *Spirited Away*, Studio Ghibli; p119 *Fantastic Mr Fox*, Twentieth Century-Fox Film; p120 *Bicycle Thieves*, Produzione De Sica; p121 *Rome, Open City*, Excelsa/Mayer-Burstyn; *Bitter Rice* poster,

Lux/De Laurentiis; p122 *Reservoir Dogs*, Live Entertainment; p123 *Slumdog Millionaire*, Film 4/Celador Films/Pathé International; *Last Year at Marienbad*, Terra/Tamara/Cormoran/Georges Pierre; p124 Taxi Driver, Columbia; p125 *Diary of a Country Priest*, U.G.C.; *Double Indemnity*, Paramount; p128 *High Noon*, Stanley Kramer/United Artists; p129 *The Hollywood Ten*; p132 Star Trek, Paramount Television; p133 *I Love Lucy*, CBS-TV; p135 *The Robe* Cinemascope Ratio, Twentieth Century-Fox; p139 3-D audience; p141 *Roman Holiday*, Paramount; p143 *Ivan the Terrible*, Mosfilm; p144 *I Was a Teenage Werewolf* poster, A.I.P.; *The Trip* poster, A.I.P.; p145 *Snakes on a Plane*, New Line/James Dittiger; p147 Alfred Hitchcock, Universal; p153 Brigitte Bardot at the 1953 Cannes Film Festival, Bob Hawkins; p156 *Play Time*, Specta; p157 *The Desperate Hours*, Paramount; p158 *Shirin*, BFI; p158 *The Searchers*, Warner Bros.; p160, *A bout de souffle* poster, SNC; Anna Karina and Jean-Luc Godard, Georges Pierre; p164 *Nanook of the North*, Flaherty; p165 *Bowling for Columbine*, Alliance Atlantis/Dog Eat Dog/United Broadcasting; p166 *Saturday Night and Sunday Morning*, Woodfall/British Lion; *We Are the Lambeth Boys*, Graphic Film; p168 *Cyclo*; *The Time That Remains*, Canal+; Antonio das Mortes, Glauber Rocha/Mapa; p169 *The Cow*, Iranian Ministry of Culture; p172 *The Motorcycle Diaries*, Film Four/South Fork/Senator Film; p173 *It Happened One Night*, Columbia; p174 Shaft, MGM; p175 *Super Fly* poster, Warner Bros.; p176 *Last Tango in Paris*, Pea; p177 *The Idiots*, Zentropa Entertainments; p179 White Material, Canal+; p180 *Star Wars*, Lucasfilm/Twentieth Century-Fox; *The Godfather*, Paramount; p181 *Duel in the Sun*, Selznick/RKO/Lacy, Madison; p182 Jack Pierce and Boris Karloff, Universal; p183 *Nosferatu*, Gaumont; Max Factor and Clara Bow, Culver; p186 *Love Finds Andy Hardy*, MGM; p187 *Rebel Without a Cause*, Warner Bros.; p188 *Spider-Man*, Marvel/Sony Pictures; p189 *The Son of the Sheik*, United Artists; *Fallen Angels*, Jet Tone Productions; p190 *Psycho* (1998), Universal; *Psycho* (1960), Paramount; p191 *Funny Games* poster (1997), Vega Film; *Funny Games* poster (2007), Dreamachine; pp194-5 *Zidane: A 21st Century Portrait*, Canal+; *The Oberwald Mystery*, RAI; p198 *Stranger Than Paradise*, Cinethesia-Grokenberger/ZDF; *Yiddle with His Fiddle*, Green-Film; p199 *The Blair Witch Project*, Artisan Films; p200 *Bad Education*, Canal+/TVE; Hamam, Sorpasso Film; p201 *Mädchen in Uniform*, Deutsche Film/Limot; p202 *A Room with a View*, Merchant Ivory/Goldcrest; p203 *Jean de Florette*, Renn-Films/A2/RAI2; p205 *Russian Ark*, Fora Film/Hermitage Bridge Studio; p206 Yoda, Lucasfilm/Twentieth Century-Fox; p207 *Titanic*, Twentieth Century-Fox/Paramount.

Courtesy of The Ronald Grant Archive: p2 *Cinema Paradiso*, Cristaldi Film; p12 Kinetoscope line drawing; p15 *L'Arroseur arrosé*, Lumière; p13 Black Maria; p31 *Memento*, Newmarket Capital Group; p32 *Rear Window*, Paramount Pictures; p32 *Carrie*, Twentieth Century-Fox Corporation; p36 *Intolerance*; p38 *Gone with the Wind*, Selznick/MGM Pictures; p42 *Barton Fink*, Working Title Films; p45 *Raging Bull*, MGM Pictures; p46 *The Perils of Pauline*; p47 *Flash Gordon*, Universal Pictures; p48 Charles Chaplin and Max Linder; p51 *Steamboat Bill Jr.*; p53 *Rinty of the Desert* poster; p56 Darryl F. Zanuck; p58 Warner Bros. logo; p58 Universal logo; p58 Paramount logo; p59 Columbia logo; p59 MGM logo; p59 Twentieth Century-Fox logo; p60 Aerial photograph RKO and Paramount Studios; p65 *The Leopard*, Titanus; p67 *Cinema Paradiso*, Cristaldi Film; p71 Marlon Brando; p76 *Blade Runner*, Warner Bros.; p76 *Suspicion*, Warner Bros.; p79 *The Cabinet of Dr. Caligari* poster; p82 *Raise*

the Red Lantern, Era International; p84 *Battleship Potemkin*; p97 *King Kong*; p98 Robinson Crusoe titles; p100 Pathé News logo; p104 *The Birth of a Nation* poster; p106 *The Long Day Closes*, BFI; p110 *Cat People* poster; p113 *Harry Potter and the Philosopher's Stone*, Warner Bros.; p115 *The Music Box*, Hal Roach/MGM; p117 *Mighty Mouse*, Twentieth Century-Fox Corporation; p126 *Le Samouraï*, Compagnie Industrielle et Commerciale Cinématographique (CICC); p130 *A Streetcar Named Desire*, Warner Bros.; p130 *Way Down East*; p131 *Raging Bull*, MGM Pictures; p138 *House of Wax* poster; p139 *Avatar*, Twentieth Century-Fox Corporation; p142 *Ben Hur*, MGM; p143 *Mother India* poster; p161 *Day for Night*, Les Films du Carrosse; p166 *The Lacemaker*, Action Films; p174 *Jackie Brown*, Miramax Films; p178 Dorothy Arzner; p185 Our Gang; p186 *The Breakfast Club*, Universal Pictures; p187 *New Moon*, Summit Entertainment; p191 *Dark Water* (2005), Touchstone Pictures; *Dark Water* (2002), Toho Company.

Courtesy of BFI Stills Collection: p19 *The '?' Motorist*; *A Trip to the Moon*; p20 *The Passion of Joan of Arc*, Artificial Eye; p24 *In the City of Sylvia*, Eddie Saeta S.A.; p38 *Greed*, MGM Pictures; p51 *Stagecoach*, Warner Bros.; p57 Louis B. Mayer and MGM stars, MGM Pictures; p65 *The Innocents*, Twentieth Century-Fox Corporation; p66 *The Poor Little Rich Girl* poster; p68 Sight and Sound Vol.18 Issue 9; p73 *A Matter of Life and Death*, Columbia Picture Industries; p73 *The White Ribbon*, X-Filme Creative Pool; p74 *The Ten Commandments*, Paramount Pictures; p78 *Dracula*, Universal Pictures; p86 *Earth*, Mosfilm; p88 *Un Chien andalou*, Contemporary Films; p90 *Meshes of the Afternoon*; p92 *Dr Jekyll and Mr Hyde*, Paramount Pictures; p102 *The Outlaw*, RKO/George Hurrell; p107 *Quai des brumes*, Studio Canal; p117 *The Adventures of Prince Achmed*; p118 *The Wrong Trousers*, Aardman Animations; p119 *Metropolis*; p127 *The Big Combo*, Allied Artists Pictures Corporation/Security Pictures Inc./Theodora Productions; pp134-5 *Napoleon*; p135 BFI IMAX; p136 *In the Mood for Love*, Block 2 Pictures/Jet Tone Productions; p136 *Les Parapluies de Cherbourg*, Parc Film/Madeleine Films/Beta Film; p137 *The Wizard of Oz*, MGM Pictures; p140 *Crouching Tiger, Hidden Dragon*, Good Machine International; p149 *Decasia*; p154 Cahiers du Cinéma No.31; p156 *Red Desert*, Film Duemila/Federiz/Francoriz Productions; p159 *Peeping Tom*, Michael Powell (Theatre); p162 Lars Von Trier; p163 *Antichrist*, Zentropa Entertainments; p163 *Jules et Jim*, Les Films du Carrosse; p171 *Easy Rider*, Columbia Pictures; p172 Paris, Texas, Road Movies Film Produktion; p173 *La Strada*, Ponti-De Laurentiis Cinematografica; p177 *Ai No Corrida*, Oshima Productions; p184 *The Red Balloon*, Films Montsouris; p203 *Babette's Feast*, Panorama Film A/S; p204 *Collateral*, Paramount Pictures; p205 *Russian Ark*, Fora Film/Hermitage Bridge Studio; p206 *The Lady and the Duke*, Pathé Image/Compagnie Eric Rohmer.

Courtesy of The Bill Douglas Centre: p8 Enamelled toy magic lantern; p9 Alice in Wonderland magic lantern slides; p11 Phenakistoscope and magic disks; Musée Grevin poster; p14 Cinématographe Lumière poster; *L'Arroseur arrosé* poster; p34 Mabel Normand; p37 Queen Elizabeth; p40 Odeon organ; p185 Rank Saturday show card.

Courtesy of akg-images: p71 26th Academy Awards.

Courtesy of Alamy: p55 Hollywood sign © Eric Ju.

Courtesy of Alexander Ballinger: p68 Cahiers du Cinéma No.180; Première No. 318; p155 The American Cinema cover art, with thanks to Derek Kendall.

Courtesy of Artificial Eye: P103 *Certified Copy*.

Courtesy of Bloomsbury Publishing: p64 J.K. Rowling, *Harry Potter and the Philosopher's Stone* cover image, with thanks to Bloomsbury Publishing, The Christopher Little Literary Agency and Derek Kendall.

Courtesy of Chicago Architectural Photographing Company Collection, The Theatre Historical Society of America: p41 The Paradise Theatre, Chicago.

Courtesy of The Cinema Store (www.thecinemastore.co.ukn): p69 Film magazines, with thanks to Graham at The Cinema Store and Derek Kendall.

Courtesy of The Cinema Theatre Association: p192 Warner Village Cinema, Preston, Cinema Theatre Association Archive.

Courtesy of the Cinémathèque Française: p150 Claude Chabrol and Jean-Luc Godard; p151 Cinémathèque Française exterior.

Courtesy of David Parkinson: p147 Cigarette Cards.

Courtesy of Empire Magazine: Empire Magazine cover Art, June 2010, with thanks to Ian Freer.

Courtesy of the Estate of Stan Brakhage and Fred Camper (www.fredcamper.com): p91 *Mothlight*.

Courtesy of The Kinepolis Group: p193 Kinepolis, Brussels.

Courtesy of Ocho y Medio (www.ochoymedio.com): p68 CineArte, Nùmero 11; Cahiers du Cinéma No. 41 in Spanish, with thanks to Jesus Robles.

Courtesy of The Reel Poster Gallery (www.reelposter.com): p63 *Psycho* (1960) poster; p152 Cannes Film Festival 1953 poster.

Screengrabs: p16 *The Magic Box*, with thanks and acknowledgement to The Festival Film Production; p18 *That Fatal Sneeze*, with thanks and acknowledgement to Hepworth; p22 *The 400 Blows*, with thanks and acknowledgement to Les Films du Carrosse; p23 *Cries and Whispers*, with thanks and acknowledgement to Cinematograph AB/Svenska Filminstitutet; *The 39 Steps*, with thanks and acknowledgement to Gaumont British Picture Corporation; p26 *Touch of Evil*, with thanks and acknowledgement to Universal International Pictures; p30 *Rescued by Rover*, with thanks and acknowledgement to Hepworth; p33 *2001: A Space Odyssey*, with thanks and acknowledgement to MGM; p39 *Berlin Alexanderplatz*, with thanks and acknowledgement to Bavaria Media GMBH; p85 *The Untouchables*, with thanks and acknowledgement to Paramount Pictures Corporation; p99 *Letters from Iwo Jima*, with thanks and acknowledgement to Warner Bros.; p146 *Pépé le Moko*, with thanks and acknowledgement to Studio Canal; p148 *Persona*, with thanks and acknowledgement to Svensk Filmindustri; p149 *Inglourious Basterds*, with thanks and acknowledgement to Universal; p165 *Grey Gardens*, with thanks and acknowledgement to Maysles Films Inc.; p170 *Vertigo*, with thanks and acknowledgement to Universal Studios; p171 *Barry Lyndon*, with thanks and acknowledgement to Warner Bros.; p195 *Sex, Lies, and Videotape*, with thanks and acknowledgement to Outlaw Productions (I)/Virgin; p196 *Fanny and Alexander*, with thanks and acknowledgement to Cinematograph AB/Svenska Filminstitutet; p197 *Jacquot de Nantes*, with thanks and acknowledgement to Canal+.

Acknowledgements

My involvement with this book is entirely due to Alexander Ballinger. We were going to write it together but, after we had collaborated on a list of headwords, Alex was forced to withdraw. However, few can match his knowledge of and enthusiasm for cinema and he continued to provide encouragement and insight as well as doing a magnificent job in researching the illustrations.

Many thanks are owed to Philip Cooper and Sophie Wise at Laurence King Publishing, who respectively developed the project and edited it, with the contributions of Robert Shore and Jon Allan and the expert guidance of Laurence King.

I should also take this opportunity to thank everyone at *Empire* and *Radio Times* for keeping me gainfully employed while I was working on the manuscript, as well as my family back on Merseyside, Marie Wright, Mike Nottage, Kim Thompson, Nick Dawson, Anna Lea, Adam Smith, Justin Hopper, Graeme Hobbs, Moira Rhodes, Jason Freeman, Judith Paskin, Chris Chambers, Abigail Ballinger, Andrew Lockett and Laura Morris for keeping either me or my laptop going throughout.

However, I am most indebted to Siobhan Lancaster and she knows why.

David Parkinson

Oxford, March 2011

LAURENCE KING

First published in 2012
This edition published in 2019
by Laurence King Publishing Ltd
361–373 City Road
London EC1V 1LR

tel +44 20 7841 6900

e-mail: enquiries@laurenceking.com
www.laurenceking.com

Text © 2012 David Parkinson

This book was designed and produced by
Laurence King Publishing Ltd, London.

The right of David Parkinson to be identified as
the author of the work has been asserted by him
in accordance with the Copyright, Designs and
Patents Act of 1988.

All rights reserved. No part of this publication
may be reproduced or transmitted in any form or
by any means, electronic or mechanical, including
photocopy, recording or any information storage
and retrieval system, without prior permission in
writing from the publisher.

A catalogue record for this book is available from
the British Library.

ISBN: 978-1-78627-486-1

Design: TwoSheds Design
Picture research: Alexander Ballinger
Senior editor: Sophie Wise
Printed in China

David Parkinson is a film critic for *Radio Times* and *The Oxford Times*, and a contributing editor on *Empire*. In addition to writing regularly for the BFI website and several other online outlets, he is also the author of several books including *A History of Film*, *The Young Oxford Book of Cinema*, *The Rough Guide to Film Musicals* and *Oxford At the Movies*. He also edited *Mornings in the Dark: The Graham Greene Film Reader*.